# Education, Unemployment, and Economic Growth

# Education, Unemployment, and Economic Growth

**Alan L. Sorkin**
Johns Hopkins University
School of Hygiene and Public
Health

**Lexington Books**
D.C. Heath and Company
Lexington, Massachusetts
Toronto          London

**Library of Congress Cataloging in Publication Data**

Sorkin, Alan L.
    Education, unemployment, and economic growth.

    Includes bibliographical references.
    1. Labor supply—United States. 2. Unemployed—United States. 3. Occupational training—United States. I. Title.
HD5724.S635       331.1'26      73-11656
ISBN 0-669-85498-0

Published simultaneously in Canada.

Printed in the United States of America.

International Standard Book Number: 0-669-85498-0

Library of Congress Catalog Card Number: 73-11656

# Contents

HD
5724
S635

v

# List of Figure and Tables

# Preface

In recent years there have been a considerable number of highly technical, econometrically oriented volumes published in the fields of labor and manpower economics. While these books have provided important contributions to knowledge, they were often unintelligible to non-specialists or even to specialists with less than formidable quantitative skills.

This is not a technical book. It can be used for a variety of purposes. Thus, an undergraduate taking his first course in labor or manpower economics could utilize it as a supplementary text. The book could also hopefully be useful to business or government economists who must make decisions based on a thorough understanding of labor market dynamics and current manpower development programs. Finally, perhaps those members of the general public with an interest in labor problems will find the book worthwhile reading.

Chapter 1 discusses the basic labor force concepts such as employment and unemployment. The second chapter focuses on the job structure of the U.S. economy as well as analyzing changes in the labor force participation rates of various worker groups. The next three chapters are concerned with the nature and composition of postwar unemployment. The controversy regarding whether the excessive unemployment of the late 1950s and early 1960s was due to a deficiency in aggregate demand or associated with structural changes in job requirements is carefully considered in the light of recent unemployment experience. Chapter 6 focuses on the interrelationships between unemployment, economic growth, and poverty. In addition, the recent shift in the Phillips Curve and attendant policy implications are discussed. The next chapter presents an evaluation of several major federal manpower programs whose goal is to provide training and education for the disadvantaged. The concluding chapter is concerned with labor force and employment projections for the year 1980. The accuracy of past manpower projections is also considered.

The author is grateful to the following authors, publishers, and journals for permission to quote copyrighted material: *Journal of Human Resources*; the McGraw Hill Book Company; the Johns Hopkins Press, *Education, Training and the Urban Ghetto* by Bennett Harrison; and the *Industrial and Labor Relations Review*, "The Jobs Corps Transition" by Joseph Pichler.

John Owen, Carl Schramm, and Martin Sorkin read the entire manuscript and their constructive comments are gratefully acknowledged, if not always heeded. Mrs. Peggy Bremer expertly typed the several drafts of the manuscript in a most expeditious manner. Sylvia Dovner edited the manuscript, and William C. Kiessel prepared the index. Finally, I wish to thank my wife Sylvia not only for encouraging me to undertake and complete this book, but for her patience during the many hours I was involved in the research and writing. It is to her that this book is dedicated.

**Education, Unemployment,
and Economic Growth**

# 1 The Anatomy of Employment and Unemployment

This chapter focuses on the major labor force concepts, such as employment and unemployment, which will be used throughout the book, and which are constantly referred to in the popular press and magazines. In addition, the various types of unemployment will be described.

It has been said that the unemployment rate is the most important single statistic published by the federal government. As stated by President Kennedy in 1961:

These [labor] statistics are of vital importance as measures of the economic health and well-being of the nation. They serve as guides to public policy in the development of measures designed to strengthen the economy, to improve programs to reemploy the unemployed, and to provide assistance to those who remain unemployed.[1]

This information is also useful to state and local governments as well as to business firms, labor unions, and various research and planning organizations.

During the mass unemployment of the 1930s widely differing estimates of the level of joblessness indicated the urgent need for reliable information on the number of employed and unemployed persons. A small group of economists and other social scientists in the Works Progress Administration developed an objective national survey measure of labor force behavior based on actual activity during a specified week.[2] Responsibility for the national sample survey (begun in 1940) was ultimately given to the Bureau of the Census, and the survey, known as the Current Population Survey, has remained the basis from which national statistics on employment and unemployment are derived.

The Current Population Survey is a monthly sample obtained by personal interview of approximately 50,000 households. In any month, the sample contains 8 groups, distinguished by the number of times the household has appeared in the survey. Each household included in the sample appears for 4 consecutive months, is dropped for 8 months, and then appears again for 4 consecutive months.

The survey is conducted by the Bureau of the Census for the Bureau of Labor Statistics. Persons are classified through a series of questions as to whether they held a job; and, if not, whether they were looking for employment or were not in the labor force. The data relate to the labor force status of individuals in the week that includes the 12th day of the month (the survey week) and are collected in the subsequent week (the interview week).[3]

3

Employed persons include those who undertake at least one hour's work for pay or profit during the survey week, as well as those absent from a job or business for such reasons as illness, vacations, or strikes. Moreover, those individuals who work 15 hours or more per week without pay in a family farm or business are also classified as employed.

To be counted as unemployed the individual cannot have worked at all during the survey week. In addition, he must have made a definite attempt to gain employment during the past four weeks. This could include applying directly to an employer or a private or public employment agency. It could also include checking out job possibilities with friends and relatives, and being available for work at the time of the survey. Persons who are on temporary layoff or who are waiting to begin a new job (within 30 days) need not meet these job search requirements in order to be classified as unemployed.

An individual who is unable to work is not counted as unemployed, even though he would like to work. Thus, persons who are mentally retarded, who suffer from severe emotional or psychological problems, or who are physically handicapped are generally excluded from the labor force.

The total labor force consists of the total of all individuals, 16 years of age and over, classified as employed or unemployed according to the above definitions. Those persons who are neither employed or unemployed are classified as "not in the labor force." Because the work ethic is thought to be deeply entwined within American cultural patterns, it is unlikely that many out-of-work men in the prime working ages (25 to 64) would readily admit to an interviewer that they have made no attempt to find employment or would not take a job if one were made available. Thus, in some circumstances it would take a highly trained interviewer to determine whether an individual was actually unemployed or simply not in the labor force. However, it is worth noting that at no time during the course of the interview is the term "unemployed" used, and as a consequence, the respondents themselves frequently do not know how they will be classified. Furthermore, no individual is asked whether or not he has applied for or is currently receiving unemployment compensation payments.

From the sample of 50,000 households, projections are made for the level and rate of unemployment in the United States. Since each individual in the sample represents 1,300 persons in the total population, a total of 5 million unemployed (the average level in 1972) would be represented by 3,800 individuals. At first glance, this appears to be a very small sample for obtaining nationwide employment statistics. However, the labor force survey is the largest monthly household survey in the world—50 times larger than many of the national public opinion polls—and is a scientifically selected sample that is studied and reviewed on a continuous basis.[4] In addition, the sample does yield consistent results month after month, which tends to lend credence to the sampling procedure. However, because these labor statistics are based on a sample survey, one must recognize that a degree of error does exist.

The statistics concerning employed and unemployed persons, as well as participation and non-participation in the labor force, are tabulated on the basis of a wide variety of characteristics such as sex, age, color, and level of educational attainment. Information is also collected on whether the employed individual works on a full or part-time basis; and for the unemployed, the duration of his unemployment as well as his reasons for being unemployed. Moreover, statistics are collected regarding the industry and occupation of both the employed and unemployed. Cross tabulations of a number of these latter characteristics are also available, on the basis of such attributes as race, sex, and age. However, a relatively high unemployment rate based on these statistics does not necessarily indicate that any one identifying characteristic is the explanation. Individuals of any given age, sex, or race group have many other attributes besides those enumerated that affect their relative employment status. For example, the unemployment rate for blacks is considerably higher than for whites; however, blacks have fewer years of schooling than whites, which thus limits their employability and accounts for their unemployment in addition to the race factor.

Sampling variability can be measured by determining the "standard error"—that is, the variations that might occur by chance because only a fraction of the population is surveyed. The chances are roughly 2 out of 3 that a sample estimate would differ from the results of a total count by less than the standard error; the chances are 9 out of 10 that it would differ by less than 1.6 times the standard error; the chances are 19 out of 20 that the difference would be less than twice the standard error. In its analysis of labor force data, the Bureau of Labor Statistics uses 1.6 times the standard error as the criteria for determining whether or not changes in the figures are statistically significant. For example, a variation in the level of total unemployment must exceed 150,000 from one month to the other in order to be considered statistically significant. Similarly, the national unemployment rate would have to change by 0.2 percentage point or more on a monthly basis to be significant. Movements that are smaller than these can reasonably be attributed to sampling variations.

Although "significant" is a statistical and therefore technical term in the interpretation of labor force developments, the word is frequently used in a more general sense, and there may be instances in which confusion arises over its use. If the overall unemployment rate declines by 0.2 percentage point from one month to the next, this is a "significant" change statistically. However, the decline would not be significant in the sense of being an important change. Thus, users of labor force statistics should consider the multiple meanings of this word when examining the data on employment and unemployment.

How does one determine which labor force changes are important? Several factors are considered. First, it is necessary to identify the groups in the work force that have the greatest economic or social significance, both in general and for a particular period. If employment in a major industry or important occupation is changing rapidly, the jobless rate for this industry or occupation should be carefully examined. Trends among a number of worker groups should also be given close attention—for example, married men and women, blue-collar workers, manufacturing workers, full-time workers, as well as those workers recently laid off.

In addition, the analyst studies those sectors of the labor force with higher than average unemployment rates. This is the case for black workers, teenagers, women, and construction workers. For example, the rate of black unemployment is nearly double that of white workers, and for a variety of reasons including the effectiveness of government anti-discrimination programs, this situation is carefully watched.

Finally, it is important to view changes in unemployment not only by considering the single month being examined, but also from a longer-term perspective. For example, during the recession of 1969-70, the rate of increase in joblessness among adult men greatly exceeded that among other age-sex groups, even though the rate was relatively low and many of the individual monthly changes were small. Because of the family responsibilities of these workers, any rise in their level of joblessness has considerable importance.

**Gross Flows**

Monthly statistics of the labor force and unemployment conceal a vast degree of movement between labor force categories. Generally, about half of the unemployed in one month will find jobs or leave the labor force in the next month, and about an equal number will be newly unemployed. Thus, in 1970, a year of rising unemployment, more than 14.5 million persons experienced at least one spell of joblessness, although the annual average was only 4.1 million. Similarly, there are many people moving into and out of the labor force each month. (See Table 1-1.) These statistics illustrate the March-April 1971 changes in the employment status of the population, 16 years of age and over.

Labor force statistics are frequently presented in the form of rates or percentages in order to facilitate understanding or comparison of changes. The unemployment rate refers to the percentage of the labor force that is jobless. For example, if a labor market contained 12,000 workers with 800 of them jobless, the unemployment rate would be 7.2 percent. This implies that the employment rate would be 92.8 percent (100 minus the unemployment rate). Labor force participation statistics can also be presented in the form of rates. The total population (16 years of age and over) was 146 million in 1972, of whom 89 million were in the labor force. Thus, the labor force participation rate in 1972 was approximately 61 percent.

**Table 1-1**

**Gross Flows in the Employment Status of Persons 16 Years and Over, Between March and April 1971 (Thousands)**

| Employment Status | March | | | April |
|---|---|---|---|---|
| | Employed | Unemployed | Not In Labor Force | |
| Employed | 74,240 | 1,508 | 2,660 | 78,409 |
| Unemployed | 1,018 | 2,409 | 1.067 | 4,494 |
| Not in Labor Force | 2,566 | 1,182 | 52,553 | 56,302 |

Source: John E. Bregger, "Unemployment Statistics and What They Mean," *Monthly Labor Review*, Vol. 94, No. 11, November 1971, p. 26.

**Criticisms of Unemployment Concepts and Statistics**

During the early 1960s as business conditions improved following the recession of 1960-61, unemployment rates remained relatively high. This situation led to criticism among both businessmen and academicians that the official figures on employment and unemployment were unreliable and misleading.

In November, 1961, President Kennedy appointed a committee of technical experts, chaired by Dr. Robert Gordon, to appraise the official figures on employment and unemployment and recommend any improvements they believed were required.[5]

The Gordon Committee found that there was no basis in fact for allegations that the official series on the labor force or the rates of employment and unemployment were unreliable; that the concepts used were inappropriate; or that the methods of data collection and statistical procedures were faulty or careless. They found that the figures were not misleading, provided that they were interpreted in the context of the concepts and definitions used. The Committee made no recommendations for major changes in concepts or statistical procedures. However, it did suggest that additional information on the labor force and labor market be gathered and published regularly to permit a more thorough analysis. For example, the Committee noted the absence of a useful set of job vacancy statistics and recommended that the Department of Labor initiate a program of research leading to the development of a comprehensive measure of job vacancies.[6] Such information would be useful both in developing job training programs related to actual manpower needs and in leading to more accurate measures of the demand for labor. Since 1969 this recommendation has been partially implemented in that the Department of Labor has been publishing a monthly series on job vacancies in manufacturing.

The Gordon Committee also recommended that information be collected, on a quarterly basis, regarding those persons not in the labor force. This survey would not only determine the characteristics of such persons but would also explain why they are not looking for work. While this suggestion has resulted in the collection of some information concerning these individuals, surveys of the non-labor force participants have not been undertaken on a quarterly basis. The data has been collected only occasionally for a portion of those not in the work force.[7]

Another important Committee recommendation was that labor statistics be made available on a comparable basis with those of other major industrialized countries. This suggestion has been implemented by an occasional Bureau of Labor Statistics study, but such projects have not been a regular undertaking.

In spite of the Gordon Committee's generally favorable conclusions regarding the overall adequacy of U.S. labor statistics, some important criticisms of current procedures can be made. First, one wonders whether it is necessary to rely so heavily on *sample* surveys. Could not these figures be supplemented by a complete biennial or triennial census of employment or unemployment? At present our only complete census of employment is taken from the decennial census of population. It is of interest that data obtained from the 1970 census indicate that prior estimates of the civilian labor force were 775,000 persons too low and that total employment levels were actually 300,000 above the estimates based on Bureau of Labor Statistics household surveys.[8]

A further criticism directed at the employment statistics is that the particular definitions adopted in the survey understate the true volume of unemployment by failing to include the "invisible unemployed." The "invisible unemployed" fall into several major categories:

1. *Persons working part-time but wishing full-time employment, if it could be obtained.* These individuals are considered underemployed. The additional hours these persons would work if they could find full-time employment represent a surplus of labor that is not indicated by the official unemployment rate. The reason is that the government figures include in the "employed" category anyone who has worked at least one hour for pay in the week preceding the survey. In 1972, there were almost 2.5 million workers employed part-time for economic reasons, of whom about 1.2 million normally work full-time but were unable to find full-time jobs.[9]

2. *Persons looking for work and, unable to find it, dropping out of the labor force.* When the rate of unemployment rises, many jobless workers become discouraged about employment prospects and cease to make a minimum effort to find work. Thus, in Great Britain during early 1972, the level of unemployment would have been 600,000 higher if the labor force dropouts had been included among the unemployed.[10]

3. *Seasonal workers wishing year-round employment, if it were available.* The

Bureau of the Census does not include seasonal workers in the labor force if they were neither working nor seeking work in the survey week. While many in this group may desire employment only on a part-year basis, there are no doubt many others who would prefer year-round employment but do not look for it because of their belief, based on past experience, that opportunities for their particular skills are lacking on an annual basis.

4. *Persons with physical and mental handicaps.* As indicated earlier, these individuals are generally treated as unemployable rather than unemployed and are excluded from the labor force. However, experiences during World War II and the activities of such organizations as Good Will have convinced employers that there is a definite place in industry for the blind, the crippled, and the mentally retarded. The U.S. Department of Labor has estimated that there are about 5 to 7 million handicapped workers who could be placed in industrial occupations. In considering statistics of unemployment, it is important to remember that concepts of employability are a function of the changing needs of the economy and that in the future we may consider persons to be unemployed who today are deemed unemployable.

Finally, the current concepts and methods can be criticized on a broad conceptual basis. According to contemporary economic thought in the United States, the basic economic agent from the production standpoint is the individual. Employment theories and policies, as well as employment objectives and manpower planning, all relate almost exclusively to the individual, apart from occasional references to the obstacles constituted by families to the geographic mobility of labor.

According to Mouly, an economic advisor to the International Labor Office, this orientation is questionable with reference to the industrialized economies of the Western World. Consider the two following examples:

1. In some cases employment is a group phenomenon—that is, the work is performed by all the members of the family together in accordance with their ability to be useful. This is true, for example, of family-owned shops in which each member specializes to a greater or lesser degree; it also applies to small holdings generally.

2. Even when there is no family business and the members of the restricted family all have separate occupations, decisions as to the employment of each individual are necessarily affected by the employment of the others. This is particularly apparent, for example, when one of the jobs is only a supplementary source of income; the conditions in which it is performed are then entirely "dominated" by the conditions in which the principal job is performed. It is probable that this "domination" which implies a principal job, is bound up with the quantitative relationship between the principal and supplementary incomes, and that the greater the gap, the more marked the domination.[11]

While such criticisms may have relevance for certain employment policies or income objectives, it is not clear that the employment definitions presented above would need to be modified to meet Mouly's criticisms, as far as industrialized countries are concerned. For example, as indicated earlier, unpaid family workers are counted as employed if they work for 15 hours a week or more. Moreover, while family employment decisions are not mutually exclusive the fact remains that it is the *individual worker* who holds a particular job, is unemployed or not in the labor force. Finally, while Mouly objects to the present "individual" orientation of labor force statistics he provides no guidance as to how these concepts would be refined if labor force statistics were collected on a "family"-oriented basis.

## Types of Unemployment

There are a number of categories of unemployment. These include cyclical, seasonal, frictional, as well as several other types of joblessness. Such a classification has relevance for public policy, and it enables economists, trade union officials, and government officials concerned with the problem of unemployment to formulate appropriate strategies to reduce it.

### Frictional Unemployment

Frictional unemployment consists of unemployed new entrants to the labor force, the seasonally unemployed, as well as those individuals who voluntarily quit one job and are presently unemployed because they have not been able to find another position. Thus, much of frictional unemployment is independent of the movement of the general business cycle; but certainly not all, since voluntary quit rates as well as labor force participation rates of secondary earners are positively related to overall economic activity.

There has been remarkably little research regarding the magnitude and other aspects of frictional unemployment. A special study carried out by the Bureau of Labor Statistics in the mid-1950s concluded that frictional unemployment during those years amounted to 2.4 percent of the civilian labor force. The 1955 to 1957 period was one characterized by high levels of economic activity with unemployment averaging around 4 percent of the work force. This implies that during periods of low unemployment over half of all *measured* unemployment is frictional.

More specifically, the Bureau of Labor Statistics found that voluntary shifts from one job to another accounted for roughly 10 percent of the unemployed. The continuing entry of new workers into the labor market (including those who re-entered after a period of being outside the labor force) made up an additional 20 percent of the unemployed. In addition, seasonal unemployment accounted for 20 percent of all the unemployed.[1][2]

There is no evidence to suggest that the rate of frictional unemployment has increased over time. A study published in 1966 concluded that there had been little change since the mid-1950s.[13]

Much of the joblessness occurring among women and teenagers is frictional. The great bulk of teenage unemployment (about 66 percent in 1972) consists of new entrants and re-entrants into the labor force. More than half of these in 1972 wanted only temporary work.[14] Moreover, nearly half of adult female unemployment in 1972 consisted of new workers and re-entrants, with slightly more than half being job losers or job leavers.[15]

The volume of frictional unemployment to some extent reflects the ability of workers to withstand some unemployment while they are looking for a job. The relatively high earnings of American workers permit many families to build up sufficient savings so that economic pressure does not force an individual to take the first position available. However, measures that improve the mobility of labor, such as employment exchanges, aptitude testing, and the collection of adequate job vacancy information, will tend to reduce the volume of frictional unemployment because workers will be better informed and less likely to quit one job before they have obtained another.

*Seasonal Unemployment*

Seasonal unemployment results from changes in business activity during the year caused by climatic or other seasonal changes in supply. It is also related to varying seasonal demands reflecting custom, habit, or religious observances. The agricultural industry, for example, reflects the direct influence of the weather and is therefore strongly susceptible to seasonal variation in output and employment. Moreover, a number of industries involved in agricultural processing are likewise subject to seasonal fluctuation in employment due to the availability or non-availability of the raw material upon which their enterprise depends. As the importance of agricultural employment in our economy has declined, this major component of seasonal change has diminished in importance. (However, migratory farm workers, who suffer acutely from seasonal unemployment, still present an unsolved social problem because of their low incomes and shameful housing conditions.)

Focusing on seasonal variation in demand, these changes are particularly evident in those industries that produce consumption goods for sale at a particular time of the year. Christmas decorations and Easter clothes are but two examples. Many retail establishments account for nearly 50 percent of their total sales in the 4 weeks between Thanksgiving and Christmas and, as a result, must hire extra sales personnel on a temporary basis.

The largest seasonal employment upsurge occurs between May and June with nearly 2 million young people entering the labor market at the end of the school year. To determine the economic meaning of a month's unemployment data relative to the previous month or months, it is essential to differentiate between the change that actually occurs in the month and the change, if any, that exceeded the normal, or expected change. Therefore, all of the major labor force estimates are "seasonally adjusted" to permit an easy and more revealing comparison of data for one month with any other.[16]

Without the separation of the seasonal component from other changes in labor statistics, the continuing trend in the labor market situation would be very difficult to discern. Moreover, since most other economic statistics such as Gross National Product and industrial production, are widely used in seasonally adjusted form, the adjusted labor force data are made comparable with them.

*Cyclical Unemployment*

Cyclical unemployment reflects changes in the number of jobless workers as a result of fluctuations in overall economic activity. During a period of recession or depression most unemployment is of a cyclical nature as opposed to prosperity when the majority of job seekers can be classified as frictionally unemployed. Table 1-2 indicates changes in the level of unemployment by quarter for the period of 1957 to 1959. This period encompasses the recession of 1957-58, the nation's most severe postwar recession. (This recession com-

**Table 1-2**
**Unemployment Rates by Quarter, 1957 to 1959**

| Year | | Unemployment Rate |
|------|-----|------------------|
| 1957 | I | 4.1 |
| | II | 4.1 |
| | III | 4.3 |
| | IV | 4.9 |
| 1958 | I | 6.5 |
| | II | 7.2 |
| | III | 7.4 |
| | IV | 6.4 |
| 1959 | I | 6.0 |
| | II | 5.0 |
| | III | 5.4 |
| | IV | 5.6 |

Source: Computed from U.S. Department of Commerce, *Economic Report of the President, 1960*, (Washington, D.C.: U.S. Government Printing Office, 1960), Table D-17, p. 175.

menced in August 1957, and the economy reached a low point in April 1958, after which a recovery began that continued through the remainder of 1958 and all of 1959.)

Although production levels reached a low point in April 1958, unemployment reached a postwar high of 7.5 percent in August 1958. Typically the downturn in unemployment lags several months behind the upswing in production. This phenomena occurs because employers are reluctant to recall laid-off workers until they are fairly certain that business conditions have improved. Moreover, there is the normal growth in the labor force that must be absorbed as well as the rehiring of the employees who were laid off during the recession period.

The burden of cyclical unemployment is not spread evenly. Some industries and occupations suffer major declines in employment while others are essentially insulated from variations in overall economic activity. Employment in manufacturing, especially durable goods manufacturing, is quite sensitive to business fluctuations. However, employment in the service industries has shown a persistent upward trend for many years that is relatively unaffected by changes in economic conditions. Because our economy has gradually shifted from goods producing to services, shifts in economic conditions have a smaller effect on employment levels than previously.

## Structural Unemployment

Discussions regarding structural unemployment engender considerable controversy regarding its relative magnitude as well as the attendant policy implications. (The policy implications of a high level of structural unemployment are discussed in some detail in Chapter 5.) Basically, structural unemployment results from a mismatching of the skills and abilities of the unemployed in comparison with the employment requirements of industry. This mismatching is generally attributed to various changes in the job structure of the United States' economy. For example, workers in Appalachia may remain unemployed because they are unable or unwilling to accept employment outside the region. Poorly educated workers continue jobless because available jobs require a high school diploma. Automation may lead to layoffs of production workers whose specialized skills are obsolete and not necessarily transferable to other jobs. While most economists would accept the fact that there is some structural unemployment, there is considerable disagreement about its magnitude and social significance. However, there is no doubt that there is a structural unemployment problem for certain types of workers. Thus, in 1972 the unemployment rate for 16 to 19 year olds was 16.2 percent, compared to a rate of 2.8 percent for married males; in 1969, a year of very tight labor markets, the rate for teenagers was 12.2 percent, compared to 1.5 percent for married males.[17] The persistence of this large differential in both good times and bad suggests that factors other than the lack of aggregate demand (cyclical unemployment) cause the differential.

### Disguised Unemployment

With respect to industrialized countries, there is a type of *qualitative* unemployment in which an individual holds a position that does not require full utilization of his skills or training. For example, during the depression of the 1930s many college graduates accepted clerical and sales positions because these were the only jobs available.

In underdeveloped economies disguised unemployment is generally associated with the existence of surplus labor in the agricultural sector. Thus, it is argued that the agricultural labor force could be appreciably reduced without changing the total volume of agricultural output. In effect, this implies that the marginal productivity of these "surplus" workers is zero.

The densely populated countries of Southeast Asia probably have high levels of disguised unemployment. A United Nations report of the early 1950s indicates that in many regions of the Philippines, Pakistan and India, the surplus of population is 20 to 25 percent.[18] A general estimate is that 25 percent of the population of this region represents surplus labor.[19] A recent study by Robinson indicates that between 1951 and 1961 the degree of disguised unemployment in Bangladesh increased sharply amounting to some 20 percent of the 1961 labor force.[20] However, Schultz questions the existence of this underemployment and states that it probably does not exceed 5 percent of the labor force.[21] Although there is certainly a need for more and better empirical evidence, most observers do believe that labor is usually the most wasted resource in most poor countries.

### Discouraged Workers (Hidden Unemployment)

Discouraged workers are those persons outside the labor force who want work but are not actively looking for a job because they think their search would be in vain.[22] In order to identify discouraged workers, the interviewer asks first whether the persons not in the labor force "want a regular job now, either full-time or part-time." If the answer is yes, or even a tentative yes, there is a follow-up question asking the reasons they are not looking for work. In order to be classified as discouraged, a person's principal reasons for not looking for work must fall into one of the following five categories:

1. Believes no work available in line of work or area;
2. Has tried out but could not find work;
3. Lacks necessary schooling, training, skills, or experience;
4. Employers think too young or too old;
5. Other personal handicap in finding a job.[23]

Table 1-3 indicates the relationship between the overall unemployment rate and the number of discouraged workers. Despite the positive relationship between the rate of unemployment and the number of discouraged workers, the two series did not correlate very highly with each other. The coefficient of correlation between monthly changes in the two variables was only 0.53.

Since it may be assumed that changes in the number of discouraged workers lag behind the fluctuations in the unemployment rate, one can relate variations in the number of discouraged workers to the unemployment rate 3 and 6 months later. This raises the correlation coefficient to 0.61 in both cases—again indicating only a moderately strong relationship.[24]

It is not clear why there is not a closer relationship between changes in the number of discouraged workers and the overall unemployment rate. Perhaps the survey questions fail to determine the actual number of discouraged workers or that a large proportion of discouraged workers are so classified because of structural changes in the economy and not as a result of relatively short-term economic fluctuations.

Most discouraged workers are women and teenagers who are generally under less economic pressure than adult males to persist in a seemingly futile job hunt. In 1971 these groups constituted three-quarters of all discouraged workers.[25]

**Table 1-3**
**Unemployment Rate and Number of Discouraged Workers, 1967 to 1972**

| Year | Discouraged Workers (Thousands) | Unemployment Rate (Percent) |
|------|---------------------------------|-----------------------------|
| 1967 | 732 | 3.8 |
| 1968 | 667 | 3.6 |
| 1969 | 574 | 3.5 |
| 1970 | 638 | 4.9 |
| 1971 | 774 | 5.9 |
| 1972 | 765 | 5.6 |

Source: Data for Discouraged Workers from Paul O. Flaim, "Discouraged Workers and Changes in Unemployment," *Monthly Labor Review*, Vol. 96, March 1973, p. 11. Data on overall unemployment rate from U.S. Department of Labor, *Manpower Report of the President, March, 1973*, (Washington, D.C.: U.S. Government Printing Office, 1973), Table A-18, p. 180.

Also included in this category are elderly persons who might be induced out of retirement if they had a high probability of obtaining employment.

The number of discouraged workers should be added to the number classified as unemployed to determine the *total* under-utilization of manpower accompanying a recession. However, as indicated in Table 1-3, the increase in the number of discouraged workers, as currently defined, was relatively small when compared with the magnitude of the changes in unemployment. This being the case, it would be unreasonable to assume that the return of these workers to the job market as economic conditions improve could be of such magnitude as to act as a major break against the lowering of the unemployment rate.

## Summary

Labor statistics are derived from a large-scale household survey conducted each month. Information is collected on the employment status of the individual as well as a number of other characteristics such as age, race, occupation, and industry, which facilitates the study of employment changes among various worker groups.

A number of criticisms of labor force concepts were discussed. While some of the Gordon Committee's recommendations have been implemented, there is considerable scope for broadening the data base (e.g., job vacancy statistics) as well as carrying out in depth studies of particular employment phenomena such as the level and comparability of international labor force statistics with United States' data.

The various types of unemployment were described. It was observed that during recessions cyclical unemployment constitutes a high proportion of total unemployment, but during prosperity frictional unemployment accounts for a major share of joblessness.

# 2 The American Labor Force

This chapter concentrates on labor force developments that have taken place in the past 25 years. Employment and unemployment changes, as well as shifts in the job structure of the work force, are noted. In addition, considerable attention focuses on the labor force participation rates of various worker groups, particularly married women.

The most positive labor force development of the postwar period has been the strong upward trend in total employment. (See Table 2-1.) In fact, during the last 25 years total employment has failed to increase above the previous year's level only four times. Moreover, the annual declines that did occur were fairly small. In no case did employment fall by more than 1.8 percent. Finally, each annual decline was followed by a strong upturn in employment the following year.

In retrospect it seems clear that at no time between the end of World War II and 1973 did a major decline in economic activity and employment appear imminent. While recessions did occur in 1948-49, 1953-54, 1957-58, 1960-61, and 1969-70, these declines in economic activity were relatively mild and of short duration in comparison to prewar business fluctuations. Prompt use of some of the discretionary tools of macroeconomic policy probably contributed to both the mildness and the brevity of the recessions; but no important new policy tools were adopted for the purpose of moderating them, nor were the existing measures always applied vigorously.

The annual unemployment rate has never risen to 7 percent in the postwar period, in contrast to the much higher rates prior to World War II. For instance, in early 1933 nearly 25 percent of the labor force was unemployed, and the rate of joblessness did not fall below 15 percent for the remainder of that decade. This postwar decline in unemployment rates, however, does not mean that unemployment has not been a problem. First, a moderate or low overall rate can be associated with very high unemployment levels for specific groups. (See Chapter 3.) Secondly, while unemployment has not approached the levels of the depressed 1930s, there have been relatively few peacetime years in which jobless rates have been as low as 4 percent—the level that many economists consider a "full-employment" unemployment rate. Thus, between 1948 and 1972, the annual unemployment rate was near or below the 4 percent level 11 times, but during 7 of those years the United States was involved in major wars (Korea and Vietnam). Therefore, during only 4 of the 18 peacetime years that have elapsed since 1948 was the goal of "full employment" achieved. However, in 1958 and

**Table 2-1**

**Employment Status of the Non-Institutional Population 16 Years and Over: Annual Average 1948 to 1972**

| Year | Total (Thousands) | Civilian Labor Force (Thousands) | | | | Not in Labor Force (Thousands) |
|---|---|---|---|---|---|---|
| | | Employed | | Unemployed | | |
| | | Number | Percent of Labor Force | Number | Percent of Labor Force | |
| 1948 | 60,621 | 58,344 | 96.2 | 2,276 | 3.8 | 42,447 |
| 1949 | 61,286 | 57,649 | 94.1 | 3,637 | 5.9 | 42,708 |
| 1950 | 62,208 | 58,920 | 94.7 | 3,288 | 5.3 | 42,787 |
| 1951 | 62.017 | 59.962 | 96.7 | 2,055 | 3.3 | 42,604 |
| 1952 | 62,138 | 60,254 | 97.0 | 1,883 | 3.0 | 43,093 |
| 1953 | 63,015 | 61,181 | 97.1 | 1,834 | 2.9 | 44,041 |
| 1954 | 63,643 | 60,110 | 94.5 | 3,532 | 5.5 | 44,678 |
| 1955 | 65,023 | 62,171 | 95.6 | 2,852 | 4.4 | 44,660 |
| 1956 | 66,552 | 63,802 | 95.9 | 2,750 | 4.1 | 44,402 |
| 1957 | 66,929 | 64,071 | 95.7 | 2,859 | 4.3 | 45,336 |
| 1958 | 67,639 | 63,036 | 93.2 | 4,602 | 6.8 | 46,088 |
| 1959 | 68,369 | 64,630 | 94.5 | 3,740 | 5.5 | 46,960 |
| 1960 | 69,628 | 65,778 | 94.5 | 3,852 | 5.5 | 47,617 |
| 1961 | 70,459 | 65,746 | 93.3 | 4,714 | 6.7 | 48,312 |
| 1962 | 70,614 | 66,702 | 94.5 | 3,911 | 5.5 | 49,539 |
| 1963 | 71,833 | 67,762 | 94.3 | 4,070 | 5.7 | 50,583 |
| 1964 | 73,091 | 69,305 | 94.8 | 3,786 | 5.2 | 51,394 |
| 1965 | 74,455 | 71,088 | 95.5 | 3,366 | 4.5 | 52,058 |
| 1966 | 75,770 | 72,895 | 96.2 | 2,875 | 3.8 | 52,288 |
| 1967 | 77,347 | 74,372 | 96.2 | 2,975 | 3.8 | 52,527 |
| 1968 | 78,737 | 75,920 | 96.4 | 2,817 | 3.6 | 53,291 |
| 1969 | 80,733 | 77,902 | 96.5 | 2,831 | 3.5 | 53,602 |
| 1970 | 82,715 | 78,627 | 95.1 | 4,088 | 4.9 | 54,280 |
| 1971 | 84,113 | 79,120 | 94.1 | 4,993 | 5.9 | 55,666 |
| 1972 | 86,542 | 81,702 | 94.4 | 4,830 | 5.6 | 56,784 |

Source: Council of Economic Advisors, *Economic Report of the President, 1973* (Washington, D.C.: U.S. Government Printing Office, 1973), Table C-24, p. 220.

1961 when the average annual unemployment rates were the highest of the postwar period (see Table 2-1), the total employment rate was over 93 percent. Thus, even in recession years, over 9 out of 10 Americans in the labor force had jobs. (Because the data in Table 2-1 are annual averages, they obscure the fact that during any given year many more individuals experience one or more spells of unemployment than are indicated by the yearly statistics. For example, during 1970 the average monthly level of unemployment was 4.1 million, but 14.5 million persons experienced some unemployment in 1970.)

**The Changing Job Structure**

In this section attention is focused on *characteristics of the jobs* held by workers in the postwar period. One major employment change that has occurred is the large decline in the number of agricultural workers. (See Table 2-2.) Although total employment increased by more than 23 million between 1948 and 1972, the number of persons employed in agriculture declined by 4.5 million. In 1972 only about 5 percent of all persons had jobs in agriculture, compared to 14 percent in 1948. While the decline in agricultural employment has been continuous, there is some evidence that the exodus from farm employment tends to accelerate when job opportunities in the non-agricultural sector of the economy are more plentiful; it tends to decelerate when job opportunities in the non-agricultural sector become scarce. This may explain the relatively small employment decline in 1971-72, but the high prices for farm products and concomitant increases in farm income may also be partly responsible.

Traditionally, most farms in the United States have been classified as family farms—that is, the bulk of the labor is supplied by the owner and his family. Thus, the postwar reduction in the number of persons employed in agriculture is attributable primarily to a decrease in the number of farms. The proportion of all employed persons who have jobs as wage or salary workers in agriculture has always been small, and this has not changed very much from 1948 to 1972. Over the same period the number of self-employed workers in agriculture declined by

**Table 2-2**
**Average Agricultural and Non-Agricultural Employment, 1947 to 1972**

| Years | Total Employment (Thousands) | Agricultural | Non-Agricultural |
|---|---|---|---|
| 1947-49 | 57,675 | 7,725 | 49,950 |
| 1950-52 | 59,713 | 6,796 | 52,917 |
| 1953-55 | 61,155 | 6,305 | 54,850 |
| 1956-58 | 63,636 | 5,939 | 57,697 |
| 1959-61 | 65,384 | 5,408 | 59,976 |
| 1962-64 | 67,924 | 4,718 | 63,206 |
| 1965-67 | 72,771 | 4,048 | 68,723 |
| 1968-70 | 77,483 | 3,628 | 73,855 |
| 1971-72 | 80,411 | 3,430 | 76,981 |

Source: Council of Economic Advisors, *Economic Report of the President, 1973* (Washington, D.C.: U.S. Government Printing Office, 1973), p. 220.

approximately 3 million and the number of unpaid family workers declined by approximately 1 million.

The decrease in the number of self-employed and unpaid family workers in agriculture has not been offset by comparable increases in the number of these workers employed in non-agricultural industries. The proportion of unpaid family workers in non-agricultural industries has only increased slightly, while the proportion of self-employed workers in non-agricultural industries has also declined.

Thus, as agricultural employment fell, both the proportion of self-employed and unpaid family workers in the total labor force declined. The proportion of wage and salary workers rose, however, from 78.3 percent of all workers in 1948, to 90.1 percent in 1972.[1] The increasing fraction of wage and salary workers has economic significance because these workers are more vulnerable to spells of unemployment than self-employed individuals or unpaid family workers.

## Employment by Industry

The percentage distribution of workers by major industry groups from 1947 to 1972 is shown in Table 2-3. The increase in the relative importance of government employment is indicated by the nearly 50 percent increase in the percentage of workers employed by government agencies. Most of this increase can be accounted for by the rapid growth of employment in state and local government. The total number of such employees has nearly tripled since 1947.

The second largest increase occurred in the services industries, which employed nearly 17 percent of all workers in 1972, compared to 11.5 percent in 1947. This sector encompasses such rapidly growing fields as health services and education. The percentage of employees working in wholesale and retail trade, as well as contract construction, have remained constant, while the proportion employed in manufacturing has declined.

The effect of these changes in the industrial structure of employment is a relative decrease in the proportion of jobs in the goods-producing industries and a relative increase in the proportion of jobs in the service-producing industries. Thus, in the period of 1947 to 1949, 41.2 percent of the non-agricultural work force was employed in goods-producing industries, compared to 58.8 percent in service-producing industries. In the period 1971 to 1972, the percentage of workers in the latter had increased to 68.2 percent. A closely related phenomenon has also occurred within the goods-producing industries themselves. In most of these industries the proportion of jobs directly related to production has decreased since the end of World War II, while the percentage of non-production workers has increased. In manufacturing, for example, non-production employees constituted 16.4 percent of all employees in 1947, as compared with

**Table 2-3**
**Major Industry Group of Employed Persons, Non-Agricultural Establishments, 1947 to 1972**

| Year | Mining | Contract Construction | Manufacturing | | Transportation and Public Utilities | Wholesale and Retail Trade | Finance Insurance and Real Estate | Services | Government |
| --- | --- | --- | --- | --- | --- | --- | --- | --- | --- |
| | | | Durable Goods | Non-Durable Goods | | | | | |
| 1947-49 | 2.2 | 4.7 | 18.2 | 16.1 | 9.3 | 20.8 | 4.1 | 11.7 | 12.8 |
| 1950-52 | 1.9 | 5.3 | 18.7 | 15.3 | 8.8 | 20.6 | 4.2 | 11.8 | 13.4 |
| 1953-55 | 1.6 | 5.3 | 19.2 | 14.7 | 8.3 | 20.7 | 4.5 | 12.1 | 13.5 |
| 1956-58 | 1.6 | 5.5 | 18.2 | 13.9 | 7.9 | 20.7 | 4.7 | 12.9 | 14.5 |
| 1959-61 | 1.3 | 5.4 | 17.3 | 13.5 | 7.4 | 21.0 | 5.0 | 13.8 | 15.5 |
| 1962-64 | 1.1 | 5.2 | 17.0 | 13.0 | 6.9 | 20.8 | 5.1 | 14.7 | 16.3 |
| 1965-67 | 1.0 | 5.1 | 17.4 | 12.4 | 6.5 | 20.8 | 4.9 | 15.0 | 16.9 |
| 1968-70 | 0.9 | 4.8 | 16.6 | 11.8 | 6.3 | 20.9 | 5.1 | 16.0 | 17.5 |
| 1971-72 | 0.9 | 4.6 | 15.0 | 11.3 | 6.3 | 21.5 | 5.4 | 16.9 | 18.2 |

Source: U.S. Department of Labor, *Manpower Report of the President, March, 1973* (Washington, D.C.: U.S. Government Printing Office, 1973), Table C-1, p. 215.

26.9 percent in 1972. Moreover, in mining, the number of production workers declined by over 400,000 in the postwar period, while the number of non-production workers *rose* by over 60,000.[2]

## Occupational Distribution of Employed Workers

The occupational distribution of workers in 1940, 1960, and 1970 is presented in Table 2-4. The major change that has occurred is the threefold increase in the percentage of professional and technical workers in the labor force. One causal factor is the large increase in consumer incomes and leisure time and improvement in living standards, which has permitted persons to spend more on education, health, entertainment, recreation, and other professional services. Another reason for this rapid employment growth is the increasingly complex and scientific character of industrial operations, as well as a major increase in government sponsored research. Both of these developments require large numbers of research scientists, engineers, and technical assistants to undertake basic and applied research.

**Table 2-4**

**Occupational Composition of the United States Labor Force, 1940, 1960, and 1970**

| Occupational Group | 1940 | 1960 | 1970 |
|---|---|---|---|
| Professional, Technical, and Kindred Workers | 4.6 | 11.4 | 14.2 |
| Farmers and Farm Managers | 17.3 | 4.2 | 2.2 |
| Managers, Officials, and Proprietors, Except Farm | 7.2 | 10.7 | 10.5 |
| Clerical and Kindred Workers | 5.5 | 14.8 | 17.4 |
| Sales Workers | 5.0 | 6.4 | 6.2 |
| Craftsmen, Foremen, and Kindred Workers | 11.7 | 13.0 | 12.9 |
| Operatives and Kindred Workers | 14.1 | 18.2 | 17.7 |
| Service Workers | 9.6 | 12.2 | 12.4 |
| Farm Laborers and Foremen | 13.4 | 3.6 | 1.7 |
| Laborers, except Farm and Mine | 11.6 | 5.4 | 4.7 |

Source: Data for 1940 from U.S. Bureau of the Census, 1940 Census of Population, *The Labor Force* (Washington, D.C.: U.S. Government Printing Office, 1943), Table 62, pp. 88-89; data for 1960 and 1970 from U.S. Department of Labor, *Manpower Report of the President, 1972* (Washington, D.C.: U.S. Government Printing Office, 1972), Table A-11, p. 172.

The sustained decline in the percentage of farmers and farm workers is partly due to the rapid pace of farm mechanization and the productivity gains in agriculture that have caused a drastic decrease in agricultural manpower requirements. In addition, the incomes of farm operators have lagged far behind those earned by individuals employed in non-agricultural occupations, thus providing a strong incentive for individuals to leave agriculture. For example, in 1970 the median earnings of all males was $7,685 compared to only $1,776 for all farm workers.[3]

There has been a rapid growth both in the numbers and proportion of workers classified as clerical employees. Almost three-fourths of these workers are women, and this occupational group has shown the greatest increase in female employment. The large increase in the number of clerical jobs reflects the expansion of service industries—government, finance and insurance, trade, and communications—in which clerical workers are especially important. It also reflects the growing size, complexity, and mechanization of industrial operations, all of which require more and more people to distribute and keep records on the goods that fewer and fewer workers are producing. This employment increase in clerical jobs has occurred despite the labor-saving effects of computers and new office equipment and indicates the mounting volume of paper work in business and government.

Despite fears that the advent of mass production and automation would reduce the need for skilled manual workers, blue-collar employment (craftsmen, operatives, and non-farm laborers) has continued to grow (in absolute terms) with the largest increase among craftsmen and foremen. Manufacturing employs a greater number of craftsmen than any other industry group; but in construction, craftsmen form a higher proportion of the work force—one-half, compared with one-fifth in manufacturing and transportation and fewer than one-tenth in other industries.[4] Operatives and kindred workers, or semiskilled employees, remain the largest single occupational group, with about 14 million workers in 1970, or almost one-fifth of all employment. Operatives in factories account for every three out of five semiskilled workers; among the non-factory operatives, the largest group are drivers of trucks, buses, and taxicabs. Over the first half of this century operatives' employment increased sharply as technological innovations caused industries to use mass production processes that demanded many operative level workers. As these processes became well established, more sophisticated advances, including automation, gradually slowed down the employment growth.

**Labor Force Participation**

Previously, attention has been focused on the types of jobs held by American workers. Let us now consider the *characteristics of the job holders.* One approach is to examine changes in the labor force participation rates of various groups of workers in the labor force.

Statistics on labor force participation rates by age and sex and the proportion of each age-sex group in the total work force are indicated in Table 2-5. The major change of the postwar period has been a sharp increase in the labor force participation rates of women, with the greatest increase occurring among women in the 35 to 64 age group. During the 1960s women entered the labor force three times faster than men, and for the first time, married men—the group that had previously constituted the bulk of the labor force—dropped to less than half of all workers. A large share of newly married women are working; an increasing number of married women return to work while their children are relatively young.

In 1947, female labor force participation rates peaked at age 18 to 19 and declined steadily thereafter. However, in 1972, female participation rates varied

**Table 2-5**

**Participation Rates and Percentage Distribution of the Civilian Labor Force, 1947 and 1972, by Age and Sex**

| Age-Sex | 1947 | | 1972 | |
|---|---|---|---|---|
| | Participation Rate | Percent of Labor Force | Participation Rate | Percent of Labor Force |
| Total | 58.9% | 100.0% | 60.9% | 100.0% |
| Male | 86.6 | 72.6 | 79.7 | 61.5 |
| 16-17 | 52.2 | 1.9 | 48.3 | 2.2 |
| 18-19 | 80.5 | 3.1 | 72.0 | 2.9 |
| 20-24 | 84.9 | 8.4 | 85.9 | 7.7 |
| 25-34 | 95.8 | 17.4 | 95.9 | 14.1 |
| 35-44 | 98.0 | 15.8 | 96.5 | 11.9 |
| 45-54 | 95.5 | 12.9 | 93.3 | 12.0 |
| 55-64 | 89.6 | 9.3 | 80.5 | 8.2 |
| 65 and over | 47.8 | 3.9 | 24.4 | 2.3 |
| Female | 31.8 | 27.4 | 43.9 | 38.5 |
| 16-17 | 29.5 | 1.0 | 36.6 | 1.7 |
| 18-19 | 52.3 | 2.0 | 55.6 | 2.4 |
| 20-24 | 44.9 | 4.5 | 59.1 | 6.1 |
| 25-34 | 32.0 | 6.2 | 47.6 | 7.5 |
| 35-44 | 36.3 | 6.0 | 52.0 | 7.0 |
| 45-54 | 32.7 | 4.5 | 53.9 | 7.6 |
| 55-64 | 24.3 | 2.5 | 42.1 | 4.9 |
| 65 and over | 8.1 | 0.7 | 9.3 | 1.3 |

Source: U.S. Department of Labor, *Manpower Report of the President, March, 1973* (Washington, D.C.: U.S. Government Printing Office, 1973), p. 128.

little for women between the ages of 18 and 54. Since the beginning of this century, labor force participation rates of women have doubled.[5]

There are two important factors that have increased the labor force participation rates of women generally. First, there has been an increase in the productivity of women in the household as a result of the proliferation of household appliances and the availability of manufactured food and clothing, as well as services, bought by the female homemaker. This productivity increase has freed the homemaker from some of the drudgery involved in housework and allowed more time to be made available for employment outside the home.

Secondly, the secular increase in female labor force participation is associated with the reduction in the length of the work week. A shorter work week has permitted an increasing number of women to maintain a home at the same time that they hold a full- or part-time job. Clarence Long found a close association between the reduction in the average full-time work week for all major industry groups and the increase in female labor force participation.[6] This relationship was observed in both urban and rural areas.

For males there has been a decline in labor force participation rates among teenagers, reflecting a lengthening of the time spent in school. A decline in participation has also occurred among men over 45. (See Table 2-5.) This latter decline is partly due to the growth of governmental as well as private pension plans, including some union provisions for early retirement at nearly full pay. Because of a decline in participation rates of younger and older males, their proportion in the labor force has declined slightly despite an increase in the number of such males in the total population.

Adult men reach a peak participation rate of about 97 percent in their mid-20s, and this percentage remains roughly constant until age 55. Job stability increases as the male worker matures. A 55-year-old man can be expected to stay on the same job over 7 years, or about 1.5 times longer than a man of 20.

In spite of shifts in the age-sex composition of the labor force, overall labor force participation rates have been essentially unchanged since World War II. Since that time, annual labor force participation rates have fluctuated narrowly, between 59 and 61 percent of the total non-institutional population of the United States. During the same period, male rates have declined steadily from 87 to 80 percent, while the comparable rates for women rose from 32 to 44 percent.

Excluding the 3.2 million in the armed forces, the civilian labor force totaled 83 million in 1972. This left 56.8 million outside the work force. (See Table 2-1.) Surveys taken from 1967 to 1972 indicate that about 90 percent of all non-participation was voluntary—that is, the individual interviewed did not want a full- or part-time job.[8] This latter group included full-time students, housewives, and retired workers. Ten percent of those interviewed were reported as wanting a regular full- or part-time job but most were indecisive as to whether they would look for work in the near future. When these "involuntary" non-participants were asked why they were not looking for work, 60 percent of the men cited ill health or the fact that they were in school. For women, about one-half cited family and child-care responsibilities. The "involuntary" non-participants were poorly educated. Only a third were high school graduates (compared with about 50 percent of all non-workers) and also disproportionately black (23 percent compared to only 10 percent of all non-participants).[9]

## Labor Force Participation Rates of Married Women

Over the past 25 years the labor force participation rates of married women have doubled. However, this rapid increase is actually the continuation of a change that began at the turn of the century. Since that time, participation rates of married women have increased fivefold, and their share of the labor force has risen sixfold to about one-fifth.[10]

Before analyzing the factors accounting for the increase in the labor force participation rates of married women over time, let us examine this phenomenon as it occurs at any given moment of time. (See Table 2-6.) The statistics indicate that the higher the husband's income, the higher the wife's participation, up to the $5,000 to $7,000 income level, at which the rate is 47 percent. Thereafter, the percentage of wives at work outside the home falls rapidly to a low of 18 percent for those with husbands earning $25,000 or more.

**Table 2-6**
**Labor Force Participation of Wives, March 1969, by Earnings of Husband in 1968**

| Earnings of Husband | Percent of All Wives in Labor Force |
|---|---|
| <$1,000 | 33 |
| $1,000-2,000 | 38 |
| 2,000-3,000 | 42 |
| 3,000-4,000 | 44 |
| 4,000-5,000 | 45 |
| 5,000-6,000 | 47 |
| 6,000-7,000 | 47 |
| 7,000-8,000 | 45 |
| 8,000-10,000 | 41 |
| 10,000-15,000 | 35 |
| 15,000-25,000 | 26 |
| 25,000 & over | 18 |

Source: Herman P. Miller, "Profile of the Blue Collar American," in *Blue-Collar Worker*, edited by Sar Levitan, (New York: McGraw Hill, 1971).

From their 1964 survey, Morgan, Baerwaldt, and Sirageldin found a similar relationship between the percentage of wives who worked for money and the income of their husbands. Specifically, for all wives under 65 years of age, the variation was as follows: 37 percent of the wives whose husbands' incomes were $3,000, or less, worked in 1964; 55 percent, with husbands' incomes of $3,000 to $7,500; 42 percent with $7,500 to $10,000; and 32 percent, with $10,000 or more.[11] Thus, wives are less likely to work if their husbands' incomes are very high or very low. The latter probably reflects to some extent low labor force participation rate of women in rural areas since most of the very low male earners were engaged in agricultural occupations.

Thus, excluding those males with below average earnings, the evidence indicates that at any point in time, the higher the husband's income, the less likely is the wife to work outside the home. Through time, however, husbands' incomes have risen but *at the same time* wives' labor force participation rates have also increased. How are we to explain this seemingly paradoxical situation? The different implications of cross-section and time-series data was first resolved by Jacob Mincer who showed that while husbands' earnings have been rising, wives' earning potentials have also been increasing. The positive correlation of wives' desire to work with their own potential earnings more than offsets the negative impact of their husbands' higher incomes, with the result that increasing proportions of wives have joined the labor force each year.[12] This factor has also been verified by Cain whose findings about female educational attainment add supporting evidence of two sorts. First, a positive effect of education on the labor force participation of wives was established with cross-section data, and the increase of both education and participation over time is consistent with this finding. Second, the hypothesis of a large potential wage effect for wives is supported since education is a variable that is not only associated with higher earnings but reflects partly the non-money returns to labor such as the level of fringe benefits and pleasant working conditions.[13]

Another factor increasing the labor force participation rate of married women is the trend toward smaller families. The decline in birth rates that dates from the late 1950s and the emergence of the two-child norm for American families have reduced the burden of child-care responsibilities.

The contribution of wives' earnings to the rising standard of living of American families is substantial. For those families with incomes above the median, the earnings of wives account for about a quarter of the family's total income. Considering families with lower incomes, wives' earnings account for about one-sixth of total family income.[14]

The studies of labor force participation of women undertaken by Long, Mincer, Cain and Bowen and Finegan, emphasized the role of supply factors (such as education and husbands' earnings) in raising female labor force participation. A recent survey by Oppenheimer has examined the influence of the demand for women workers. For the 1950 to 1960 decade, she found that almost half of the net increase in the numbers of employed females occurred in occupations in which at least 70 percent of the workers were women, and almost 60 percent of the increase occurred in occupations that had a majority of women. She concludes that "there is substantial evidence that the demand for female labor has been increasing over the years. Furthermore, this rising demand can, to a large extent, be attributed to a rise in the demand for workers in typically female occupations—clerical work and several occupations in the professional and service categories. On the whole, this suggests that perhaps the best explanation for the overall increase in female labor force participation in recent years is that there has been an increase in the *demand* for female workers, which has, in turn, stimulated an increase in the *supply* of women to the labor market."[15] Moreover, she argues that the rapid increase in the labor force participation rates of older and married women has been in response to a shortage of younger, single women, who had been traditionally given hiring preference by employers. Oppenheimer can be criticized for over-emphasizing the demand factor. Thus, as Kreps has noted, "the availability of low-priced female labor, both skilled and unskilled; women's reliance on the utilization of skills acquired in the course of performing their traditional roles; lack of pre-job training for women, their geographical immobility, and most of all, perhaps the attitudes of both sexes as to what constitutes appropriate male and female jobs are all supply factors which cannot be neglected.[16]

*Day-Care Centers*

Although the presence of children under 6 years of age greatly reduces the likelihood of a woman working, an increasing number of young mothers have entered the labor force. The number of working women with children under 6 increased by 2.5 million between 1948 and 1972, when about 3 of every 10 were in the labor force.[17]

One-fourth of all wives with children under the age of 3 are employed, as are one-third with children between the ages of 3 and 5. Estimates for the future show a continuing rising trend.

As the number of working mothers with young children rises, day-care facilities will become increasingly important. However, the types and quality of day care presently used by working mothers vary widely, with child-care centers accounting for only a minute proportion of day care. Nearly half of all children under 14 whose mothers worked full- or part-time in 1964 were cared for in their own homes, usually by relatives; about 16 percent were looked after in someone else's home. Only 2 percent of all children and 6 percent of children under 6, were in child-care centers. Most of the remainder were left to take care of themselves.[18]

Although it has been estimated that several million children need day care in licensed centers and family homes, facilities in 1971 could accommodate only 180,000 children.[19] Moreover, these limited facilities had to be shared with children who needed care because their mothers were ill or physically handicapped or because the children were orphaned or abandoned.

The cost of day care varies widely and depends on the services offered. The annual cost per child for group care averages about $400 per school-age child and $1,600 for the preschooler. The Department of Health, Education, and Welfare has estimated the annual cost per child of "acceptable" group day care (as distinct from "minimum" or "desirable" care) for 3- to 5-year-olds to be $1,862.[20] Since the proportion of working mothers is highest among families in which the husband's income is under $7,000 a year, good day-care facilities are beyond their reach if they are not subsidized by the government.

**Racial Aspects of Labor Force Participation**

Postwar trends in labor force participation rates by sex and color are shown in Table 2-7. Since the mid-1950s black males have had lower participation rates than white males. In fact, the differential has been increasing. This difference is partly due to the different marital composition of the two groups of men. Single, divorced, separated or widowed men usually have considerable lower participation rates than married men. About one-third of all black men were single in 1972 compared with one-fourth of all white men. The proportion of black men who were divorced, widowed or separated was nearly twice that of

**Table 2-7**
**Civilian Labor Force Participation Rates for Persons 16 Years and Over, by Color and Sex, 1948 to 1972**

| Year | Men | | Women | |
|---|---|---|---|---|
| | White | Black | White | Black |
| 1948-50 | 86.4 | 86.7 | 31.9 | 46.5 |
| 1951-53 | 86.3 | 86.4 | 33.5 | 45.1 |
| 1954-56 | 85.5 | 85.1 | 34.5 | 46.5 |
| 1957-59 | 84.3 | 83.9 | 35.8 | 47.6 |
| 1960-62 | 82.8 | 82.0 | 36.7 | 48.2 |
| 1963-65 | 81.1 | 79.9 | 37.6 | 48.4 |
| 1966-68 | 80.6 | 78.4 | 40.0 | 49.4 |
| 1969-72 | 79.9 | 75.5 | 42.6 | 49.3 |

Source: Computed from data contained in U.S. Department of Labor, *Manpower Report of the President, March, 1973* (Washington, D.C.: U.S. Government Printing Office, 1973), Table A-4, pp. 131-132.

white men.[21] Moreover, unemployment rates for blacks are considerably higher than for whites, thus likely discouraging some blacks—especially older, poorly educated blacks—from remaining in the labor force. In addition, there is a greater incidence of disability among non-whites. Finally, a much higher number of blacks are inmates of institutions and, by definition, excluded from the labor force. According to the 1960 census, 3.7 percent of black males 25 to 54 years of age were reported as inmates of institutions, compared with 1.1 percent of the corresponding group of white males.[22]

Over time, labor force participation rates of black women have increased much more slowly than for white women. Cain indicates that one important factor is the higher proportion of the non-white female labor force in domestic service—a declining occupation. With the number of workers in domestic service dropping rapidly, these poorly educated women have few other employment opportunities and tend to withdraw from the labor force.[23] In addition, the labor force participation rates of black married women are more closely associated (inversely) with increases in husband's incomes than white women. Since the earnings of black men have been rising somewhat more rapidly in the last decade than those of white men, this has tended to cause a narrowing of the difference in labor force participation between black and white women.

Although black women have not increased their labor force participation rates as rapidly as white women, an important difference in participation remains. (See Table 2-7.) Several factors seem relevant. First, poorer housing conditions, smaller dwelling units, and a greater incidence of doubling up of families among blacks, are all generally conducive to more market work and less home work for black women in comparison with white women. Moreover, the relative instability of non-white families influences black women to maintain closer ties with the labor market. This tendency is reinforced by their typically low-income status and limited chances of obtaining alimony or adequate financial support for their children. Finally, the black husband may face greater discrimination in the labor market than the wife, leading to some substitution in market work between them. Annual earnings statistics indicate that from 1939 to 1959 the income of black men and women increased at the same rate, but that during the 1960s the income of black women increased much faster. Thus, while non-white women earned only 39 percent as much as non-white men in 1959, the earnings of the former rose to 60 percent of the earnings of the latter in 1970.[24]

In addition, during the latter 1960s the proportion of Negro women who were single spurted upward. The larger share exerted a downward pull on the overall rates because participation rates for single black women were lower than for those who were married. At the same time, the proportion of white women who were single increased slightly, but did not materially effect the overall rate for white women.

### Educational Attainment of the
### Labor Force

Before considering the association between educational attainment and labor force participation, it is important to briefly analyze the trend in the level of schooling of the labor force. Statistics on the educational achievement of the work force from 1940 to 1972 are presented in Table 2-8.

While there have been major increases in the educational attainment of both male and female labor force participants, it is clear that whether we focus on the median years of schooling of the work force, or the upper end of the educational distribution, male educational attainment is increasing faster than female. There are several reasons why the educational attainment of working women has fallen, relative to men. First, demographic changes that have taken place in the female work force account for part of the slower increase in the educational attainment of women workers. In 1940 nearly 70 percent of the female work force was single. In 1970, only one-fifth of the female labor force was single.[25] Since surveys have consistently indicated that single women have somewhat more education than married women, the changing marital status of the female labor

**Table 2-8**
**Education of the Labor Force, by Years of School Completed, Selected Years, 1940 to 1972 (Percent Distribution)**

| Men | 1940 | 1952 | 1957 | 1962 | 1967 | 1972 |
|---|---|---|---|---|---|---|
| Less than 5 years | 10.2 | 7.6 | 6.3 | 4.8 | 3.3 | 2.3 |
| 5-8 years | 43.7 | 31.7 | 28.2 | 23.2 | 18.7 | 13.7 |
| 9-11 years | 18.3 | 19.4 | 20.1 | 20.0 | 19.0 | 17.0 |
| 12 years | 16.6 | 24.6 | 27.2 | 29.6 | 33.7 | 36.9 |
| 13-15 years | 5.7 | 8.3 | 8.5 | 10.5 | 12.0 | 14.5 |
| 16 years or more | 5.4 | 8.3 | 9.6 | 11.9 | 13.3 | 15.6 |
| Median | 8.6 | 10.6 | 11.3 | 12.1 | 12.3 | 12.5 |
| **Women** | | | | | | |
| Less than 5 years | 6.4 | 5.2 | 3.9 | 2.8 | 1.9 | 1.2 |
| 5-8 years | 30.9 | 25.0 | 21.9 | 17.8 | 14.0 | 9.6 |
| 9-11 years | . 18.7 | 18.4 | 19.1 | 18.8 | 18.5 | 16.4 |
| 12 years | 28.6 | 34.7 | 37.3 | 39.7 | 43.8 | 47.1 |
| 13-15 years | 8.8 | 9.0 | 9.3 | 11.2 | 11.9 | 13.9 |
| 16 years or more | 6.6 | 7.7 | 8.4 | 9.7 | 9.9 | 11.8 |
| Median | 11.0 | 12.0 | 12.1 | 12.3 | 12.4 | 12.5 |

Source: William V. Deutermann, "Educational Attainment of Workers, March, 1972," U.S. Department of Labor, Special Labor Force Report No. 148 (Washington, D.C.: U.S. Government Printing Office, 1972), Table A, p. A-7.

force has "retarded" slightly the increase in the educational attainment of female workers.

Moreover, in the postwar period there has been a major increase in the labor force participation rates of women 45 to 64 years of age. (See Table 2-10.) These women have less education than younger female workers, and fewer of the former have college training. Since 45- to 64-year-old female workers are an increasing proportion of the female work force, they also "retard" somewhat the educational gains of working women as a whole. In contrast, the labor force participation rates of older men, who have less education than the typical male worker, are declining, thus "raising" the educational achievement of the average male worker.

However, the impact of demographic factors has been moderate. If the 1970 female labor force had the same proportion of single women as in 1940, and if the 1940 labor force participation rates for 45- to 64-year-old women had prevailed, the average educational attainment of the 1970 female labor force would have been approximately 0.5 year higher.[a]

A second reason why the educational attainment of working women has fallen, relative to men, is that the rate of return to investment in higher education is probably greater for men than for women and the former are therefore more likely to make the investment. Becker, citing evidence by Mincer and Renshaw, has indicated that the rate of return received by white college women is several points lower than that received by white men.[26]

Finally, in 1969 the median age of first marriage for women was 20.8 years, with relatively little change having taken place for some time.[27] In contrast, the average age of marriage for men was 23.2, a difference of 2.4 years. For a number of reasons, including the possible support of a graduate student husband, marriage while attending college is often followed by the female student's leaving college before graduation. Men, on the other hand, are more likely not to marry until at least undergraduate studies are completed. Thus, as rising family income as well as a growing number of scholarship and loan programs have made college attendance and graduation feasible for a greater number of men and women, a relatively early age of marriage has limited the educational gains of women in comparison with men.

## Education and Labor Force Participation

There is a strong positive relationship, at a moment of time, between the educational attainment of an individual and his propensity to be in the labor

[a]This estimate is calculated on the basis of data contained in C.C. Long, *The Labor Force* . . . , Tables A-4 and A-6, pp. 295-297; and U.S. Department of Labor, Special Labor Force Report No. 103, "Educational Attainment of Workers, 1968," (Washington, D.C., U.S. Government Printing Office, 1969), Tables D, E, F, G, and H, pp. A-8 to A-12. Because of the much greater difference in the educational attainment of single as compared to married women in 1940 than exists presently, the educational attainment of the 1940 female labor force would have been 1.5 years lower had the proportion of married women in the labor force been the same as in 1970.

force. (See Table 2-9.) For men, this relationship is especially strong for individuals above the age of 45. Among those males 65 years of age and over, those with college training are twice as likely to be in the labor force as those with only an elementary school education. This presumably reflects the greater availability of jobs for older workers who have achieved relatively high levels of schooling. Moreover, when an older worker is laid off, he is less likely to remain in the labor force if he is poorly educated. For example, in a special study of older workers—conducted by the Bureau of Labor Statistics in 1962—examining displaced workers in the petroleum refining, foundries, manufacturing of automobile equipment, glass jars, and floor covering industries, the Labor Department concluded "Displaced workers who were not seeking employment were primarily the less-educated groups who gave up in view of their combined handicap of age and inadequate education."[28] R.C. Wilcock and Walter Franke in their studies of six midwestern cities in 1960 to 1962, reported similar findings.[29]

For women the relationship between education and labor force participation

**Table 2-9**
**Labor Force Participation Rates of the Population, by Sex, Age, and Years of School Completed, March 1972**

| 1972 | Total 16 Years and Over | 16-19 Years | 20-24 Years | 25-34 Years | 35-44 Years | 45-54 Years | 55-64 Years | 65 Years and Over |
|---|---|---|---|---|---|---|---|---|
| Men | 78.2 | 52.4 | 81.7 | 95.7 | 96.3 | 93.6 | 81.3 | 24.7 |
| Less than 5 years | 47.7 | – | 63.6 | 79.0 | 79.1 | 78.5 | 63.0 | 15.9 |
| 5-7 years | 63.0 | 54.3 | 88.2 | 93.0 | 90.8 | 87.5 | 71.7 | 18.6 |
| 8 years | 65.2 | 46.1 | 85.3 | 92.6 | 95.0 | 90.4 | 78.5 | 23.7 |
| 9-11 years | 71.5 | 47.8 | 90.6 | 95.5 | 95.8 | 93.8 | 70.1 | 26.4 |
| 12 years | 88.5 | 68.0 | 91.4 | 97.7 | 97.5 | 95.5 | 86.4 | 29.6 |
| 13-15 years | 81.3 | 49.6 | 67.4 | 94.1 | 97.3 | 96.0 | 88.3 | 35.2 |
| 16 years | 89.9 | – | 83.8 | 97.3 | 99.7 | 97.1 | 88.4 | 31.6 |
| 17 years or more | 90.2 | – | 74.3 | 93.3 | 98.3 | 97.5 | 90.4 | 45.5 |
| Women | 43.6 | 41.7 | 57.0 | 47.9 | 52.7 | 54.7 | 42.7 | 9.5 |
| Less than 5 years | 17.3 | – | – | 26.4 | 30.7 | 34.1 | 24.8 | 5.3 |
| 5-7 years | 26.2 | 27.4 | 40.0 | 38.3 | 38.2 | 44.6 | 33.6 | 7.2 |
| 8 years | 27.9 | 18.4 | 39.5 | 39.1 | 46.3 | 46.7 | 36.0 | 8.4 |
| 9-11 years | 38.6 | 35.4 | 35.4 | 40.8 | 53.2 | 50.2 | 40.9 | 8.9 |
| 12 years | 50.5 | 59.2 | 60.4 | 47.3 | 54.3 | 58.0 | 47.8 | 11.5 |
| 13-15 years | 49.0 | 46.5 | 56.6 | 49.9 | 52.6 | 59.0 | 47.6 | 11.8 |
| 16 years | 57.4 | – | 80.1 | 57.8 | 56.3 | 63.0 | 57.1 | 15.5 |
| 17 years or more | 68.2 | – | 82.9 | 70.7 | 72.6 | 80.6 | 69.2 | 28.6 |

Source: William V. Deutermann, "Educational Attainment of Workers, March, 1972," U.S. Department of Labor, Special Labor Force Report No. 148 (Washington, D.C.: U.S. Government Printing Office, 1972), Table E, p. A-11.

is even stronger than for men. Females who have schooling beyond the bachelors degree are four times as likely to be in the labor force than women with less than five years of schooling. (The low rate of labor force participation observed for all poorly educated workers is not due simply to lack of education per se; many of these individuals lack the mental ability or emotional stability to function in either a school or employment situation.)

Wives' earnings are correlated with their educational achievement (as is the case for males); hence, the higher the level of education the higher are wives' earnings and their rates of labor force activity. Moreover, highly educated women are more likely to work outside the home, whether or not they are married. These women earn reasonably good salaries and can choose from a greater variety of positions than less-educated women. In 1969, for example, women 25 years and over with eight years of schooling had a median income of $1,991 compared to $3,759 for high school graduates and $5,635 for college students.[30] Thus, the positive effect of high potential income more than offsets the negative effect on participation resulting from the tendency of better-educated women to marry men with high incomes. This latter factor would be expected to discourage wives from working. The availability for market work of ever increasing numbers of educated women therefore makes it likely that the upward drift of female labor force activity will continue as long as the economy continues to demand workers of progressively higher educational achievement.

*Education and Labor Force*
*Participation Over Time*

The percentage changes in male and female labor force participation rates by age and sex from 1952 to 1972 are indicated in Table 2-10. Let us first consider the data for males. There is a much more rapid decline in the labor force participation rate of less-educated males than those whose educational attainment is above average. Even when we examine the relationship between education and changes in the participation rate for males in the prime working ages (25 to 44 years of age), this relationship exists. The likely explanation for this phenomena is that as the average level of schooling and work-related training in the labor force has increased, these poorly educated individuals found it progressively more difficult to compete for the available jobs. As a result of repeated spells of unemployment of a progressively longer period, these males became discouraged about job prospects and left the labor force. Some evidence confirming this argument is that from 1940 to 1972, the average educational attainment of male labor force participants increased by 4 years, while the average educational attainment of male non-labor force participants increased by less than 2 years.

For females there is also a strong positive relationship between educational

**Table 2-10**

**Percentage Change in Labor Force Participation Rates by Sex, Age, and Years of Schooling From 1952 to 1972**

| Men | Total 18 Years and Over | 25-34 Years | 35-44 Years | 45-64 Years | 65 Years and Over |
|---|---|---|---|---|---|
| Less than 5 years | −35 | −17 | −16 | −20 | −55 |
| 5-7 years | −23 | − 3 | − 5 | −13 | −53 |
| 8 years | −26 | − 6 | − 4 | −10 | −48 |
| 9-11 years | −22 | − 3 | − 2 | − 8 | −44 |
| 12 years | − 5 | − 1 | 0 | − 3 | −37 |
| 13-15 years | − 5 | − 2 | 0 | − 3 | −39 |
| 16 years or more | + 3 | + 4 | + 1 | − 1 | −29 |
| **Women** | | | | | |
| Less than 5 years | −38 | −33 | −29 | −16 | −32 |
| 5-7 years | − 4 | +16 | + 6 | +28 | − 7 |
| 8 years | −11 | + 6 | +18 | +21 | − 8 |
| 9-11 years | +10 | +10 | +31 | +31 | − 2 |
| 12 years | +24 | +33 | +30 | +35 | −22 |
| 13-15 years | +30 | +38 | +41 | +21 | − 6 |
| 16 years or more | +25 | +48 | +20 | +17 | +16 |

Source: Computed from U.S. Department of Commerce, Current Population Reports, Series P-50, No. 49, "Educational Attainment and Literacy of Workers: October, 1952," (Washington, D.C.: Government Printing Office, October 1953), Table 5, p. 11; William V. Deutermann, "Educational Attainment of Workers, March, 1972," U.S. Government Department of Labor, Special Labor Force Report No. 148, (Washington, D.C.: U.S. Government Printing Office, 1972), Table E, p. A-11.

attainment and changes in overall labor force participation rates. Only those women with fewer than 5 years of schooling showed declines in participation at all ages. However, there was little relationship between schooling and participation for women 45 to 64 years of age, (except for the 0 to 4 years of schooling group). This would imply that job opportunities for older women are relatively abundant, irrespective of their level of education.

In Long's extensive study of the American labor force, he advanced the thesis that better-educated women were squeezing the relatively poorer-educated males out of jobs. Certainly Long did not mean that females were actually taking over jobs formerly held by males, since the principal decline in male employment has taken place in jobs requiring some degree of manual labor, whereas female employment has been expanding in clerical and sales positions that do not require heavy labor.[31] However, is the proposition true in a demographic sense? The answer is yes, but only partially. While better-educated women did increase their participation rates quite rapidly, there was still an influx of less-educated women 25 to 64 years of age. Many of these individuals obtained low-paying employment as factory operatives and service workers. Perhaps these women workers were hired instead of males with similar levels of schooling because it was possible to maintain a lower wage scale in an industry dominated by poorly educated female employees as compared to less-educated males.

## Labor Force Participation and Unemployment

There are two important hypotheses concerning the response of labor force participation rates to changes in employment. One, known as the additional worker hypothesis, is that large numbers of dependents enter the labor force because of widespread joblessness of family breadwinners during recession or depression. The other, known as the discouraged worker hypothesis, is that many persons of borderline employability or inclination to work are drawn into the labor force by the good wages and other job attractions that prevail during high employment but leave the labor force when business conditions worsen and the rate of unemployment rises.

With respect to severe depressions, the statistics strongly indicate that more people have been driven out of the labor force by the unavailability of jobs (or by the unrewarding and exacting nature of the only ones available to secondary workers) than have been driven into it by joblessness of family breadwinners.[32]

However, the economic fluctuations experienced in the United States since World War II have been much milder than the depression of the 1930s or most of the other prewar fluctuations in business activity. Is there any evidence verifying the additional worker hypothesis during relatively mild recessions? Cain, utilizing census data from the 1940, 1950 and 1960 Census of Population found that the effect of the male unemployment rate in cities or metropolitan areas was significantly negative with respect to the labor force participation rate of wives. This indicates that the higher the male unemployment rate the less likely for females to be in the work force,[b] lending credence to the discouraged worker hypothesis. This result is corroborated by the findings of Mincer as well as Bowen and Finegan,[33] who estimated that in 1960 a 1 percent increase in the total unemployment rate is associated with a two-thirds of a percentage point fall in the total labor force participation rate. Mooney examined the labor force participation rates of urban black married women. He found that their labor

---

[b]Cain, *Married Women* . . . , p. 62. However, Katz found that the labor force participation rate of married women increased the longer the husband was unemployed and the greater the decline in income relative to the preceding year. He found that participation of secondary workers increases more when family income expectations are disappointed. See Arnold Katz, "Cyclical Unemployment and the Secondary Family Worker," (unpublished manuscript).

force participation rate rises by approximately three percentage points with a one percentage point fall in the overall unemployment rate.[34] Thus, the combination of rising wages on the part of the employed husband and increased labor force participation on the part of the wife during prosperity greatly improved the chances of a black urban family earning an income above the poverty level.

The additional worker hypothesis was revived in 1970, when the nation was experiencing a combination of inflation and recession. The selective decline in economic activity still left job vacancies for secondary workers, especially married women, who might have sought employment to maintain family income eroded by inflation and reduced opportunities to work overtime. The net effect was an expansion of the total labor force accompanied by rising unemployment rates. However, as the recession continued, the labor force participation rate declined, and the labor force expansion reflected only population growth.

## Summary

The past 25 years have witnessed major changes in the American labor force. Agricultural employment has fallen precipitously as the number of farms and agricultural manpower requirements have declined sharply. In relative terms government and service industry jobs have increased sharply while those in manufacturing, mining and transportation and public utilities have declined. Moreover, while there have been substantial increases over the past generation in the proportion of professional and clerical workers, the percentage of workers classified as laborers and operatives has fallen.

Labor force participation rates among worker groups have experienced some important changes in the postwar period. For example, male labor force participation rates have declined while those of women—especially married women—have shown a considerable increase. The increase in the participation rate of women is associated with a shorter work week, thus allowing the woman to do housework as well as engage in paid employment, the increased education of women that increases their potential earnings, and an increase in the demand for workers in certain occupations that have had a high proportion of female employees.

Workers with high levels of education are more likely to be in the labor force than their less-educated counterparts. There is considerable statistical evidence of declines in the labor force participation rates of less-educated workers due to a paucity of employment opportunities for workers with little schooling.

The empirical data available support the discouraged worker hypothesis and reject the additional worker hypothesis.

# 3 The Nature and Composition of Postwar Unemployment

This chapter focuses on shifts that have taken place since World War II in the incidence of unemployment among different segments of the work force, such as blacks, women, teenagers, and the "less-educated." Moreover, the reasons for these changes are indicated in some detail.

Although it is important to know the direction and magnitude of the total level of unemployment, it is also necessary for policy purposes to examine variations in its composition. What groups of workers are most likely to be jobless? Are they concentrated in certain industries or occupations? Do they reside in certain geographic locations? Are they primarily the less-educated or the more highly skilled? How long have they been out of work?

Answers to questions such as these are required to thoroughly understand the existing unemployment problem. Moreover, an in depth study of sector unemployment rates is essential to formulating appropriate manpower strategies aimed at reducing the incidence of joblessness among those subgroups of the population in which this problem is most severe.

## Unemployment by Occupation and Industry

The unemployed person is likely to be unskilled. As shown in Table 3-1, for example, the unemployment rate for non-farm laborers is greater than that of any occupational group. This proportion has occurred whether the overall unemployment rate was high or low, and it reflects the chronic relative lack of employment opportunities for laborers. Another occupational group whose jobless rate generally exceeds the national average is operatives and related semiskilled workers. By contrast the unemployment rate for managers and professional workers has generally been less than two percent. However, these rates rose sharply in the period of 1970 to 1971, reaching 3.4 percent for professional workers in March 1971. This was the highest level recorded since these statistics became available in 1958.[1] These increased rates of unemployment, which fell only slightly in 1972, reflect sharp cutbacks in defense and aerospace production and in government financed research.

The percentage of jobless workers varies greatly by industry. For example, the construction sector has an unemployment rate nearly double that for all workers. (See Table 3-1) Construction is subject to sharp seasonal as well as cyclical variations in employment; projects are often of short duration and the worker has only a passing attachment to any particular employer.[2]

39

**Table 3-1**

**Unemployment Rates by Occupation and Industry, 1969 to 1972**

| Occupation | Annual Averages | | | | 1972 Seasonally Adjusted Quarterly Averages | | | |
|---|---|---|---|---|---|---|---|---|
| | 1969 | 1970 | 1971 | 1972 | 1st | 2nd | 3rd | 4th |
| White-Collar | 2.1 | 2.8 | 3.5 | 3.4 | 3.5 | 3.3 | 3.4 | 3.3 |
| Professional and Technical | 1.3 | 2.0 | 2.9 | 2.4 | 2.6 | 2.2 | 2.4 | 2.5 |
| Managers (except Farm) | .9 | 1.3 | 1.6 | 1.8 | 1.8 | 1.6 | 1.8 | 1.9 |
| Sales Workers | 2.9 | 3.9 | 4.3 | 4.3 | 4.1 | 4.0 | 4.5 | 4.4 |
| Clerical Workers | 3.0 | 4.0 | 4.8 | 4.7 | 4.8 | 4.9 | 4.7 | 4.4 |
| Blue-Collar | 3.9 | 6.2 | 7.4 | 6.5 | 7.0 | 6.6 | 6.3 | 5.8 |
| Craftsmen | 2.2 | 3.8 | 4.7 | 4.3 | 4.4 | 4.4 | 4.2 | 4.1 |
| Operatives | 4.4 | 7.1 | 8.3 | 6.9 | 7.7 | 7.2 | 6.7 | 6.0 |
| Non-Farm Laborers | 6.7 | 9.5 | 10.8 | 10.3 | 11.6 | 10.4 | 9.9 | 9.1 |
| Service Workers | 4.2 | 5.3 | 6.3 | 6.3 | 6.2 | 6.1 | 6.6 | 6.3 |
| Farm Workers | 1.9 | 2.6 | 2.6 | 2.6 | 2.4 | 2.6 | 2.5 | 2.9 |
| Industry | | | | | | | | |
| Non-Agricultural Private Wage and Salary Workers | 3.5 | 5.2 | 6.2 | 5.7 | 6.0 | 5.8 | 5.7 | 5.4 |
| Construction | 6.0 | 9.7 | 10.4 | 10.3 | 10.1 | 10.5 | 10.5 | 10.2 |
| Manufacturing | 3.3 | 5.6 | 6.8 | 5.6 | 6.2 | 5.8 | 5.4 | 4.7 |
| Durable Goods | 3.0 | 5.7 | 7.0 | 5.4 | 6.3 | 5.9 | 5.2 | 4.2 |
| Non-Durable Goods | 3.7 | 5.4 | 6.5 | 5.7 | 6.1 | 5.8 | 5.6 | 5.4 |
| Transportation and Public Utilities | 2.2 | 3.2 | 3.8 | 3.5 | 3.8 | 3.4 | 3.9 | 2.9 |
| Wholesale and Retail Trade | 4.1 | 5.3 | 6.4 | 6.4 | 6.4 | 6.3 | 6.6 | 6.3 |
| Finance and Service Industries | 3.2 | 4.2 | 5.1 | 4.8 | 5.1 | 4.7 | 4.6 | 4.8 |
| Government Workers | 1.9 | 2.2 | 2.9 | 2.9 | 2.9 | 2.8 | 3.1 | 3.0 |
| Agricultural Wage and Salary Workers | 6.0 | 7.5 | 7.9 | 7.6 | 7.6 | 7.5 | 7.1 | 8.4 |

Source: U.S. Department of Labor, *Manpower Report of the President, March, 1973* (Washington, D.C.: U.S. Government Printing Office, 1973), p. 17.

.  However, the high rate of unemployment among agricultural workers reflects a long-term reduction in farm jobs, which has been attributable to mechanization as well as past government production control programs. Even though jobless rates are high and incomes are low, many farm workers are reluctant to leave agricultural employment because they lack the education and training that would qualify them for other kinds of jobs.

In manufacturing, changes in unemployment rates depend critically on fluctuations in overall economic activity. Since durable goods purchases, such as air conditioners or freezers, can be postponed more rapidly than non-durable goods purchases, unemployment rates generally rise more sharply in the former as compared to the latter during time of recession. As business conditions improve and consumers are more willing to undertake purchases on installment credit, employment expands rapidly in the durable goods industries.

### Unemployment Differences Between Men and Women

Women workers have generally experienced higher unemployment rates than male workers. (See Table 3-2.) One reason why unemployment rates are higher for women than men at a moment of time is that a greater number of the former are re-entering the labor force or changing jobs, thus leading to a higher level of frictional unemployment for women workers.

However, the statistics presented in Table 3-2 indicate a secular increase in the relative unemployment rates of women. These data must be interpreted cautiously since there is a tendency for unemployment rates of men and women to diverge during prosperity and converge during recession (when frictional unemployment is a smaller proportion of total unemployment). Thus, our comparisons must be confined to periods when overall unemployment rates are similar. The ratio of female to male unemployment was 135 in 1951-53 and 158 in 1966-68. During both periods the overall unemployment rate was less than 4 percent. Similarly, the ratio of female to male unemployment increased from 111 in 1959-61 to 133 in 1971-72. Unemployment during these years averaged

Table 3-2
Unemployment Rates, by Sex, 1947 to 1972

| Year | Male | Female | Ratio of Female to Male |
|------|------|--------|-------------------------|
| 1947-49 | 4.5 | 4.6 | 102 |
| 1950-52 | 3.6 | 4.6 | 131 |
| 1953-55 | 4.1 | 4.7 | 114 |
| 1956-58 | 4.9 | 5.4 | 111 |
| 1959-61 | 5.7 | 6.3 | 111 |
| 1962-64 | 5.0 | 6.3 | 126 |
| 1965-67 | 3.4 | 5.2 | 153 |
| 1968-70 | 3.4 | 5.1 | 159 |
| 1971-72 | 5.1 | 6.8 | 133 |

Source: Computed from data contained in U.S. Department of Labor, *Manpower Report of the President, March, 1973* (Washington, D.C.: U.S. Government Printing Office, 1973), Table A-15, p. 147.

6.0 percent of the labor force. These calculations indicate a moderate secular deterioration in employment opportunities for women.

One of the major factors accounting for this upward shift in relative female unemployment rates has been the important changes occurring in the labor force participation rates of men and women. As indicated in Chapter 2, during the postwar period the male labor force participation rate has declined moderately, while there has been a substantial increase in the female labor force participation rate. Because the range of occupations open to women has historically been somewhat limited, the additional supply of female labor has been concentrated primarily in a relatively few traditional female occupations.[3] This has tended to depress income gains for women as well as to contribute to the rising unemployment of female workers relative to male workers. (If male labor force participation rates had not declined slightly in the 1947 to 1972 period, the deterioration in the employment status of women would have been even greater.)

### Racial Differences in Unemployment

In part skill differentials and educational differences are the cause of substantially higher levels of unemployment among blacks than among whites. (See Table 3-3.) However, regardless of educational achievement or work experience, blacks are more likely than whites to be jobless. Discrimination accounts for a significant part of these differences.

Ever since the middle 1950s the unemployment rate for black workers has been approximately double that of white workers, which was not always the situation. (The data analyzed in this section pertain to non-whites; but since blacks comprise about 95 percent of the non-whites in the country, it is assumed that what is given for non-whites is applicable to blacks.) The statistics indicate that during the 1930s the black unemployment rate was actually *lower* than the white rate. The difference in the occupational distribution of white and non-white workers is a likely explanation for this phenomenon. For example, in 1940, 41.1 percent of all non-whites were employed in agricultural pursuits compared to 21.1 percent of whites.[4] Since measured (but not disguised) unemployment rates are usually lower in agriculture than in other sectors of the economy, the higher proportion of blacks in farming was the major reason why unemployment rates for blacks were lower than for whites before World War II.

It is difficult to state what happened to the white/black unemployment ratio during World War II since unemployment statistics classified by race were not collected at that time. Ross points out that although the U.S. Employment Service had a formal policy of non-discriminatory referrals, "community customs" and employment hiring patterns were honored in practice so that Negroes were only sent out to openings where they were likely to be hired. Then

**Table 3-3**
**Unemployment Rates, by Race, 1947 to 1972**

| Year | White | Black | Ratio of Black to White |
|------|-------|-------|-------------------------|
| 1930 | 6.6[a] | 5.8 | 88 |
| 1940 | 13.9[b] | 12.0 | 86 |
| 1948-50 | 4.7[c] | 7.9 | 168 |
| 1951-53 | 2.9 | 5.1 | 176 |
| 1954-56 | 4.2 | 9.0 | 214 |
| 1957-59 | 4.9 | 10.4 | 212 |
| 1960-62 | 5.3 | 11.2 | 211 |
| 1963-65 | 4.6 | 9.5 | 207 |
| 1966-68 | 3.3 | 7.1 | 215 |
| 1969-72 | 4.5 | 8.6 | 191 |

[a]1930 data for workers 10 and over.

[b]1939 data for workers 18 to 64.

[c]Data for 1948 to 1972 for workers 16 and over.

Source: Data for 1930 from U.S. Bureau of the Census, *1930 Census of Population*, Volume 2 (Washington, D.C.: U.S. Department of Commerce, 1930), Table 10, p. 251. Ratios for 1939 computed from *1940 Census of Population*, Volume on Education (Washington, D.C.: Department of Commerce, 1943), Tables 17 and 20, pp. 75 and 99. Ratios for subsequent years computed from data contained in U.S. Department of Labor, *Manpower Report of the President, March, 1973* (Washington, D.C.: U.S. Government Printing Office, 1973), Table A-14, p. 145.

on the grounds that it was difficult to place Negroes in war industries, they were excluded from training programs. The inevitable consequences in many communities was severe labor shortages for war production combined with heavy relief loads.[5] While this situation may have prevailed in some localities, Robert Weaver points out that wartime prosperity permitted more industrial and occupational advancement for Negroes than had occurred in the preceding 75 years.[6]

The relative black unemployment rate increased during the first 10 years of the postwar period and then stabilized. (See Table 3-3.) However, very recently there has been a moderate drop in the relative unemployment rate for blacks, which has been attributed to the layoff of highly skilled production workers as well as highly paid scientific and technical personnel. These employment cutbacks were due to the recession of 1969-70 and declines in defense spending and government sponsored research. The affected occupations employed very few blacks so that the white unemployment rate rose faster than the black unemployment rate.

Two factors that have an important bearing on the total level of Negro unemployment can be discussed. The first factor is education. It has often been stated that one of the most important methods of minority group advancement into the mainstream of American economic life is via a high level of educational attainment.[7] Additional years of schooling, it is argued, enhance one's skills and productivity, provide the key to a higher income, and reduce the probability of unemployment. Let us examine the gains in white and black levels of education and determine whether these gains have been directly associated with changes in the black/white unemployment ratio. Table 3-4 indicates the distribution of schooling of blacks and whites for 1952 and 1972, as well as the percentage change in the various educational categories.

The data presented indicate that black educational attainment has risen at a much faster rate than white schooling levels during the 1952 to 1972 period. For example, the proportion of black high school graduates increased by 207 percent while the proportion of white high school graduates increased by only 44 percent. Moreover, the number of black college graduates increased by 215 percent from 1952 to 1972 compared to 74 percent for whites over the same period.

One would expect that since non-white schooling levels rose much more rapidly than white educational attainment, the relative unemployment rate for blacks would decline. However, as the statistics in Table 3-3 indicate, no such tendency was observed for the twenty-year period under consideration.

Migration is also considered as a possible partial explanation for the unfavorable employment status of the black worker. During the 1940 to 1970 decade 1,600,000 blacks moved from the South to the North. This figure has changed only slightly thereafter. Thus, in the 1950 to 1960 and 1960 to 1970 decades 1,500,000 blacks migrated from the South.[8]

There are several ways in which migration could affect the total level of black

Table 3-4

**Percentage Distribution of Labor Force 18 Years and Older, by Years of Schooling, 1952 and 1972**

| Years of School | 1952 | | 1972 | | Percent Change 1952-1972 | |
|---|---|---|---|---|---|---|
| | Black | White | Black | White | Black | White |
| 0-4 | 26.7 | 5.2 | 6.2 | 1.6 | −77 | −69 |
| 5-8 | 38.7 | 29.3 | 18.7 | 12.4 | −52 | −58 |
| 9-11 | 15.9 | 18.7 | 24.1 | 15.7 | +52 | −16 |
| 12 | 10.8 | 28.3 | 33.2 | 40.9 | +207 | +44 |
| 13-15 | 3.7 | 8.8 | 9.6 | 14.6 | +159 | +40 |
| 16 or more | 2.6 | 8.5 | 8.2 | 14.8 | +215 | +74 |
| Median | 7.6 | 11.4 | 12.0 | 12.5 | +58 | +10 |

Source: U.S. Department of Labor, *Manpower Report of the President, March, 1973* (Washington, D.C.: U.S. Government Printing Office, 1973), Table B-9, p. 177.

unemployment. First, the majority of black migrants have moved from rural agricultural-oriented occupations to urban non-agricultural pursuits. Partly as a result of this movement, 77 percent of all blacks lived in urban areas in 1970 compared to 48 percent in 1940. The measured unemployment rates in non-agricultural occupations tend to be higher than in agricultural pursuits, meaning that movement from the latter to the former would tend to cause an increase in the total level of black unemployment. For example, in 1950 the measured unemployment rate for black farmers and tenants, farm managers, and farm labor was 2 percent; however, as mentioned previously, agricultural areas suffer from problems of seasonal unemployment and chronic underemployment.

Secondly, there is a significant differential between the educational attainment of southern black migrants and northern blacks and whites. Thus, the migrant would be at a competitive disadvantage to the extent that education is considered by employers in choosing their work force.[a] However, had he remained in the South, his principal competition (partly because of employment discrimination) would have come from other poorly educated blacks. Moreover, not only are the years of schooling of the southern black deficient in comparison with northern whites and blacks, but the quality of southern black education has traditionally been inferior. (For example, a 1960 survey of accreditation status of black and white schools in six deep South states indicated slightly over half of the white schools were accredited compared to one-fifth of the black schools.)[9] Furthermore, not only do non-whites who migrate from the South to the North face potential employment problems because of deficiencies in the quantity and quality of their education, but also because the social minimum wage is higher in the North than in the South.[10] (The social minimum wage is a function of welfare payments, legal minimum wage rates, levels of unemployment compensation, as well as prevailing wages for unskilled labor.) Many southern blacks have been employed in farm related occupations where coverage by statutory minimum wage laws and unemployment insurance is of very recent origin. However, in the North, non-whites may seek employment in occupations covered by the minimum wage or in strongly unionized industries where relatively high wages force employers to hire the most productive people. Moreover, one requirement for entry into some occupations in the North is union membership. Some of these unions continue to practice discrimination against blacks and thus effectively freeze them out of that occupation. However, in the South that same occupation may have a preponderance of non-union workers giving blacks a somewhat better opportunity for employment. Thus, for example, union restrictions have minimized the number of black bricklayers in

---

[a]A special survey conducted in 1967 by the Office of Economic Opportunity indicated that the median years of schooling for rural blacks was 8.0 years, compared to 8.8 years for rural-urban migrants, and 10.9 years for blacks born in urban areas and presently residing there. For further information, see Calvin L. Beale, "Rural-Urban Migration of Blacks: Past and Future," paper presented at the American Agricultural Economics Association Meeting, Detroit, Michigan, December 29, 1970.

the North, but in the South where there is a smaller proportion of union bricklayers the percentage of blacks is far higher.

So far we have indicated that non-white migration *could* cause higher black unemployment rates, but what of the evidence? The 1950 Census of Population contains information on the employment status of individuals who migrated between state economic areas in 1949. The data indicate that non-migrant whites residing in these areas experienced about 4 to 5 percent unemployment; black non-migrants about 9 to 10 percent; white migrants approximately 7 to 8 percent; and finally black migrants, 20 to 25 percent.[11] One would expect that migrants would have relatively high unemployment rates since many of them had moved into the area only a few months before the survey and were experiencing the frictional unemployment associated with job changing. However, recent migration per se does not explain the difference in unemployment rates between white and black migrants. Thus, the relative employment position of black migrants is much worse compared to non-migrant blacks than is the case of migrant whites compared to non-migrant whites. In fact, migrant whites were less likely to be unemployed than non-migrant blacks. One reason is that white workers often move from one place to another because of a job transfer; blacks are less likely to have a job "in hand" at the time of migration.

An analysis of information obtained from the 1960 Census of Population regarding the employment status in 1960 of individuals residing in selected standard Metropolitan Statistical Areas, and who migrated to these areas from 1955 to 1960, yields results similar to those presented above.[12] Of the 10 major SMSAs receiving large numbers of migrants from 1955 to 1960, the exclusion of migrants from the unemployment statistics significantly lowers the ratio of black to white unemployment in 8 of them.

The 1970 Census results indicate that the unfavorable employment status of the black migrant has continued. (See Table 3-5.) One might wonder what is the incentive for blacks to migrate if they experience such high unemployment rates. A partial answer is that while their probability of being unemployed is greater after moving than previously, total income may be higher after migrating in spite of periodic spells of unemployment. For example, a 1967 survey conducted by the Office of Economic Opportunity indicated that rural blacks in 1966 had a median income of $2,778, compared to $5,116 for blacks that had migrated from rural or urban areas.[13] Kaun found that Negro migrants were more likely to move to regions where incomes were high but that unemployment levels did not influence the pattern of migration.[14]

**Unemployment by Age**

Unemployment rates for teenage workers are considerably higher than unemployment rates for adult workers. (See Table 3-6.) There are several major

**Table 3-5**

**Unemployment Rates, Black and White Males, by Age and Migration Status, 1970**

| | 16 Years and Over | | 16-24 | | 25-34 | | 35-44 | | 45-64 | | 65 and Over | |
|---|---|---|---|---|---|---|---|---|---|---|---|---|
| | White | Black | White | Black | White | Black | White | Black | White | Black | White | Black |
| Migrant[a] | 4.3 | 8.3 | 6.8 | 20.0 | 2.8 | 7.0 | 2.7 | 7.1 | 4.3 | 12.5 | 3.3 | 7.2 |
| Non-Migrant[b] | 3.5 | 4.8 | 8.5 | 13.5 | 3.3 | 3.8 | 1.9 | 4.1 | 2.0 | 3.2 | 3.6 | 5.0 |

[a]A migrant is defined as one who resided in his state of birth in 1965 but not in 1970.

[b]A non-migrant is defined as one who resided in his state of birth in 1965 and 1970.

Source: U.S. Bureau of the Census, 1970 Census of Population, Subject Report PC(2)-2D, *Lifetime and Recent Migration* (Washington, D.C.: U.S. Government Printing Office, 1973), Table 3, pp. 11-22.

**Table 3-6**
**Unemployment Rates, by Age and Sex, 1947 to 1972**

| | Total 16 Years and Over | 16 and 17 Years | 18 and 19 Years | 20-24 Years | 25-34 Years | 35-44 Years | 45-54 Years | 55-64 Years | 65 Years and Over |
|---|---|---|---|---|---|---|---|---|---|
| | | | | MEN | | | | | |
| 1947-49 | 4.5 | 11.4 | 11.8 | 8.6 | 3.8 | 3.1 | 3.1 | 3.8 | 3.8 |
| 1950-52 | 3.6 | 11.1 | 8.9 | 5.5 | 3.0 | 2.5 | 2.9 | 3.4 | 3.8 |
| 1953-55 | 4.1 | 11.7 | 10.4 | 7.8 | 3.4 | 3.1 | 3.3 | 3.9 | 3.6 |
| 1956-58 | 4.9 | 13.1 | 13.5 | 9.1 | 4.4 | 3.5 | 3.9 | 4.2 | 4.0 |
| 1959-61 | 5.7 | 16.5 | 15.4 | 9.1 | 5.1 | 4.0 | 4.4 | 4.9 | 4.6 |
| 1962-64 | 5.0 | 17.3 | 14.8 | 8.6 | 4.2 | 3.3 | 3.6 | 4.3 | 4.4 |
| 1965-67 | 3.4 | 14.8 | 11.0 | 5.2 | 2.5 | 2.1 | 2.1 | 2.8 | 3.1 |
| 1968-70 | 3.4 | 14.9 | 10.8 | 6.2 | 2.4 | 1.8 | 1.8 | 2.2 | 2.8 |
| 1971-72 | 5.1 | 18.4 | 14.5 | 9.8 | 4.1 | 2.9 | 2.8 | 3.2 | 3.5 |

FEMALE

| | Total 16 Years and Over | 16 and 17 Years | 18 and 19 Years | 20-24 Years | 25-34 Years | 35-44 Years | 45-54 Years | 55-64 Years | 65 Years and Over |
|---|---|---|---|---|---|---|---|---|---|
| 1947-49 | 4.6 | 11.3 | 8.5 | 5.6 | 4.6 | 3.5 | 3.2 | 3.4 | 2.8 |
| 1950-52 | 4.6 | 11.1 | 8.1 | 5.3 | 4.6 | 3.7 | 3.5 | 3.7 | 2.8 |
| 1953-55 | 4.7 | 11.1 | 8.7 | 5.9 | 5.1 | 3.9 | 3.5 | 3.6 | 2.2 |
| 1956-58 | 5.4 | 14.1 | 10.7 | 7.1 | 5.8 | 3.6 | 4.6 | 3.9 | 3.2 |
| 1959-61 | 6.3 | 16.0 | 13.7 | 8.7 | 6.5 | 5.4 | 4.5 | 4.0 | 3.2 |
| 1962-64 | 6.4 | 18.6 | 14.6 | 8.9 | 6.6 | 5.1 | 4.1 | 3.5 | 3.6 |
| 1965-67 | 5.2 | 16.2 | 13.3 | 6.9 | 5.2 | 4.1 | 3.1 | 2.5 | 2.8 |
| 1968-70 | 5.1 | 16.3 | 13.0 | 7.0 | 5.0 | 3.7 | 2.8 | 2.4 | 2.7 |
| 1971-72 | 6.8 | 18.8 | 15.7 | 9.4 | 6.6 | 5.1 | 3.8 | 3.3 | 3.5 |

Source: U.S. Department of Labor, *Manpower Report of the President, 1973* (Washington, D.C.: U.S. Government Printing Office, 1973), Table A-15, p. 147.

reasons for this occurrence. First, as indicated in Chapter 1, teenagers include a large proportion of new entrants into the job market, and they customarily experience a period of frictional unemployment associated with searching for a satisfactory position. Moreover, many begin their wage earning activities by accepting part-time employment on a temporary or seasonal basis. Since young people generally have fewer family responsibilities than adult workers, they experience higher job turnover rates in searching for the "right" job and are unlikely to accept a position paying a relatively low wage even if they have been without work for some time. In addition, teenagers experience higher unemployment rates than older workers because they lack experience and on-the-job training, and they tend to be vulnerable to layoffs because of a lack of seniority.

Throughout much of the postwar period there has been a steady increase in the unemployment rates of teenagers in comparison to adults. Thus, in the mid-1950s white teenagers experienced unemployment rates about triple that of white adults; in the early 1970s the relative unemployment rate of teenagers was quadruple that of white adults. For black teenagers the deterioration in employment opportunities has been even greater. In the mid-1950s the black teenage unemployment rate was double that of black adults; in the early 1970s the relative unemployment rate of black teenagers was nearly five times that of black adults. With nearly one out of every three black youths unemployed, the potential for violence and juvenile delinquency in our central cities is greatly heightened.

Part of the increase in teenage unemployment rates may be explained by demographic factors. The high birth rates that prevailed in the first 10 postwar years meant that during the 1960s and early 1970s there would be a rapid increase in the number of teenagers coming into the labor market. For example, between 1956 and 1959, the total number of teenagers in the labor force increased only 4.6 percent. However, the figure rose to 11.6 percent between 1959 and 1962; 15.3 percent from 1962 to 1965; 17.2 percent from 1966 to 1969; and increased 17.1 percent from 1969 to 1972. Thus, it is likely that the teenage labor force has increased more rapidly than the rate at which workers of this age group can be absorbed into productive employment. Moreover, because of a variety of demographic changes, the number of young blacks aged 14 to 24 is increasing about twice as fast as the total black population of our central cities.[15] At the same time, the decline in draft calls and the recent cutbacks in manpower programs has made the surplus of youth in the civilian labor market even more acute.

However, as pointed out by Gallaway and Dyckman, birth rates have been dropping steadily since the late 1950s. On the basis of their calculations regarding the relationship between teenage employment and increases in GNP, the economy would only have to grow at the rate of 2.7 percent per year from 1970 to 1980 to cause the teenage unemployment rate in 1980 to return to the level that prevailed in 1953. This is primarily because the recent low birth rates will reduce the number of teenage entrants to the labor force during the 1970s. If the Gallaway-Dyckman study is correct, the relative unemployment rates of teenagers have peaked and will decline substantially in the near future.[16]

 In recent years there has been an increasing amount of evidence that federal minimum wage laws have been a major contributing factor to the very high levels of teenage unemployment. Yale Brozen studied changes in the unemployment rates before and after increases in the federal minimum wage. He compared the unemployment rate the month before a change in the minimum took place with the jobless rate for the month in which the increase became effective. He found, in the eight cases studied, that the seasonally adjusted unemployment rate of 16 to 19 year olds rose in six cases, fell in one, and remained the same in the other.[17] Arthur F. Burns developed regression equations relating the teenage unemployment rates to the jobless rate of adult males and to the minimum wage, (as a percent of average hourly earnings in manufacturing).[18] He observed a statistically significant relationship between the level of the minimum wage and teenage unemployment. The relationship was most powerful in the case of Negro teenagers. The Kosters-Welch study related the employment rates of teenagers to the minimum wage (as a percent of average hourly earnings in manufacturing) as well as the extent of minimum wage coverage. The results indicated that increases in the effective minimum wage would increase the vulnerability of teenage employment to cyclical fluctuations and would also decrease the teenage share of total employment. In addition, the authors found that a disproportionate share of these disemployment effects fell on black teenagers.[19]

However, not all investigators have concluded that minimum wage laws have had adverse effects on teenage employment. For example, Kalachek related teenage unemployment to a number of variables including a dummy variable representing the presence of a state minimum wage. He concluded that the minimum wage had no impact regarding state differences in teenage unemployment rates.[20]

The major policy implication of these findings is fairly clear. Since teenagers are probably vulnerable to the level and extent of coverage of the federal minimum wage, it would appear advisable to lower somewhat the minimum wage for teenage workers, or more realistically, to increase the minimum for them at a slower rate than for adults. This would help to provide jobs for teenagers in the youth intensive industrial and service sectors (such as entertainment or retail sales) either by displacing adult workers who are at or above the minimum, or by increasing total employment in these sectors. However, if the teenage minimum were below the lowest acceptable wage for many workers in this age group, the positive employment effects would be correspondingly reduced.

## Unemployment of Vietnam Veterans

A special category of young workers, whose unemployment problems must be given particular consideration, is the over 4 million Vietnam veterans who have returned to civilian life. In February 1971, the seasonally adjusted unemployment rate for veterans 20 to 29 years old was 11.1 percent versus 8.7 percent for non-veterans of comparable age.[21]

It would be expected that unemployment rates for veterans would be higher than those for non-veterans. Most non-veterans had been employed in the immediate past, while the returning veteran was entering the civilian labor force as employment cutbacks were spreading as a result of the recession of 1969-70.

Moreover, Vietnam veterans are eligible for unemployment insurance regardless of prior work experience, and this income may have tended to cause them to be more selective regarding the positions they would accept. However, many young non-veterans did have enough wage credits to obtain unemployment compensation while they looked for work and therefore may have been more inclined to take whatever jobs were available.[22]

Since February 1971, the gap between the unemployment rates of Vietnam-era veterans and non-veterans has closed dramatically. By June 1971, the gap had fallen to two percentage points, and to only one percentage point by February 1972. In January 1973, the two rates were virtually identical.[23]

The reduction in the veteran's unemployment rate, which reflects in part the general upturn in employment from 1971 to 1973 and decline in joblessness, is also linked to other factors. An important one is the recent decline in the number of newly discharged veterans—those most prone to civilian unemployment because of their youth and lack of civilian employment experience. Thus, the number of discharges during 1972 fell from nearly 100,000 in January to about 50,000 in December. In addition, a growing percentage of the Vietnam veterans in the civilian labor force during 1972 had been out of the service for several years, and thus had time to establish themselves in jobs. Moreover, they were in the older age groups (25 to 29 and 30 to 34) where unemployment rates are much lower than for men under 25. (See Table 3-6.) These factors combined with federal efforts to improve veterans job counseling, placement, and training benefits, all contributed to lowering the unemployment rate for Vietnam-era veterans.

Traditionally the federal government has given veterans preferential treatment when competing for positions classified under the civil service. This factor appears to provide a special source of employment for black veterans. In 1972, 22 percent of the employed black veterans 20 to 29 years old, worked for federal, state, or local governments, compared to 12 percent of the white veterans.[24]

## Older Workers

Unemployment rates of older workers are considerably less than for younger workers. (See Table 3-6.) The principal factor that results in low jobless rates is the long job tenure or seniority of the older worker. Seniority can be broadly defined as a labor practice where employees in a plant receive preference in layoffs, rehiring, promotion and choice of work assignment in the order in which they were hired. Of 1743 major union-management agreements (each covering 1,000 workers or more) studied by the Bureau of Labor Statistics in 1954-55, less than one-fourth, predominantly in non-manufacturing industries, failed to provide for consideration of length of service in determining the order of layoff.[25] Moreover, consideration of length of service in layoffs was reported by 95 percent of 110 non-union companies surveyed in 1950 by the National Industrial Conference Board.[26]

Because of the job security that accrues from seniority and since most private pensions are nonvested (cannot be transferred from one company to another), older workers are less likely than young workers to change jobs and thus possibly experience the attendant frictional unemployment. While in some cases this may restrict the older workers' opportunity for advancement, it also tends to maintain the unemployment rate for older workers at fairly low levels.

Once an older worker loses his job he is apt to be restricted to a variety of low-paying temporary positions. Not only are there age barriers in hiring, but older workers—particularly the less-educated ones—often lack adequate training for today's technical jobs. Older workers are thus much more likely than their younger colleagues to have frequent spells of unemployment and to spend many more weeks searching for employment. (See Table 3-7.) As a result of this experience many older workers simply withdraw from the labor force. This labor force withdrawal lowers the measured unemployment rate for older workers. However, these individuals often suffer a sharp decline in their standard of living as a result of their "retirement."

**Education and Unemployment**

Workers with fewer years of formal schooling tend to have considerably higher rates of unemployment than workers with above average levels of education. (See Table 3-8.) Workers who have only attended grammar school have unemployment rates nearly twice the average for all males 25 to 64 years of age, while those workers who have attended college have a much lower probability of

**Table 3-7**
**Frequency and Duration of Unemployment of Persons with Work Experience, by Age, During 1970**

| Age (Years) | Percent with Unemployment | Percent With | | Percent Unemployed | |
|---|---|---|---|---|---|
| | | 2 Spells | 3 or More Spells | 15 to 26 Weeks | 27 Weeks or More |
| 25-34 | 15.0 | 16.2 | 15.2 | 19.6 | 8.9 |
| 35-44 | 11.1 | 15.4 | 17.8 | 21.3 | 10.8 |
| 45-54 | 9.4 | 15.8 | 19.0 | 22.1 | 12.6 |
| 55-64 | 9.3 | 16.8 | 20.9 | 24.2 | 14.0 |
| 65 and over | 4.6 | 14.5 | 34.6 | 26.2 | 28.0 |

Source: U.S. Bureau of Labor Statistics, "Work Experience of the Population in 1970," Special Labor Force Report No. 141 (Washington, D.C.: U.S. Government Printing Office, 1972), Table C-1, p. A-19.

**Table 3-8**

**Education and Unemployment, March 1972, Males, 25 to 64**

| Years of School Completed | | Unemployment Rate (Percent) |
|---|---|---|
| Elementary: | 0-4 years | 6.8 |
| | 5-7 | 5.3 |
| | 8 | 6.1 |
| High School: | 1-3 years | 4.7 |
| | 4 | 3.5 |
| College: | 1-3 years | 3.0 |
| | 4 years or more | 1.8 |
| Total | | 3.8 |

Note: Workers aged 16 to 24 years are excluded from this table because their employment problems are associated with their age and lack of experience as much as with fewer years of schooling.

Source: Computed from data contained in William V. Deutermann, "Educational Attainment of Workers, March, 1972," U.S. Department of Labor, Special Labor Force Report, No. 148 (Washington, D.C.: U.S. Government Printing Office, 1972) Table K, p. A-18.

becoming unemployed. One important reason for the higher unemployment rates occurring among less-educated workers is that these persons tend to be employed in unskilled or semiskilled jobs, or in occupations that are sensitive to fluctuations in overall economic activity. However, workers who have achieved above average levels of formal schooling are more likely employed in white-collar occupations, which are generally shielded from business fluctuations and where extensive training costs incurred by employers make layoffs unlikely in all but the most severe situations.

Over the years, the unemployed have had fewer years of schooling than the employed. Nevertheless, the gap between the educational level of the two groups has been narrowing since 1957. While the median years of school completed by both employed and unemployed persons has been rising, the increase for the latter group has been more rapid. Thus, in 1957 the median years of schooling for employed workers was 11.7 years compared to 9.4 years for unemployed workers.[27] However, in 1972, the median years of schooling for employed workers was 12.4 years compared to 12.0 years for unemployed workers.[28] The rapid increase in the level of schooling of the unemployed reflects the unusually high jobless rate for well-educated persons such as engineers, technical personnel and other white-collar workers previously employed by the defense and aerospace industries. (See Table 3-1.) Moreover, the high rate of unemployment among young high school graduates has contributed to this phenomenon. In October 1971, for example, the unemployment rate of individuals not enrolled in college who graduated from high school in June, 1971, was 17.2 percent; for those who graduated in June, 1970, the unemployment rate was 12.4 percent; and for those completing high school in June, 1969, the unemployment rate was 7.8 percent. In addition, many older workers with limited formal schooling are leaving the labor force after a long period of continuous unemployment. This trend has accelerated in recent years.

The college graduate in our society can still look forward to a career marked by less unemployment than the high school graduate, primarily because of the difference in occupations to which the two groups will gravitate. Nevertheless, recent trends support the argument that the educational distribution of workers and the job mix are temporarily out of balance, for it is an unfortunate fact that a humanities major with a Ph.D. may have as much difficulty in finding satisfactory employment as a recent high school graduate.

The data presented in Table 3-8 imply that lack of education per se is associated with higher unemployment rates. However, is it only the lack of formal schooling which determines this relationship? Let us assume that an individual's general ability level can be measured by an I.Q. test. Table 3-9 shows the association between educational attainment and I.Q. scores based on a number of surveys undertaken by the Commission on Human Resources and Advanced Training in 1953. These data indicate that those individuals who achieve a limited amount of formal schooling also tend to be of relatively low mental ability; and it is difficult, if not impossible, to determine whether lack of schooling per se or limited mental ability (as represented by I.Q.) is more responsible for their more frequent spells of unemployment. This problem actually tends to be more complicated because I.Q. tests are not purely aptitude examinations but also reflections of educational achievement. Thus, two individuals with the same native "intelligence" tend to obtain different test scores if they have achieved dissimilar amounts of formal education.

**Table 3-9**
**Average I.Q. Test Scores for Individuals Achieving Various Educational Levels, 1950**

| Level of Schooling (Years) | Mean I.Q. Score |
|:---:|:---:|
| 0-8 | 82 |
| 9-11 | 91 |
| 12 or more | 111 |
| 12 only | 107 |
| 16 or more | 120 |

Source: Computed from Dael Wolfle, *America's Resources for Specialized Talent* (New York: Harper and Brothers, 1954), p. 314.

## Long-Term Unemployment

The Bureau of Labor Statistics classifies an individual who has been unemployed for 15 weeks or more as having experienced a period of long-term unemployment. The change that has occurred in the structure of employment and unemployment over the past decade has had an effect upon the volume of long-term joblessness in the American economy. In 1972 there were 1.2 million persons unemployed 15 weeks or longer, representing about 24 percent of all unemployed. This compares to 1.1 million long-term unemployed in 1962, which totaled 29 percent of all unemployed workers.[30] (The total unemployment rate in 1962 and 1972 was virtually identical, and at both times recovery from a recent recession was underway.) A major reason for the decline in the incidence of long-term unemployment is the increasing importance of teenagers and women in the labor force. These two groups typically have high job turnover, high mobility, and relatively short durations of unemployment. As these two groups have come to represent a larger segment of the labor force, there has been an increase in the relative number of workers who experience unemployment for short periods of time. Thus, the proportion of total unemployment represented by long-term jobless workers has declined.

While there has been a drop in the incidence of long-term unemployment, (as a percentage of total unemployment), the fact remains that during the recession phase of the business cycle, long-term unemployment rises faster than the overall unemployment rate. Thus, in 1969, when the overall unemployment rate was only 3.5 percent, long-term unemployed workers numbered 375,000 or 11 percent of all unemployed. During 1970, unemployment averaged 4.5 percent of the labor force and long-term unemployment rose to 662,000 or 16 percent of the unemployment total. In 1971, the annual unemployment rate reached 5.9 percent, a 10 year high, and long-term joblessness rose to 1.2 million or 24 percent of all unemployment. One major factor accounting for the rising proportion of long-term unemployed during a recession is that many of them were previously employed in cyclically sensitive manufacturing industries. These industries do not rehire workers until business conditions show a definite improvement. Thus, many of these persons remain unemployed for several months joining the ranks of the long-term unemployed. In addition, it is much more difficult for a laid-off worker to find another job when the total unemployment rate is rising than when the level of unemployment is steady or declining.

## Long-Term Unemployment and Education

During most of the 1960s there was a fairly close relationship between educational attainment and duration of unemployment—that is, individuals who were out of work for 15 weeks or more and 27 weeks or more (very long-term unemployment) tended to have fewer years of schooling than individuals who had been unemployed for only a few weeks. (See Table 3-10.) While this inverse relationship between educational attainment and duration of unemployment prevailed during 1966, it is clear that by 1972 workers who had been unemployed for six months or longer had as much education on the average as individuals who had been out of work for only a few weeks.

There are several reasons why the traditional inverse relationship between educational attainment and duration of unemployment no longer prevails. First, while an increasing proportion of the short-term unemployed are comprised of well-educated women and young people, the recession of 1969-70 and its cutbacks in research and defense spending have caused substantial increases in the long-term unemployment rates of well-educated professional and technical workers. For example, between 1968 and 1971 the unemployment rate for engineers quadrupled from 0.7 percent to 2.9 percent, and stood at 2.8 percent in March 1972.[31] Professional and technical workers composed nearly 9 percent of all long-term unemployed in 1971, nearly twice the proportion three years earlier.

Moreover, many of the less-educated older workers have been withdrawing from the labor force after experiencing a period of long-term unemployment. These individuals, the majority of whom have 8 to 11 years of schooling, are relatively unlikely to change their geographic location or occupation in order to find work. Moreover, their age and lack of schooling make it very difficult for them to find jobs, especially when the labor market is relatively slack as has been the case since 1970. However, as these individuals withdraw from the labor force, they cease to be included in the unemployment statistics and help to "raise" the median educational level of the long-term unemployed.

**Table 3-10**
**Duration of Unemployment by Years of School Completed, 1966 and 1972**

| Duration of Unemployment | Median School Years Completed | |
|---|---|---|
| | 1966 | 1972 |
| 1-4 weeks | 11.7 | 12.0 |
| 5-14 weeks | 11.4 | 12.1 |
| 15-26 weeks | 10.4 | 11.8 |
| 27 weeks or more | 10.2 | 12.1 |
| Total | 11.2 | 12.0 |

Source: Data for 1966 from Harvey R. Hamel, "Educational Attainment of Workers, March, 1966," U.S. Department of Labor, Special Labor Force Report No. 83 (Washington, D.C.: U.S. Government Printing Office, 1967), Table M, p. A-16; data for 1972 from William V. Deutermann, "Educational Attainment of Workers, March, 1972," U.S. Department of Labor, Special Labor Force Report No. 148 (Washington, D.C.: U.S. Government Printing Office, 1972), Table M, p. A-20.

## The Full-Employment Unemployment Rate

What is full employment? Gordon defines aggregate full employment as "the lowest level to which it is feasible to reduce the overall unemployment rate given both the amount of frictional (including seasonal) unemployment and also the structural factors which make some sectors of the labor force more vulnerable to unemployment than others."[32] This definition takes the amount of frictional and structural unemployment as given. Most economists believe that when the economy is operating at full employment levels the unemployment rate is approximately 4 percent. In other words, 4 percent is the full-employment unemployment rate.

As indicated earlier there have been significant increases in the unemployment rates of teenagers and women workers. Because of demographic shifts and changes in labor force participation rates, young workers and women now make up a larger portion of the work force than formerly. Because their unemployment rates are higher than the rates for adult males, the composition, as well as the overall rate of unemployment, has been affected. For example, it has been estimated that if the age-sex distribution of the labor force had been the same in 1971 as it was in 1961, the overall unemployment rate would have been 5.5 percent in 1971, rather than 5.9 percent.[33] This calculation assumes that the rates for each age-sex group would be the same as those actually recorded in 1971.

Thus, the changing composition of the work force can result in a gradually rising level of unemployment even though economic activity is at a sustained high level. The Council of Economic Advisors estimated that the unemployment rate would have risen from 4.1 percent in 1956 (a year of peacetime prosperity) to 4.5 percent in 1971 even if business activity had been as great in relation to productive capacity in 1971 as was the case in 1956. Since, as indicated above, 4 percent has been accepted by most economists as the full-employment unemployment rate, it appears that this policy goal should be adjusted upward to reflect the changing composition of the employed. An alternative would be to establish employment targets for each of the sectors of the labor force, but this implies a level of government intervention in selected labor markets that the present administration would likely consider excessive.

Earlier it was noted that the decline in birth rates, which has occurred from 1958 to 1972, should cause a future decline in the teenage unemployment rate. However, the evidence points to increases in the labor force participation rates of women—many of whom will be seeking full-time jobs. Whether this pattern will result in higher unemployment rates for women depends on the rate of expansion in the occupations that employ large numbers of female workers, as well as the success of women in securing entrance into occupations that have traditionally hired male workers.

### International Unemployment Differences

The unemployment rates for the United States and eight other industrialized countries are presented in Table 3-11. All of the unemployment statistics have been adjusted to conform to United States employment concepts. Over the entire 12-year period, the United States and Canada have systematically had the highest unemployment rates, while Japan and West Germany have had the lowest proportion of jobless workers. Sharp increases in unemployment have occurred in a number of countries since 1969. For example, in Great Britain the unemployment rate has more than doubled since 1966. After the British government's wage and price freeze in July 1966 and accompanying deflationary policies, unemployment rose to 4.0 percent by 1970 and then jumped to 5.3 percent by 1971, as British firms engaged in the biggest work force cutbacks since the depression of the 1930s.[34] The drastic layoffs were in response to sharply rising labor costs and slackening demand. Some of the cutbacks were viewed as a delayed reaction to the slow growth of output in the late 1960s. Unemployment in Britain rose throughout 1971 and into early 1972. In February 1972, millions of additional workers were laid off as the coal strike caused the government to decree emergency power cuts for factories.[35]

In Canada, unemployment climbed sharply in the early 1970s. The 1971 rate of 6.4 percent was nearly double the rate that prevailed 5 years earlier. In the second half of 1971, the situation worsened and unemployment reached a

### Table 3-11
### Unemployment Rates in Nine Countries, 1959 to 1971

| Year | United States | Australia | Canada | France | West Germany | Great Britain | Italy | Japan | Sweden |
|------|------|------|------|------|------|------|------|------|------|
| 1959 | 5.5 | — | 6.0 | 2.4 | 1.7 | 3.1 | 5.7 | 2.3 | — |
| 1960 | 5.5 | — | 7.0 | 2.2 | 0.8 | 2.3 | 4.3 | 1.7 | — |
| 1961 | 6.7 | — | 7.1 | 1.9 | 0.5 | 2.1 | 3.7 | 1.5 | 1.5 |
| 1962 | 5.5 | — | 5.9 | 1.9 | 0.4 | 3.0 | 3.2 | 1.3 | 1.5 |
| 1963 | 5.7 | — | 5.5 | 1.9 | 0.5 | 3.8 | 2.7 | 1.3 | 1.7 |
| 1964 | 5.2 | 1.4 | 4.7 | 1.6 | 0.3 | 2.6 | 3.0 | 1.2 | 1.6 |
| 1965 | 4.5 | 1.3 | 3.9 | 1.8 | 0.3 | 2.3 | 4.0 | 1.2 | 1.2 |
| 1966 | 3.8 | 1.5 | 3.6 | 1.8 | 0.3 | 2.4 | 4.3 | 1.4 | 1.6 |
| 1967 | 3.8 | 1.6 | 4.1 | 2.3 | 1.0 | 3.8 | 3.8 | 1.3 | 1.7 |
| 1968 | 3.6 | 1.5 | 4.8 | 2.7 | 1.2 | 3.7 | 3.8 | 1.2 | 2.1 |
| 1969 | 3.5 | 1.5 | 4.7 | 2.1 | 0.8 | 3.7 | 3.7 | 1.1 | 1.8 |
| 1970 | 4.9 | 1.4 | 5.9 | 2.2 | 0.5 | 4.0 | 3.4 | 1.2 | 1.5 |
| 1971 | 5.9 | 1.6 | 6.4 | 2.7 | 0.7 | 5.3 | 3.4 | 1.3 | 2.6 |

Source: Constance Sorrentino, "Unemployment in Nine Industrialized Countries," *Monthly Labor Review* 95 (June 1972): 30.

seasonally adjusted level of 7.1 percent in September. This jump was related to the adverse effects on Canadian industry that resulted from the United States' 10 percent surcharge on certain dutiable imports. As an emergency measure, the Canadian government undertook to defray two-thirds of the surcharge cost to affected firms so that they would not be forced to lay off workers.[36] Moreover, job-creating public works projects were also instituted, as the government came under increasing pressure to combat rising unemployment. In the last quarter of 1971, the jobless rate declined and by December stood at 6.3 percent.

Why is unemployment so much higher in the United States than in most other industrialized countries? It seems probable that the higher percentage of wage and salary workers and concomitantly lower proportion of self-employed individuals, accounts for much of the difference between unemployment rates in the United States and a number of Western European nations. Yet, Great Britain, where the proportion of wage and salary workers is even higher than the United States, has generally had markedly lower unemployment rates.[37] Secondly, job turnover rates tend to be lower in Western Europe, and employment exchanges and job vacancy information are more effectively utilized in Western Europe than in the United States. Thus, although precise figures are not available, the level of frictional unemployment is likely lower in Western Europe than in this country.

Moreover, lower wage rates in Western Europe have permitted these countries to be highly competitive in international trade. This has contributed to a relatively high rate of economic growth that has tended to result in low unemployment rates. (The interrelationship between unemployment and economic growth will be discussed in some detail in Chapter 6.)

Finally, it is probable that institutional factors, not generally amenable to quantitative measurement, are also important in determining international differences in unemployment rates. For example, differences between nations in customs, in union strength and labor legislation cause variations in the proportion of workers who are dismissed from their jobs and in the proportion who voluntarily quit one job before they have obtained another. Differences in wage rates and levels of unemployment compensation, which affect the ability of a jobless worker to be selective in evaluating employment opportunities, also impinge on overall unemployment levels.

## Summary

Unemployment rates are higher in unskilled as compared to skilled occupations. This occurs partly because of a long-term decline in the relative number of unskilled jobs, which results from advancing technology.

Black unemployment rates have been approximately double those of whites throughout much of the postwar period. The large scale migration of blacks from the South to the North has put considerable upward pressure on the overall black unemployment rate.

Throughout much of the 1950s and 1960s the teenage unemployment rate has risen in comparison with jobless rates for adults. Minimum wage laws and demographic factors are closely associated with this phenomenon. The decline in the birth rate, which has been observed since 1957, will result in fewer teenagers entering the labor force in the 1970s, likely causing a fall in their relative unemployment rate.

There is an inverse relationship between education and unemployment—that is, those with fewer years of schooling are more likely to be jobless. However, because lack of schooling is associated with lack of ability, one cannot attribute the higher unemployment rates of the less-educated solely to lack of education per se.

Unemployment rates in most other industrialized countries are lower than in the United States. Higher rates of economic growth, a higher proportion of self-employed individuals and lower job turnover rates in these countries appear to account for much of the difference.

# 4

## The Geographic Incidence of Unemployment

The previous chapter focused on the unemployment rates of various sectors of the labor force, analyzing overall national statistics. In this chapter attention is given to unemployment in local or regional labor markets. Thus, the spatial aspects of unemployment are considered.

If the rate of unemployment were the same throughout the United States, appropriate policies would be formulated to deal with the problem on an aggregate nationwide basis. However, since the end of World War II, the geographic incidence of joblessness has varied greatly with some areas having very tight labor markets, while others have suffered from chronic high unemployment.

A local unemployment rate may differ from the national average for a variety of reasons. Areas in which a single industry—such as munitions—predominates are particularly likely to experience substantial unemployment if there are cutbacks in military expenditures. Moreover, suppose one area has a concentration of firms—such as Pittsburgh's steel industry—that tend to produce goods whose output levels are sensitive to fluctuations in overall economic activity; the unemployment rate in such an area is likely to exhibit much sharper fluctuations than the overall jobless rate.

Also significant is the case in which high local unemployment rates are unrelated to cyclical fluctuations but tend to persist even when tight labor markets generally prevail. This situation may exist because of the depletion of a natural resource, as has happened in the iron mining areas of northern Michigan and Minnesota or the anthracite coal fields of Pennsylvania. Chronically high jobless rates also occur because major firms move elsewhere. For example, many New England cities have suffered economically since the textile industry moved South to take advantage of the lower wage rates paid to southern workers. In addition, the heavy volume of textile imports has caused employment declines in the New England textile industry. Moreover, during most of the postwar period, bituminous coal mining areas experienced relatively high unemployment rates because an increasing preference for gas and oil kept the demand for coal from rising substantially, and rapid increases in output per man hour made it possible to obtain additional output with fewer workers.

### Regional Unemployment

Jobless rates for the 4 major geographic regions of the United States during 1963, 1968, and 1971 are presented in Table 4-1. The years 1963 and 1971 were

**Table 4-1**
**Unemployment Rates, by Region, 1963, 1968, and 1971**

|      | Northeast[a] | North Central | South | West | Total |
|------|------|------|------|------|------|
| 1963 | 6.1 | 4.2 | 5.4 | 5.7 | 5.7 |
| 1968 | 3.2 | 3.0 | 3.7 | 4.9 | 3.6 |
| 1971 | 6.4 | 4.7 | 4.6 | 6.6 | 5.9 |

[a]For an enumeration of the states located in each of the four regions, see Paul M. Schwab, "Unemployment bv Region and in Ten Largest States," *Monthly Labor Review* 93 (January 1970): 11-12.

Source: Data for 1963 and 1971 computed from U.S. Department of Labor, *Manpower Report of the President, 1972* (Washington, D.C.: U.S. Government Printing Office, March 1972), Table D-4, p. 232; data for 1968 from Paul M. Schwab, "Unemployment by Region and in the Ten Largest States," *Monthly Labor Review* 93 (January 1970): 5.

periods of almost identical national unemployment rates of nearly 6 percent, while during 1968 exceptionally tight labor markets prevailed.

An examination of these statistics indicate the unevenness of regional unemployment. Between 1963 and 1968, all regions experienced substantial unemployment declines, but the fall of the jobless rate in the West was far less than elsewhere. In fact, this 13-state area contained one-fourth of national unemployment, though only 17 percent of the nation's civilian labor force lived there. The major reason for this higher-than-average unemployment rate was the considerable migration into the region. Although many of the job seekers who arrived from other areas were often well-educated and highly skilled, they faced relocation problems and were not promptly absorbed by the local labor market. Furthermore, the region's unemployment rate also reflected the age composition of the West's labor force, which was comparatively younger than the national average.

Between 1968 and 1971 the national unemployment rate rose sharply as the manpower requirements for the Vietnam war diminished and the nation endured a thirteen-month recession. The sharp rise in unemployment in the Northeast and North Central states was due to a high concentration of cyclically sensitive manufacturing industries in those regions. These two sections contain nearly two-thirds of the nation's manufacturing workers.[1] However, these regions have not recently experienced the heavy net in-migration characteristic of the West, and the resultant unemployment normally associated with population movement.

Unemployment rose much less rapidly in the South during the period of 1968 to 1971 than elsewhere, and this region experienced the lowest unemployment rate in 1971. Because of the low proportion of manufacturing industries in the South and the concomitantly higher proportion of agricultural employment, the southern worker was less vulnerable to changing economic circumstances. In addition, the South experienced considerable out-migration of young workers— primarily blacks. This phenomenon also tended to keep the South's unemployment rate at relatively low levels.

Jobless rates rose substantially in the West during the period of 1968 to 1971. While some of the increase can be associated with employment declines in cyclically sensitive industries, as a result of the recession of 1969-70, much of it is related to major cutbacks in the highly volatile defense and aerospace industries. Thus, Washington State, which has been hard hit by such cutbacks, experienced an unemployment rate of 11.1 percent in 1971, exceeded only by Alaska and Puerto Rico. Because of the continued migration into the region unemployment rates will likely decline more slowly there than elsewhere.

### Labor Market Areas

Prior to 1948, little emphasis was given by policy makers to unemployment problems that only affected a specific local area. However, the recession of 1948-49 (the first postwar recession) demonstrated that unemployment could be a serious problem in some localities, even though the overall unemployment rate was much less than during the 1930s. For this reason, the Bureau of Employment Security decided late in 1948 to revive its wartime program of collecting and publishing data pertaining to the labor force, employment, and unemployment of selected labor market areas.[2]

A labor market area is defined by the Bureau of Employment Security as an urban area consisting of a central city or cities and the surrounding territory within commuting distance. Within a labor market area, a worker can change his job without being required to change his place of residence. The BES divides labor market areas into three size categories:

1. Major labor areas usually include a central city of 50,000 or more.
2. Smaller labor market areas have a labor force of at least 15,000, including at least 8,000 non-agricultural wage and salary workers.
3. Very small labor market areas are below the size limits for smaller labor market areas, but have a population of at least 1,500.

Each month every labor market area is classified into one of six groups (A through F) on the basis of its unemployment rate. The classification scheme is as follows:

| Labor Market Category | Description | Unemployment Rate |
|---|---|---|
| A | Overall labor shortage | less than 1.5 percent |
| B | Low unemployment | 1.5 to 2.9 percent |
| C | Moderate unemployment | 3.0 to 5.9 percent |
| D | Substantial unemployment | 6.0 to 8.9 percent |
| E | Substantial unemployment | 9.0 to 11.9 percent |
| F | Substantial unemployment | 12.0 percent or more |

This type of information is available for 150 labor market areas located in 42 states. Table 4-2 indicates the number of major labor market areas with substantial unemployment from 1957 to 1972. As one might expect, the number of labor market areas with substantial unemployment was highest in 1958, 1961, and 1971, when *total* unemployment rates were at or above 6.0 percent due to economic recession. In 1958, close to three-fifths of the labor market areas surveyed had substantial unemployment, compared to two-fifths in 1971.

The boom years of 1955 to 1957 and the period of 1965 to 1969 (when Vietnam related developments pushed overall unemployment rates below 4 percent) were intervals when the number of labor market areas with substantial unemployment fell sharply. In fact, 1971 was the first year since 1963 in which more than one major labor market area (excluding Puerto Rico) experienced unemployment rates of more than 9 percent.

More than two-thirds of the 150 major labor market areas experienced at least one year of substantial unemployment between 1957 and 1972. Some of

**Table 4-2**
**Major Labor Market Areas with Substantial Unemployment, 1957 to 1972**

| Year | Total | Major Areas With Substantial Unemployment | |
|------|-------|-------------------------------------------|--------------------------------------------|
| | | Unemployment Rate of 6.0 to 8.9 Percent | Unemployment Rate of 9.0 Percent or Higher |
| 1958 | 29 | 23 | 6 |
| 1958 | 81 | 48 | 33 |
| 1959 | 47 | 34 | 13 |
| 1960 | 50 | 43 | 7 |
| 1961 | 78 | 54 | 24 |
| 1962 | 45 | 36 | 9 |
| 1963 | 37 | 30 | 7 |
| 1964 | 33 | 32 | 1 |
| 1965 | 16 | 16 | 0 |
| 1966 | 8 | 8 | 0 |
| 1967 | 8 | 8 | 0 |
| 1968 | 5 | 5 | 0 |
| 1969 | 2 | 2 | 0 |
| 1970 | 20 | 19 | 1 |
| 1971 | 61 | 51 | 10 |
| 1972 | 48 | 38 | 10 |

Source: Data for 1957 to 1964 from U.S. Department of Labor, *Manpower Report of the President, 1965* (Washington, D.C.: U.S. Government Printing Office, 1965), Table D-7, p. 203; data for 1965 to 1972 from U.S. Department of Labor, *Manpower Report of the President, March, 1973* (Washington, D.C.: U.S. Government Printing Office, 1973), Table D-8, pp. 212-213.

them experienced only one relatively brief period of substantial unemployment; almost one-third of the total number, however experienced substantial unemployment during at least four consecutive years, and two of these areas, New Bedford, Massachusetts and Stockton, California, experienced substantial unemployment in each of the 16 years from 1957 to 1972.

However, it would be misleading to imply that in a period of continuous high unemployment it is the same labor market areas that continue to experience substantial unemployment. Thus, between 1959 and 1964 when the overall unemployment rate remained essentially unchanged (in 1959, 5.5 percent; 1964, 5.2), there were 14 fewer areas with substantial unemployment at the end of the 5-year period. Moreover, in 1959 there were 13 labor market areas with unemployment rates above 9 percent compared to only one in 1964. This implies a redistribution of unemployment from the areas of substantial unemployment to those labor markets with more moderate jobless rates. This latter phenomenon occurs because workers move from a market with excess labor supply to one with a labor shortage, either by relocating geographically or by offering a different skill. Moreover, the wage level may fall (at least relative to other wages) in markets with unemployment, stimulating demand for labor in those markets, and eventually putting the unemployed to work.

The redistribution phenomenon can be seen more clearly by examining the results of a study by Eckstein. He analyzed the distribution of unemployment by labor market areas during 1959 and 1962. These were years in which the overall unemployment rates were *identical*, and the number of areas with substantial unemployment was nearly the same. (See Table 4-2.) By 1962, fewer areas had extreme values of unemployment; for example, in 1959, 22 areas had unemployment above 8 percent, in 1962, only 14. Also, fewer of the unemployed were located in the high unemployment areas, 20 percent in locations with jobless rates above 8 percent in 1959, while only 8 percent of the unemployed were located in these high unemployment labor markets in 1962.[3]

A comparison of the ranks of these labor market areas showed some interesting changes. Of 11 areas which suffered from unemployment in excess of 10 percent in 1959, there was major improvement in 6 of them. However, of the 10 areas with unemployment below 3 percent in 1959, only 2 remained in this classification 3 years later.[4] The skeptical reader may wonder whether the tendency toward geographic redistribution of unemployment that prevailed 10 years ago would occur today. One cannot determine whether or not this phenomenon will reappear unless the relatively high unemployment rates of 1971-72 persist for another year or two.

### Urban Unemployment

In recent years it has become apparent that the most critical unemployment problems are not only associated with such predominantly rural areas as

Appalachia or the Ozarks but also occur in our decaying central cities. The economic adjustment of workers in the central cities has been further compounded by the migration of large numbers of blacks to these areas while white workers and their families moved to the suburbs. In 1960, 53 percent of blacks and only 32 percent of whites lived in central cities. By 1970 the percentage of the black population that lived in central cities had risen to 58 percent, while that for whites fell to only 28 percent.[5] Within metropolitan areas, the degree of concentration is even higher. In such areas, about 60 percent of all whites live in suburbs while close to 80 percent of the blacks reside in central cities.

Unemployment rates are higher in central cities than in the suburbs and higher in poverty neighborhoods than other portions of central cities. The level of unemployment in these three subdivisions of metropolitan areas during 1970 can be compared in Table 4-3. Negroes, Puerto Ricans, and other minority groups are heavily concentrated in poverty neighborhoods of our central cities. In New York, for example, the 1970 census data indicate that about 82 percent of the Negro population in 1970 lived in 26 officially designated poverty areas. During the 1960s there was an outflow of 1 million non-Puerto Rican whites from these poverty areas, while at the same time the black population of such depressed neighborhoods grew by more than 380,000.[6]

The critical ghetto unemployment problem is indicated in Table 4-4, which presents the measured unemployment rate and subemployment rate for 10 urban ghettos surveyed by the Department of Labor during 1966. This subemployment rate, which is derived because of the inability of the conventional measure of unemployment to capture the full force of labor market failure in the ghetto, consists of the sum of those who are actually unemployed, those working part-time but seeking full-time work, heads of households under 65 years of age earning less than $60 a week full-time, non-heads under 65 years of age earning less than $56 a week full-time, half the number of male non-participants in the labor force aged 20 to 64 and half of the "unfound" males.

**Table 4-3**
**Unemployment in Suburbs, Central Cities, and Poverty Neighborhoods, 1970**

|  | White | Black |
| --- | --- | --- |
| Suburbs | 4.5 | 7.4 |
| Central Cities | 4.9 | 8.3 |
| Poverty Neighborhoods[a] | 6.3 | 9.5 |

[a]The poverty neighborhood classification adopted by the U.S. Bureau of Labor Statistics is based on a ranking of Census tracts according to 1960 data on income, education, skills, housing, and proportion of broken families. The poorest one-fifth of these tracts in the nation's 100 largest metropolitan areas are considered poverty neighborhoods.

Source: U.S. Department of Labor, *Manpower Report of the President, 1971* (Washington, D.C.: U.S. Government Printing Office, 1971), Table 2, p. 87.

**Table 4-4**

**Unemployment and Subemployment in Ten Urban Ghettos, 1966**

| Ghetto and City | Unemployment Rate | | Ghetto Subemployment Rate |
|---|---|---|---|
| | Ghetto | SMSA | |
| Roxbury (Boston) | 6.5 | 2.9 | 24.2 |
| Central Harlem (New York City) | 8.3 | 3.7 | 28.6 |
| East Harlem (New York City) | 9.1 | 3.7 | 33.1 |
| Bedford-Stuyvesant (New York City) | 6.3 | 3.7 | 27.6 |
| North Philadelphia | 9.1 | 3.7 | 34.2 |
| North Side (St. Louis) | 12.5 | 4.4 | 38.9 |
| Slums of San Antonio | 7.8 | 4.2 | 47.4 |
| Mission Fillmore (San Francisco) | 11.4 | 5.4 | 24.6 |
| Salt River Bed (Phoenix) | 12.5 | 3.3 | 41.7 |
| Slums of New Orleans | 9.5 | 3.3 | 45.3 |

Source: Bennett Harrison, *Education, Training and the Urban Ghetto* (Baltimore, Md.: The Johns Hopkins University Press, 1972), p. 74. Copyright by The Johns Hopkins University Press.

The highest subemployment rate was found in the predominantly Mexican-American slum areas of San Antonio; nearly one of every two ghetto residents was unemployed or underemployed. The lowest subemployment rate in the sample was 24.2 percent occurring in Boston's Roxbury-South End neighborhoods.

Although later data are not available, it is likely that unemployment rates in these 10 ghettos as well as those of other major cities, such as Chicago and Los Angeles, are higher than they were when surveyed in 1966. This is because 1966 was a year of low unemployment, with the overall rate being only 3.8 percent. However, in 1972, the overall unemployment rate was 5.6 percent, or nearly 50 percent higher.

Why is unemployment so much higher in our central cities (particularly the ghettos) than in our suburban areas? The answer is not to be found in a numerical lack of jobs. The fact is that most central cities have a larger total number of jobs than the rest of the metropolitan area in which they are located. Furthermore, the percentage of jobs located in central cities is generally greater than the percentage of area's population living there. Many suburban residents commute to jobs in the central city, but there is much less reverse commutation to the expanding employment centers in the suburbs.

In a study of the hard-core unemployed in St. Louis, Kalachek concluded that the high jobless rates experienced by St. Louis blacks appear to be more the result of frequent job changes than of the inability to find employment. This is especially true of young blacks who are not willing to accept permanent positions at low wages.[7]

Furthermore, there is growing evidence that the high unemployment rates in the black ghettos are not the result of a relative lack of education and training. Data analyzed by Harrison indicate that black residents have as many years of formal schooling, on the average, as white residents of the same ghetto.[8] Moreover, data on institutional training in the ghetto areas of New York, collected during 1969, indicate that black men compared quite favorably with their white neighbors in terms of the incidence of completion of training programs.[9]

These findings strongly suggest that existing urban labor markets underutilize black workers and by discriminating against these individuals, prevent them from realizing their potential productivity. (However, because their work habits may be less acceptable in comparison to those of whites and because the former score much lower than the latter on tests of educational achievement, this conclusion should be accepted cautiously.) Thus, the remedy must be sought in opening up new job markets to the ghetto poor, markets whose jobs are physically accessible to ghetto residents, whose availability is made known to them, and whose entry level wages and promotional possibilities will in fact lead to a significant improvement in their levels of living.

Most of the businesses—finance, real estate, and business services—that have been expanding within the central cities require a preponderance of white-collar employees. However, because of discrimination, many ghetto and central city residents have been restricted to blue-collar jobs, which are declining in number in some urban areas.

## American Indian Reservations—A
## Critical Case of Rural Unemployment

There are approximately 450,000 American Indians living on federal reservations. These individuals form the most poverty-stricken minority group in the United States. Their median family income is an estimated \$4,200 per year or about one-third of non-Indian family income.[10] The critical nature of the reservation employment problem is indicated in Table 4-5. On some reservations more than half of all the Indians in the labor force are unemployed.[a] Variations

[a]The definition of unemployment adopted by the Bureau of Indian Affairs differs from that of the Department of Labor. While the Department of Labor considers as unemployed only those willing and able to work who are not employed, the Bureau of Indian Affairs counts as unemployed all those not working, with the exception of the sick, infirm, students, and housewives. Thus, the Bureau of Indian Affairs considers an individual who is able but unwilling to work as unemployed while the Department of Labor does not include him in the labor force. Although the size of the "able but unwilling to work" segment of the

**Table 4-5**

**Unemployment and Underemployment, Selected Reservations, March 1972**

| Reservation | State | Unemployment Rate | Underemployment Rate[a] | Total |
|---|---|---|---|---|
| Navajo | Arizona, New Mexico, Utah | 43 | 21 | 64 |
| Hopi | Arizona | 51 | 14 | 65 |
| Fort Hall | Idaho | 35 | 21 | 56 |
| Fond du Lac | Minnesota | 64 | 7 | 71 |
| Blackfeet | Montana | 37 | 6 | 43 |
| Crow | Montana | 27 | 23 | 50 |
| Zuni | New Mexico | 29 | 16 | 45 |
| Fort Berthold | North Dakota | 40 | 18 | 58 |
| Pine Ridge | South Dakota | 42 | 22 | 64 |
| Wind River | Wyoming | 47 | 10 | 57 |
| Alaska Natives | Alaska | 64 | 15 | 79 |
| All Reservation Indians | | 40 | 18 | 58 |

[a]Includes those who are employed on a temporary basis.

Source: U.S. Department of the Interior, Bureau of Indian Affairs, "Estimates of Resident Indian Population and Labor Force Status: March, 1972," unpublished tabulation, September 1972.

in joblessness among reservations are more a function of off-reservation employment opportunities than of differences in levels of reservation development. The employment problem is aggravated by a birthrate which is from 2 to 2.5 times the national average.[11] High birthrates coupled with swiftly falling death rates have added increasing population pressure to the already overburdened reservation economies. In addition, Indian agricultural employment, as well as the number of Indian-owned farm enterprises, have declined steadily and industrial development has occurred too slowly to provide employment opportunities for those displaced from agriculture.

An estimated 10,000 Indians leave the reservations each year to reside for varying lengths of time in major urban centers. Many of these are relocated under government assistance programs operated by the Department of Labor and the Bureau of Indian Affairs.

For example, the Indian Vocational Training Act, which was enacted in 1956, makes available a wide variety of courses which permit the Indian to up-grade his

reservation population cannot be quantified, subjective reports from Bureau of Indian Affairs reservation superintendents contained in a 1962 unemployment survey indicate that the number of such persons is small. See *Indian Unemployment Survey*, Part I, Questionnaire Returns: a Memorandum and Accompanying Information from the Chairman, House Committee on Interior and Insular Affairs, 88 Long. 1 Sess. (1963).

vocational skills. In 1972, 2,063 approved courses were available at 666 accredited vocational schools located in both urban areas and on reservations.[12] The Bureau of Indian Affairs pays the trainee's and his family's: (1) transportation to place of training and subsistence enroute; (2) subsistence during the course of training; (3) tuition, books, supplies and tools utilized in training. Upon completion of the vocational course the enrollee receives job placement services. While these relocation programs remove some of the surplus labor from the reservations, they also encourage the most ambitious and aggressive young Indians to leave their homes for the cities, thus limiting Indian community development.

## Economic Development Administration

The Economic Development Administration was established in 1965 as part of the Public Works and Economic Development Act to stimulate development in lagging regions such as Appalachia, the Ozarks, as well as depressed urban centers. Under the act, such regions may be designated as redevelopment areas eligible for a variety of assistance programs. To receive funds, they must meet one or more of the following criteria:

1. Substantial and/or persistent unemployment for an extended period.[b]
2. Median family income of less than 40 percent of the national median level.
3. An actual or threatened major rise in unemployment caused by the closing of an important job facility.[13]

In addition to meeting the above criteria for assistance, each qualified area is required to submit an Overall Economic Development Program before it can be designated as a redevelopment area eligible for EDA grants and loans. The OEDP must set forth the area's problems and potentials, goals and priorities, and finally must indicate an appropriate program of projects.

Although the most basic development unit, the redevelopment area, is the county, there are many situations in which programs must cover larger geographic areas in order to reach maximum effectiveness. Recognizing this, Congress passed legislation in 1968 authorizing a multi-county economic development district program that has been rapidly implemented.

---

[b]An area is considered to have persistent employment if:

1. Unemployment in the area is equal to 6 percent or more of its work force and has been at least 50 percent above the national average three of the preceding four calendar years.
2. Unemployment is 6 percent or more and has been at least 75 percent above the national average for two of three preceding years.
3. Unemployment is 6 percent or more and has been at least 100 percent above the national average for one of the two preceding calendar years. For further information see Bureau of Employment Security, *Area Trends in Employment and Unemployment* (1966), p. 1.

Because one of the major barriers to commercial and industrial development is the lack of an economic infrastructure, an important feature of the EDA program is grants of up to 50 percent of the costs of water, sewage disposal, and community building projects. In addition, supplementary grants of up to 80 percent of project costs are permitted for distressed communities that have difficulty raising local matching funds. Moreover, public works loans are available from EDA at an interest rate of 5.75 percent.

The EDA also makes business loans of up to 65 percent of the cost of land, buildings, machinery and equipment costs. The borrower has up to 25 years to repay. During 1971 the interest rate charged on such loans was 6.75 percent.[14] In addition to direct loans, EDA's business assistance program provides working capital guarantees of up to 90 percent. These are guarantees on the unpaid balance of private working capital loans made in connection with projects receiving direct EDA loans. Finally, EDA provides a variety of technical assistance programs ranging from planning grants to feasibility studies for sites of selected industries.

Table 4-6 indicates the number of projects and total level of expenditures for the various EDA programs from 1965 to 1971. Thus, as indicated, EDA has spent nearly $1.5 billion over a 7-year period. The bulk of the funds have been spent in low income, rural areas, particularly in the South. However, in the late 1960s an increasing number of projects were allocated to urban areas perhaps in response to the civil disturbances which occurred during the 1964 to 1969 period.

**Table 4-6**
**Economic Development Administration Expenditures and Number of Projects, 1965 to 1971**

| Type of Expenditure | Number of Projects | Level of Funding (Millions) |
|---|---|---|
| Public Works | 2,305[a] | $1,084[a] |
| Grants | | |
| Loans | | |
| Business Development | | |
| Loans | 302[b] | 263 |
| Working Capital Guarantee | | |
| Planning Grants | 574 | 26 |
| Technical Assistance | 1,431 | 65 |
| Total | 4,612 | $1,461 |

[a]Public works grants and loans.
[b]Business development loans and working capital guarantee.
Source: U.S. Department of Commerce, Economic Development Administration, *Annual Report, 1971* (Washington, D.C.: U.S. Government Printing Office, 1971), p. 87.

In spite of the large volume of expenditures, there has been little evaluation of the *effectiveness* of EDA programs by a non-governmental research agency. The Office of Management and Budget initiated a comprehensive evaluation of EDA programs in 1970 to 1971. The study reached the following major conclusions:

1. With respect to public works grants and loans, the study found that these projects generated 33,486 jobs at an average annual salary of $6,500. The total EDA public works investment in these projects was $77 million or $2,290 per job. The total cost of the 274 projects was $125 million, with the balance of the funds being provided by local, state, and other federal money. Thus, EDA's share of this cost was about 61 percent.

2. The inflow of private investment also was studied in 93 of the 274 projects. Findings indicate that these projects encouraged the location of new firms and generated private investment of $8.55 for each EDA public works dollar. EDA also conducted a separate survey of 155 industrial parks developed with EDA public work funds. These sites are occupied by 360 companies employing 34,525 persons. EDA's investments in these parks totalled $50 million. The average cost per job created was $1,434.[15]

3. An analysis was also made of the results of EDA business loans. This study indicated that the agency's cost per job created was about $1,248 and that in half the cases studied other new firms were attracted to the project site. However, one important and disappointing result is that of every 100 jobs generated through an EDA business loan only about 40 were filled by unemployed workers or those who were farm laborers, part-time workers, or individuals who were not previously members of the labor force.[16]

4. The evaluation of the impact of planning grants was favorable primarily because the funds permitted the hiring of specialized personnel who were not available locally. Moreover, planning grants helped to increase coordination and cooperation between local jurisdictions served.

It is clear that the total number of jobs created and the total appropriation for EDA is far too low to indicate a meaningful commitment to eliminating the underutilization of resources in our nation's depressed areas. Moreover, as indicated above, many of the jobs created by this agency are going to those already employed and not to those who are presently out of work. Finally, a large part of EDA's expenditures for public works grants and loans as well as industrial parks make the infrastructure more suitable for the location of business investment. However, they provide no *direct* incentive for firms to locate there.

Thus, greater efforts in regard to investment in health, education, and training of the work force in depressed areas probably would be more effective than expenditures on water and sewage facilities. Hansen points out that the unemployment problems of rural migrants are largely a function of lack of job skills and education. Moreover, the employment problems of these people will not be solved solely by improving the infrastructure in these growth centers.[17]

There are two other policies that could be employed to increase business and industrial development in depressed areas. One is to give a federal tax credit or direct payment to companies establishing new plants in such regions provided that their employment exceeded a minimum figure. (Some states do give tax credits to encourage industrial development, but these credits only apply to state taxes.) Presumably the subsidy would be granted to offset the higher production and distribution costs that result from inadequate social overhead capital and lack of demand in nearby markets.

Many economists believe that subsidies, like tariffs, are most defensible when granted to "infant" industries. In this regard, the subsidies would only be granted for a fixed period, after which the industry or business would be exposed to the full rigors of the competitive market.

Secondly, one could permit the utilization of a rapid depreciation schedule in order to attract industry with relatively high skill requirements so that the residents would have the opportunity to acquire better-paying jobs. However, the difficulty with this proposal is that by encouraging capital intensive—instead of labor intensive—industry, one is giving less consideration to the high unemployment rates that occur in depressed areas. Since labor intensive industries put more people to work per dollar invested than capital intensive ones, it would seem that rapid depreciation schedules are inefficient if maximum employment is the policy objective. (However, labor intensive industries are often vulnerable to foreign competition, especially if the item is a standard lightweight product easily produced overseas.) Moreover, if the industry is capital intensive, employment may be available only for skilled workers. But if the local unemployed workers do not possess the requisite job skills—which is likely—there will be few employment opportunities available. This would mean, of course, that the industry would bring in most of its workers from outside areas, thus leaving the local unemployment unaffected.

In comparing tax incentives with direct subsidies, many economists favor the latter. They argue that tax incentives to encourage industrial development in depressed areas involve a form of "back door" financing, which is more difficult to control than regular government expenditures. However, direct subsidies or grants are under the direct control of the Treasury and Congress.

### Summary

Unemployment varies widely by geographic region and labor market area. Factors such as the level of military expenditures, the flow of migration, and endowment of natural resources impinge on the unemployment rate in local areas.

Ghetto labor markets are characterized by extremely high levels of unemployment. Continued job discrimination against blacks combined with a movement of industry to the suburbs indicate that these jobless levels will be slow to decline.

Among the rural poor, the American Indian has endured jobless rates, year after year, which far exceed the national unemployment rate during the depression of the 1930s. Federal manpower programs have made little impact on the reservation unemployment problem.

The federal agency most concerned with improving job prospects in depressed areas is the Economic Development Administration. An evaluation of this agency indicated moderate success, but the level of expenditures and number of jobs created are far too small to make a major contribution to alleviating the employment problems of the nation's depressed areas.

# 5

## Structural Change or Inadequate Demand: Two Explanations of Excessive Unemployment

During the first 12 postwar years the unemployment rate remained relatively low, except during recession. However, from 1957 to 1964 the jobless level rose significantly. At no time during that 7-year period did the unemployment rate fall below 5 percent. A major controversy developed among economists as to the cause of the higher level of joblessness.

At one extreme was the belief that the increased levels of unemployment were attributable to an insufficiency of job opportunities. This lack of jobs was due to the failure of aggregate demand for goods and services to expand rapidly enough to absorb the new entrants into the labor force as well as those workers displaced by technological change. Moreover, because economic growth was sluggish, the unemployment rate was excessively high even at cyclical peaks, as well as during other phases of the business cycle.

The opposite position, which was taken by a number of conservative economists, was that the unsatisfactory levels of unemployment in the late 1950s and early 1960s were not primarily caused by an insufficiency of job opportunities or an underlying inadequacy of aggregate demand. Instead high unemployment was attributed to a mismatching of job seekers and job opportunities, and this mismatching was the result of recent changes in the *structure* of the American economy. In other words, the job requirements of modern industry were not consonant with the skills and abilities of the unemployed.

The policy implications of these two positions are quite different. If excessive joblessness is due to a lack of aggregate demand for goods and services, unemployment can be substantially reduced by stimulating economic activity, via the appropriate monetary and fiscal policies. For example, by changing the quantity of money in circulation (monetary policy), the government can stimulate or dampen consumer expenditures or business investment. As more money is made available, consumption tends to increase, profits go up, interest rates tend to fall, and investment rises. Conversely, as the quantity of money is reduced or prevented from growing, credit becomes restricted and business and consumer loans become more difficult to obtain. As a result, income and output grow more slowly, which tends to dominish any inflationary pressure that had previously developed. By changing its taxing and spending (fiscal policies), the government can alter the amount of cash in the hands of consumers and adjust its own demands for goods and services. Tax increases and reduced government spending will lead to a decline in total demand while tax cuts and increased government spending will tend to stimulate business activity.

However, suppose that high jobless rates are attributable to a mismatching of job seekers and job opportunities. If this disconsonance is associated with recent changes in the industrial or occupational structure of the U.S. economy, then unemployment cannot be effectively reduced by policies that stimulate aggregate demand. Indeed under these circumstances, increased economic activity may only worsen the existing imbalance between the various types of labor resulting in upward pressure on wages and prices. Moreover, serious bottlenecks may develop in some parts of the economy, preventing any increase in employment.

If the basic cause of unemployment was structural change, the primary method of reducing joblessness would be by removing a number of imperfections in the labor market. This generally entails measures that improve the efficiency of labor markets such as greater use of employment exchanges, increases in adult education classes, or expansion in the supply of skilled workers through manpower programs.

The controversy over the causes of high unemployment in the late 1950s and early 1960s subsided as joblessness fell sharply after American involvement in Vietnam increased. However, the causes of unemployment have again become important as joblessness has remained relatively high even though the economy has recovered from the recession of 1969-70. Thus, while business activity reached a low point in November 1970 and unemployment peaked at 6.4 percent in March 1971, the overall unemployment rate in 1972 was 5.6 percent and remained at 5.0 percent or slightly higher during the first half of 1973.

Most of the research undertaken in the early and middle 1960s concluded that the *primary* explanation of the prevailing high rates of joblessness was a lack of demand. Let us review some of the more important studies. This will not only improve our perspective on the controversy but will allow us to focus more sharply on the present unemployment situation.

The first major study to be analyzed was undertaken by Kalachek and Knowles for the Joint Economic Committee.[1] They examined four possible factors that could result in higher levels of structural unemployment.

1. *An acceleration in the rate of technological change.* This is important because it could indicate that rising unemployment was due to an increased displacement of workers who could not be absorbed in other sectors of the labor market.

2. *An increased concentration of gains in productivity without any acceleration of the overall rate.* This could result in higher unemployment if the layoffs were highly concentrated geographically and occupationally or the productivity gains occurred in industries for which demand was relatively inelastic. Thus, lower prices would not stimulate an increase in the quantity demanded and rising productivity would result in reduced manpower requirements.

3. *A change in the qualitative impact of productivity increases.* The authors

argued that the kind of productivity changes experienced since World War II might increase the jobless rate of semiskilled blue-collar workers in comparison to other types of labor.

4. *A declining propensity of unemployed workers to seek jobs in other occupations, industries, and geographic areas.* This decreased mobility, that could be attributed to increases in homeownership, seniority, and the growth of nonvested pension plans, would tend to result in longer average duration of unemployment for displaced workers.

Knowles and Kalachek found that each of the four possible structural causes of higher unemployment was not empirically verified. The pace of technological change had not quickened or become more concentrated. Productivity had not changed in any qualitative sense nor had workers become less mobile. Unemployment had not become concentrated among blue-collar workers. The authors concluded that structural unemployment was not the cause of persistently high unemployment rates.

This study has a number of limitations. First, it is only concerned with the 1957 to 1960 era, and therefore, is only indirectly useful in assessing the cause of the high unemployment experienced from 1960 to 1964 or any subsequent period. Secondly, the study is restricted to production workers within manufacturing industries. The fundamental shift in employment from manufacturing and other goods-producing industries to service-producing industries is ignored. Moreover, the analysis overlooks the shift in employment from production workers to non-production workers and ignores the location of employment changes.[2] Finally, concentrated productivity gains need not result in unemployment. The result would be expected only if the displaced workers (or new entrants) could not be absorbed into expanding sectors because they lacked certain qualifications.

Heller argued that if unemployment had increased since 1957 because of structural imbalances rather than because of inadequacy of total demand, one would expect to observe an increase in unfilled job vacancies concomitant with the increase in unemployment. (Of course job vacancies could not be expected to increase as much as unemployment unless increased unemployment were entirely structural.) However, if the rise in unemployment were primarily caused by a deficiency in aggregate demand, one would expect to observe a decline in job vacancies.

Using an index of job vacancies based on help wanted ads published in selected newspapers, Heller observed that for the period of 1955 to 1962 the help wanted index was inversely correlated with the unemployment rate.[3] Heller interprets this information as a rejection of the structural hypothesis since job vacancies *fell* as unemployment rose. However, he should have stated his results more cautiously. First, the index, which was compiled by the National Industrial Conference Board, only included help wanted ads in 33 labor market areas covering 44 percent of non-farm employment. Job vacancies listed with other sources such as the U.S. employment service or private employment agencies are excluded. Secondly, it is possible for the unemployment rate to increase and the number of job vacancies to increase also—not because of structural unemployment but because of an increase in *frictional* unemployment.

Several studies have focused on the geographic incidence of unemployment. Gallaway found that the labor market operated efficiently in allocating workers between regional sectors of the economy.[4] He found no tendency for unemployment to become more concentrated in certain areas of the country and observed that the unemployment rate in each of 8 geographic regions (covering the entire United States) was closely correlated with changes in the overall unemployment rate.[5] This latter finding is consistent with the inadequate demand explanation of excessive unemployment.

Mobility patterns in certain areas suffering chronic unemployment reveal that the level of in-migration into these regions is markedly less than into other similar areas with lower jobless rates. At the same time, these chronically depressed areas do not have levels of out-migration that are greater than those of other areas.[6] Thus, the net effect is one of out-migration from these depressed regions despite the fact that there is no apparent unemployment-induced increase in out-migration. However, regardless of how the transfer is effected, the impact on the labor market is the same, a redistribution of unemployment.

Eckstein focused on the distribution of unemployment by labor market areas. Examining the data for 150 labor markets for the years 1959, 1960, and 1962 (periods with almost identical unemployment rates), he points out that by 1962 fewer areas had extreme values of unemployment. For example, in 1959, 22 areas had unemployment rates above 8 percent, in 1962, only 14 labor market areas were in that category.[7] Eckstein next focuses on *insured unemployment* rates by state for the period of 1950 to 1962. His data indicate that the dispersion of unemployment rates by states as measured by the standard deviation was lower in 1962 than in either 1956 to 1950. Considerable change had occurred in the rankings of states. Thus, the New England states were the most depressed in the nation during the early 1950s but subsequently their unemployment rates fell significantly. West Virginia and Pennsylvania, relatively prosperous in 1956, were hard hit by the 1957-58 recession, but had shown significant improvement by 1962.[8] Eckstein's findings are not consistent with a structural explanation of excessive unemployment since they indicate a tendency for unemployment to become *less concentrated* over time.

A number of studies have indicated the close relationship between changes in overall unemployment rates and jobless rates in particular sectors of the economy.[9] The implication of these findings is that the close association of sectoral unemployment rates with changes in aggregate demand indicate that lack of demand (as measured by the total unemployment rate) is the primary factor causing the excessive joblessness observed from 1957 to 1964. However, suppose workers of certain skills and levels of schooling were unemployed because of structural change. Then there would be no new hirings of workers with the skills and educational levels involved and some layoffs of those currently employed with these endowments. These developments would raise unemployment rates among inadequately trained new entrants and those presently in the affected jobs. Over the course of time the displaced workers would: (1) find other jobs, (2) continue unemployed, or (3) leave the labor force. Unemployed new entrants have similar options. If (1) occurs—but the work found is only temporary—structural unemployment would exist, but the unemployed would be classified by a different occupation or industry than the one from which they originally became unemployed. If (2) occurs, the duration of unemployment in the original category would lengthen. If (3) occurs, the skill level of those outside the labor force would fall relative to those in the work force, but structural unemployment would not affect the overall jobless rate because the individuals had left the labor force. Considering the three possibilities, structural unemployment would be reflected in more concentration of unemployment only in case (2). But even in this situation, if structural changes spread from blue-collar workers to white-collar workers, more and more occupational categories would be affected and unemployment would be less, not more, concentrated.[10]

Simler noted that from 1957 to 1963 the long-term unemployment rate (those jobless 15 weeks or longer) averaged 1.69 percent of the labor force, an increase of 117 percent over the 1947 to 1957 average. Moreover, in the former period very long-term unemployment (those jobless 27 weeks or over) averaged 0.85 percent of the labor force, an increase of 158 percent over the 1947 to 1957 era. In other words, not only have long-term unemployment rates increased relative to the overall unemployment rate, but the duration of long-term unemployment has become longer.[11]

These results would appear to indicate that the relative increase in long-duration unemployment has been due to an increased structural unemployment. Moreover, because there has been a disproportionate increase in long-term unemployment rates, structural changes must have been, in whole or in part, the cause of the higher unemployment rates experienced from 1957 to 1964.[12]

However, Simler asserts that it would be possible to observe a rising proportion of long-term unemployed as a result of a condition of prolonged inadequate demand:

A hard core of long-duration unemployed workers will emerge if the probability of re-employment is a decreasing function of the duration of unemployment. Among other reasons, this will be the case if the skill level of unemployed workers is also a decreasing function of the duration of unemployment, and if the structure of wages fails to adapt to the changing structure of skills; or if unemployed workers' skills remain intact but do not advance with the increasing level of skills of the employed labor force, and if the wage structure fails to adjust to the changing skill structure. Either way, the gap between the potential productivity of the unemployed and the actual productivity of the employed widens with time; and therefore, the probability of re-employment diminishes with time.[13]

Therefore, from the mere fact that long-term unemployment has increased, one cannot logically infer the presence of underlying structural change. A disproportional rise in long-term unemployment can simply be the result of a sustained increase in overall unemployment and not in any way the cause of it.

However, Gilpatrick has shown that Simler's results are based on incomplete analysis of the existing data. She demonstrates that the increase in the number of long-term unemployed is in part, independent of overall demand conditions and thus associated with structural unemployment.[14] Moreover, on the basis of an exhaustive study of employment and unemployment in the 1948 to 1964 period, she concludes that there has been an autonomous upward shift in the unemployment rates of blacks and the inexperienced unemployed. These sectors accounted for 0.4 percent of the labor force in 1957, 0.5 percent in 1958, 1959, and 1960, and 0.7 percent in 1961, 1962, 1963, and 1964. In other words, the 5.2 percent unemployment rate experienced in 1964 could have been 4.5 percent if blacks and new entrants had experienced conditions similar to those operating before 1955. Her analysis does not consider adjustments for older workers, the poorly educated, those in distressed areas, and those with obsolete skills. Of course these categories overlap; however, she maintains that structural unemployment might account for as much as half the increase in unemployment rates above the full-employment unemployment rate with the remainder due to lack of adequate demand.[15]

Bergmann and Kaun define structural unemployment as that amount of unemployment (less minimum frictional and seasonal) that cannot be removed by monetary and fiscal policy without creating substantial, continuing inflation (as opposed to one-shot, non-repeatable price rises). On the basis of painstaking analysis they conclude that in 1964 at most, 2 percent of the labor force or 40 percent of the unemployed could be classified as jobless due to structural change.[16] One of the strengths of this study, as opposed to most others, is that the term structural unemployment is carefully defined.

On the basis of the studies reviewed, one can conclude that the higher unemployment rates experienced from 1957 to 1964 resulted primarily, but not solely, from a lack of adequate demand. While *most* of the increase is apparently associated with a relatively slow rate of economic expansion, two sectors of the labor force, young workers and the long-term unemployed, were pinpointed as having experienced increases in unemployment levels and duration, which were considerably greater than that associated with inadequate demand.

It is important to ascertain whether the higher unemployment rates experienced since the recession of 1969-70 are primarily due to inadequate demand or whether there is a structural component involved. In our investigation Gordon's definition of structural unemployment (to be presented below) will be utilized.

Suppose that the unemployment rate for a particular occupation has been increasing relative to the average rate for all workers. Moreover, assume that this occupation constitutes a steadily declining fraction of the labor force so that, despite the worsening differential rate, this group represents no larger a fraction of total unemployment than it did 10 years ago. The "structural differential" has widened, but in what sense can we say there has been an increase in "structural unemployment"?[17]

This question suggests a simple identity as a basis for studying changes in the composition of total unemployment over time. Let $U$ and $L$ represent unemployment and labor force, respectively, and let us use the subscript $i$ to represent a particular sector of the labor force when classified in a particular way (for example, by age). Then we can write:

$$\left( \frac{U_i}{L_i} - \frac{U}{L} \right) \cdot \frac{L_i}{L} = \frac{U_i}{U}$$

This formula states that the ratio of the unemployment rate in one sector to the overall unemployment rate, weighted by that sector's fraction of the total labor force, is equal to that sector's contribution to total unemployment. One can then analyze changes over time in the structure of unemployment in terms of: (1) the unweighted differential rates alone, or (2) the proportional contributions of the different sectors. If using the second type of measurement, changes are found in the proportional contributions of different sectors to total unemployment, we can then determine to what extent such changes are accounted for by variations in relative unemployment rates and to what extent by changes in the proportional size of different sectors of the work force.[18]

For example, by how much has structural unemployment among blue-collar workers increased since 1953? During 1953, blue-collar workers accounted for about 56 percent of total unemployment, but for only 40 percent of the labor force. Thus $\frac{U_i}{U} - \frac{L_i}{L} = .16$. For 1962, the same calculation yields $.48 - .36 = .12$. Thus, on the basis of Gordon's definition, the "structural component" of blue-collar unemployment declined relatively rather than increased over the decade.

Gordon's approach to the measurement of the structural component of unemployment will be utilized in examining changes in sectoral unemployment rates from 1956 to 1972. Primary attention will be focused on those sectors where unemployment rates increased and the share of the labor force accounted for by that sector did not decline. Such a sector would have represented an increasing fraction of total unemployment.

## Unemployment by Age and Sex

Let us first consider the distribution of unemployment and the labor force by age and sex presented in Table 5-1. The relative unemployment rates of teenagers rose sharply from 1956 to 1964 but have shown little change for males and a moderate decline for females since 1964. While the proportion of teenage unemployment has increased somewhat from 1964 to 1972, relative to total unemployment the increase has been due to a rising percentage of teenage workers in the labor force and is not caused by an increase in the relative unemployment rate of teenagers.

For the other age groups there are no major changes with the exception of older males. Males 45 to 64 years of age have experienced a decline in their relative rate of unemployment, as well as a drop in their proportion of the total labor force. As a result, the share of total unemployment accounted for by older males declined by one-third from 1964 to 1972. As indicated in Chapter 3, the unemployment rates of older workers are relatively low because of seniority. Moreover, labor force participation rates for older men have been decreasing in recent years, thus lowering their measured unemployment rates.

The relative unemployment rate of women remained unchanged from 1964 to 1972. However, there has been a moderate increase in the proportion of unemployment attributable to women workers due to a rise in their labor force participation rates.

## The Unemployed by Occupation

Let us now consider the occupational distribution of the unemployed. (See Table 5-2) Nearly all variants of the structural unemployment hypothesis imply that unemployment has become increasingly concentrated among blue-collar and unskilled workers. Focusing on white-collar workers, the 1956 to 1972 period has been one in which their employment opportunities have weakened. The white-collar unemployment rate, while remaining relatively low, has increased steadily. This statement is applicable to each of the four white-collar occupational categories. This unemployment increase, combined with the continued rise in the white-collar share of the labor force, has meant that these workers comprised a much larger share of total unemployment in 1972 and 1956. Over the 16-year period white-collar unemployment increased from 17.5 percent of total unemployment to 27.2 percent.

What has happened to unemployment among blue-collar workers? Over the entire 16-year period the relative unemployment rates for the different subgroups either remained constant or declined slightly. At the same time, the blue-collar fraction of the total labor force has declined slowly, which has resulted in a moderate decline in the proportion of total unemployment

**Table 5-1**

**Age-Sex Classification of the Civilian Labor Force and the Unemployed, Selected Years, 1956 to 1972**

| Age Group | Ratio of Unemployment Rate in Each Group to the National Unemployment Rate | | | | | | Percentage of Labor Force in Each Group | | | | | | Percentage of Total Unemployment in Each Group | | | | | |
|---|---|---|---|---|---|---|---|---|---|---|---|---|---|---|---|---|---|---|
| | 1956 | 1960 | 1964 | 1968 | 1971 | 1972 | 1956 | 1960 | 1964 | 1968 | 1971 | 1972 | 1956 | 1960 | 1964 | 1968 | 1971 | 1972 |
| **Male** | | | | | | | | | | | | | | | | | | |
| 16-19 | 222 | 242 | 261 | 283 | 261 | 264 | 4.2 | 4.4 | 4.7 | 5.1 | 5.1 | 5.3 | 9.8 | 11.0 | 12.9 | 15.2 | 13.8 | 14.6 |
| 20-44 | 78 | 84 | 71 | 60 | 79 | 77 | 38.7 | 37.9 | 36.7 | 35.5 | 35.1 | 35.1 | 31.5 | 33.1 | 27.3 | 22.5 | 29.2 | 28.0 |
| 45-64 | 77 | 78 | 67 | 47 | 53 | 51 | 21.8 | 22.2 | 22.1 | 21.1 | 20.3 | 19.7 | 17.7 | 17.8 | 15.3 | 10.5 | 11.1 | 10.3 |
| 65 and over | 84 | 76 | 77 | 77 | 57 | 63 | 3.7 | 3.1 | 2.8 | 2.6 | 2.4 | 2.3 | 3.3 | 2.5 | 2.2 | 2.2 | 1.4 | 1.5 |
| Total Male | 93 | 98 | 88 | 81 | 90 | 88 | 68.5 | 67.7 | 66.4 | 64.4 | 66.4 | 62.5 | 62.2 | 64.5 | 58.2 | 50.3 | 55.5 | 54.4 |
| **Females** | | | | | | | | | | | | | | | | | | |
| 16-19 | 276 | 253 | 320 | 388 | 291 | 296 | 2.7 | 2.9 | 3.1 | 3.6 | 3.7 | 4.0 | 7.7 | 7.4 | 10.2 | 14.6 | 11.4 | 12.3 |
| 20-44 | 115 | 110 | 121 | 132 | 120 | 118 | 16.8 | 16.6 | 17.2 | 18.5 | 19.5 | 20.0 | 20.3 | 19.0 | 21.6 | 25.6 | 24.2 | 24.6 |
| 45-64 | 88 | 80 | 73 | 65 | 63 | 62 | 10.0 | 11.5 | 12.0 | 12.2 | 12.4 | 12.1 | 9.2 | 8.4 | 9.1 | 8.4 | 8.0 | 7.8 |
| 65 and over | 51 | 53 | 64 | 75 | 61 | 63 | 1.2 | 1.3 | 1.3 | 1.2 | 1.2 | 1.2 | 0.7 | 0.6 | 0.9 | 1.0 | 0.8 | 0.8 |
| Total Female | 126 | 109 | 135 | 166 | 130 | 135 | 31.5 | 32.3 | 33.6 | 35.6 | 33.6 | 37.5 | 31.8 | 35.5 | 41.8 | 49.7 | 44.5 | 45.6 |

Source: Computed from U.S. Department of Labor, *Manpower Report of the President, March, 1973* (Washington, D.C.: U.S. Government Printing Office, 1973), Table A-2, p. 128 and Table A-15, p. 146.

**Table 5-2**

**Occupational Classification of the Civilian Labor Force and the Unemployed, Selected Years, 1956 to 1972**

| Occupation | Ratio of Unemployment Rate in Each Group to the National Unemployment Rate | | | | | | Percentage of Labor Force in Each Group | | | | | | Percentage of Total Unemployment in Each Group | | | | | |
|---|---|---|---|---|---|---|---|---|---|---|---|---|---|---|---|---|---|---|
| | 1956 | 1960 | 1964 | 1968 | 1971 | 1972 | 1956 | 1960 | 1964 | 1968 | 1971 | 1972 | 1956 | 1960 | 1964 | 1968 | 1971 | 1972 |
| White-Collar | | | | | | | | | | | | | | | | | | |
| Professional Technical | 24 | 31 | 33 | 33 | 49 | 43 | 9.4 | 11.4 | 12.3 | 13.6 | 14.0 | 14.0 | 2.4 | 3.4 | 3.9 | 4.5 | 6.7 | 5.8 |
| Managers, Officials, Proprietors | 20 | 25 | 27 | 28 | 27 | 32 | 10.1 | 10.7 | 10.7 | 10.2 | 11.0 | 9.8 | 2.0 | 2.5 | 2.7 | 2.7 | 2.9 | 3.0 |
| Clerical | 59 | 69 | 71 | 83 | 81 | 84 | 13.6 | 14.8 | 15.3 | 16.9 | 17.0 | 17.4 | 8.6 | 10.0 | 10.8 | 13.9 | 13.7 | 14.5 |
| Sales | 66 | 69 | 67 | 78 | 73 | 77 | 6.3 | 6.4 | 6.1 | 6.1 | 6.4 | 6.6 | 4.5 | 4.3 | 4.1 | 4.7 | 4.5 | 4.9 |
| Blue-Collar | | | | | | | | | | | | | | | | | | |
| Craftsmen, Foremen | 78 | 96 | 79 | 67 | 80 | 77 | 13.4 | 13.0 | 13.0 | 13.2 | 12.9 | 13.2 | 11.3 | 12.3 | 10.3 | 8.7 | 10.2 | 10.0 |
| Operatives | 132 | 145 | 127 | 125 | 141 | 123 | 19.7 | 18.2 | 18.6 | 18.4 | 16.4 | 16.6 | 28.5 | 27.1 | 23.9 | 23.2 | 23.7 | 20.8 |
| Laborers | 200 | 229 | 208 | 200 | 200 | 184 | 5.7 | 5.4 | 5.0 | 4.7 | 5.1 | 5.2 | 12.8 | 13.3 | 11.1 | 9.8 | 9.8 | 10.0 |
| Service | | | | | | | | | | | | | | | | | | |
| Household Workers | 102 | 96 | 103 | 108 | 76 | 71 | 3.3 | 3.0 | 2.9 | 2.3 | 1.9 | 1.8 | 3.6 | 2.9 | 3.1 | 2.5 | 1.4 | 1.2 |
| Others | 117 | 109 | 117 | 128 | 112 | 118 | 8.4 | 9.2 | 9.9 | 10.1 | 11.6 | 11.7 | 10.9 | 10.0 | 11.8 | 13.0 | 13.0 | 14.0 |
| Farm | | | | | | | | | | | | | | | | | | |
| Farmers and Farm Workers | 41 | 49 | 60 | 58 | 44 | 46 | 10.1 | 7.9 | 6.1 | 4.6 | 3.8 | 3.8 | 5.3 | 3.7 | 3.6 | 2.6 | 1.6 | 1.7 |
| No Previous Work Experience | — | — | — | — | — | — | — | — | — | — | — | — | 10.4 | 10.4 | 14.7 | 14.5 | 12.6 | 14.0 |

Source: Computed from data contained in U.S. Department of Labor, *Manpower Report of the President, March, 1973* (Washington, D.C.: U.S. Government Printing Office, 1973), Table A-17, p. 150 and Table A-11, p. 142.

attributed to blue-collar workers. Thus, from 1956 to 1972 the percentage of unemployment accounted for by blue-collar workers declined from 53 percent to 41 percent.

Let us consider the final category in Table 5-2—those with no previous work experience. ("No previous work experience" refers to people looking for their first job.) This classification could apply to either youth in school or those who have completed their education, as well as married women entering the labor force for the first time.

After 1962 the proportion of first job seekers who were teenagers exceeded 50 percent. This factor is likely responsible for the sharp rise in the proportion of unemployment in 1964 and subsequent years—that is, accounted for by first job seekers in comparison to previous periods. Moreover, the slow economic growth from 1956 to 1964 fell more heavily on those seeking their first job than on experienced (including even manual) workers. Whatever structural changes that occurred did not result in a (relatively) growing pool of experienced blue-collar workers who could not find new jobs. A variety of forms of job security tend to protect the experienced worker, and the gradual reduction in the proportions of the labor force employed in certain occupations and industries has been effected through natural attrition—retirement, death and voluntary quits—rather than wholesale firings. As a result it became increasingly difficult for new labor force entrants to obtain their first job.[19]

## Unemployment by Industry

The statistics on the distribution of unemployment by industry are given in Table 5-3. The major changes in relative unemployment rates have occurred in industries with rapidly declining labor force shares; namely, agriculture and mining. Thus, their relative improvement is not of major importance when considering the economy as a whole. The three largest industries—manufacturing, wholesale and retail trade, and service industries—have experienced little change in their relative unemployment rates from 1956 to 1972. However, the latter two industries have expanded their share of total employment and account for somewhat larger fractions of total unemployment than previously. These statistics provide no support for the hypothesis that unemployment has come to be concentrated more and more among workers displaced in particular industries—for example, mining, manufacturing, or construction. One qualification should perhaps be made. Some workers, originally displaced in these industries, may later have shown up as unemployed in trade or service industries, where they found jobs for a while before becoming unemployed again.

## Unemployment by Race

Table 5-4 indicates the distribution of unemployment by race and sex. Since 1956 there has been little change in the relative unemployment rates of white

**Table 5-3**
**Unemployment Among Experienced Wage and Salary Worker, Selected Years, 1956-1972**

| Industry | Ratio of Unemployment Rate in Each Group to the National Unemployment Rate | | | | | | Percentage of Labor Force in Each Group | | | | | | Percentage of Total Unemployment in Each Group | | | | | |
|---|---|---|---|---|---|---|---|---|---|---|---|---|---|---|---|---|---|---|
| | 1956 | 1960 | 1964 | 1968 | 1971 | 1972 | 1956 | 1960 | 1964 | 1968 | 1971 | 1972 | 1956 | 1960 | 1964 | 1968 | 1971 | 1972 |
| Agriculture | 178 | 202 | 187 | 175 | 134 | 135 | 9.9 | 8.3 | 6.5 | 5.0 | 4.3 | 4.2 | 4.5 | 4.1 | 4.1 | 3.1 | 2.0 | 2.1 |
| Mining | 166 | 172 | 129 | 86 | 70 | 57 | 1.4 | 1.2 | 1.0 | 0.9 | 0.9 | 0.8 | 1.8 | 1.5 | 1.0 | 0.6 | 0.5 | 0.4 |
| Construction | 244 | 245 | 215 | 192 | 176 | 183 | 5.1 | 4.9 | 4.9 | 4.6 | 4.6 | 4.6 | 11.4 | 12.0 | 10.3 | 9.2 | 8.5 | 9.2 |
| Manufacturing | 115 | 113 | 96 | 92 | 115 | 100 | 30.0 | 28.6 | 27.8 | 24.8 | 25.1 | 25.0 | 30.2 | 28.6 | 24.9 | 24.7 | 28.0 | 23.7 |
| Transportation and Public Utilities | 73 | 84 | 67 | 53 | 64 | 63 | 7.3 | 6.8 | 6.4 | 6.0 | 6.0 | 6.0 | 4.6 | 5.0 | 3.8 | 3.4 | 3.5 | 3.5 |
| Wholesale and Retail Trade | 110 | 107 | 110 | 111 | 108 | 114 | 18.6 | 19.4 | 19.5 | 19.7 | 20.5 | 20.7 | 16.7 | 16.5 | 17.1 | 18.3 | 18.9 | 20.4 |
| Finance, Insurance and Real Estate | 41 | 44 | 50 | 61 | 56 | 61 | 4.1 | 4.5 | 4.8 | 4.8 | 5.2 | 5.2 | 1.4 | 1.6 | 2.0 | 2.7 | 2.6 | 2.8 |
| Service Industries | 112 | 92 | 96 | 100 | 95 | 100 | 11.2 | 12.7 | 14.0 | 14.9 | 16.1 | 16.2 | 13.8 | 12.1 | 14.3 | 15.1 | 14.1 | 14.1 |
| Public Administration | 41 | 44 | 40 | 50 | 49 | 52 | 12.5 | 14.2 | 15.5 | 16.6 | 17.4 | 17.6 | 4.3 | 5.0 | 5.2 | 7.7 | 7.7 | 8.3 |

Source: Computed from data contained in U.S. Department of Labor, *Manpower Report of the President, March, 1973* (Washington, D.C.: U.S. Government Printing Office, 1973), Table C-1, p. 188 and Table A-18, p. 151.

**Table 5-4**
**Color-Sex Classification of the Civilian Labor Force and the Unemployed, Selected Years, 1956 to 1972**

| Color and Sex | Ratio of Unemployment Rate in Each Group to the National Unemployment Rate | | | | | | Percentage of Labor Force in Each Group | | | | | | Percentage of Total Unemployment in Each Group | | | | | |
|---|---|---|---|---|---|---|---|---|---|---|---|---|---|---|---|---|---|---|
| | 1956 | 1960 | 1964 | 1968 | 1971 | 1972 | 1956 | 1960 | 1964 | 1968 | 1971 | 1972 | 1956 | 1960 | 1964 | 1968 | 1971 | 1972 |
| Total White | 88 | 89 | 88 | 89 | 92 | 90 | 89.3 | 89.0 | 88.8 | 88.9 | 88.9 | 88.9 | 78.6 | 79.6 | 79.2 | 79.1 | 81.6 | 80.2 |
| Male | 83 | 87 | 79 | 72 | 83 | 80 | 61.2 | 60.0 | 58.7 | 56.6 | 55.6 | 55.4 | 49.7 | 51.6 | 47.0 | 40.5 | 46.1 | 44.6 |
| Female | 102 | 96 | 106 | 119 | 107 | 105 | 28.1 | 29.0 | 30.1 | 32.3 | 33.2 | 33.5 | 28.9 | 27.9 | 32.2 | 38.5 | 35.5 | 35.6 |
| Total Black | 202 | 185 | 185 | 187 | 168 | 179 | 10.7 | 11.1 | 11.1 | 11.1 | 11.1 | 11.1 | 21.5 | 20.4 | 20.8 | 20.9 | 18.4 | 19.8 |
| Male | 193 | 195 | 171 | 156 | 154 | 159 | 6.5 | 6.7 | 6.5 | 6.3 | 6.2 | 6.2 | 12.5 | 12.9 | 11.3 | 9.8 | 9.5 | 9.8 |
| Female | 217 | 171 | 204 | 231 | 183 | 202 | 4.2 | 4.4 | 4.6 | 4.8 | 4.9 | 4.9 | 9.0 | 7.5 | 9.5 | 11.1 | 8.9 | 10.0 |

Source: U.S. Department of Labor, *Manpower Report of the President, March, 1973* (Washington, D.C.: U.S. Government Printing Office, 1973), Table A-16, p. 148; Table A-15, p. 146; and Table A-14, p. 145.

men and white women. For blacks, however, there was significant improvement with the overall unemployment rate falling from slightly more than double the national rate in 1956 to 1.8 times the national rate in 1972. Most of this improvement occurred with respect to the black male unemployment rate, which fell sharply, in relative terms, after 1960. This phenomenon is one factor that should tend to increase black family stability.

Overall, the proportion of blacks and whites in the labor force remained constant from 1956 to 1972. Since the unemployment rate of blacks fell slightly in comparison to whites, blacks made up a somewhat smaller proportion of total unemployment in 1972 as compared to 1956. Changes in the proportion of unemployment accounted for by white men and women were a function of their varying shares of the labor force; while for black men and women, the percentage of unemployment associated with each sex group can be related to changes in labor force shares and unemployment rates.

It appears that utilizing Gordon's measures of increases in the structural component of unemployment that there is little evidence of any *major* changes from 1956 to 1972. However, there are some sectors where structural changes have occurred; namely, white-collar workers and from 1956 to 1964 the unemployment rates of young people and first job seekers. As indicated earlier, the increased proportion since 1964 of unemployed who are teenagers is solely due to their rising proportion of the labor force and not due to higher relative unemployment rates. This factor indicates that this latter unemployment problem is more demographic than an indication of structural change.

This analysis supports the view that the higher unemployment rates of 1971, 1972, and likely the first half of 1973 have been primarily due to inadequate demand as well as the changing composition of the labor force (more women and teenagers) and are not associated with an increased mismatching of vacant jobs and unemployed workers (structural unemployment). (In 1972, the rate of increase in productivity was considerably above the long-term average resulting in a slow decline in unemployment rates.)


**Education and Structural Unemployment**

This section attempts to determine whether there is any relationship between a low level of schooling and the likelihood of worsening employment prospects *over time*. In so doing, we will test empirically a hypothesis first proposed by Clarence Long in 1960, entitled "The Theory of Creeping Unemployment."

Long was seeking an explanation for the fact that from 1948 to 1960, in each period of prosperity following a recession, the rate of unemployment did not fall to a level as low as it had been in the previous business cycle. The major cause of this phenomenon, according to Long, was the inability of many members of the labor force to adapt their skills and abilities to the changing technological and educational requirements of a nuclear age. This hypothesis is clearly a structural explanation of higher unemployment rates.

This hypothesis depends upon two essential postulates. First, in a technologically advancing economy, one observes the existence of a widening productivity spread—that is, the greater the opportunity offered to the average worker to improve his personal productivity, the further some members of the labor force will fall below the average. The reasons for this are varied: some individuals lack the intelligence to absorb better training and education; others are deficient in motivation or emotional stability; still others are barred by age, color, or inferior school facilities in their locality. These workers fall behind the average; the higher the quality of the labor force, the greater the disparity of this group compared with the average.

It is much worse to have no education when the average person is a high school graduate, as was the case in 1972, than when the average educational level is only 8 years, as was the case in 1930. It is worse to be an illiterate when the average person has 8 years of education than when the average person is an illiterate.[20]

The second basic postulate in Long's hypothesis concerns the "social minimum wage." This term refers to the wage level below which workers are not employed because minimum wage legislation and union wage standards forbid it; because social security and private pensions provide an alternative to employment; or because employers themselves set minimum scales to impede unionization, to avoid a reputation as a sweatshop, or to maintain employee morale.

Long argued that the social minimum wage rose at least as fast as the average wage—for which fact there is considerable empirical evidence—and that average wage increased at the same rate as average productivity.[21] The productivity of the uneducated or otherwise poorly equipped worker lags behind both average productivity and the social minimum wage. It becomes unprofitable to hire these low productivity workers with the result that they become unemployed or leave the labor force. Whether unemployment rises or the labor force shrinks depends on whether the stragglers are replaced in the labor force by persons formally outside whose productivity rises at a rate equal to or faster than the social minimum wage.

Long considered education the best single indicator of an individual's productivity.[a] Thus, a person with less than a high school education is not very well equipped to compete with his better educated and more productive counterparts in the labor market.

The Long hypothesis can be analyzed by examining the relationship between education and unemployment over time. The Gordon definition of structural

[a]This view was certainly not shared by all economists. For example, Hans Staehle and Vladamir Woytinsky believed that personal productivity was primarily a function of ability. See Hans Staehle, "Ability, Wages and Income," *Review of Economics and Statistics* 25 (1943); and W.S. Woytinsky, *Earnings and Social Security in the United States* (Washington, D.C.: Social Science Research Council, 1943).

unemployment will be utilized in this investigation as a basis for determining whether there is an increase in the structural component of unemployment among the less-educated.

Statistics on the distribution of education and unemployment for males in 1950, 1960, and 1972 are presented in Table 5-5. These are years with similar

**Table 5-5**

**Years of School and Rates and Proportions of Unemployment, 1950, 1960, and 1972 (Males 25 and Over)**

| Years of School | | Relative Rate of Unemployment | Proportion in Labor Force 25 and Over | Percentage of Total Unemployment |
|---|---|---|---|---|
| **1950** | | | | |
| Elementary: | 0 | 136 | 1.7 | 3.5 |
| | 1-7 | 113 | 24.6 | 34.4 |
| | 8 | 89 | 19.6 | 23.1 |
| High School: | 1-3 | 70 | 17.7 | 18.5 |
| | 4 | 53 | 22.4 | 13.3 |
| College: | 1-3 | 47 | 7.6 | 4.5 |
| | 4 or more | 26 | 7.8 | 2.7 |
| **1960** | | | | |
| Elementary: | 0 | 149 | 1.3 | 2.5 |
| | 1-7 | 129 | 17.0 | 30.2 |
| | 8 | 100 | 16.1 | 21.4 |
| High School: | 1-3 | 87 | 20.2 | 22.4 |
| | 4 | 51 | 25.8 | 15.5 |
| College: | 1-3 | 45 | 9.6 | 5.2 |
| | 4 or more | 20 | 10.0 | 3.0 |
| **1972** | | | | |
| Elementary: | 0 | 138 | 0.5 | 1.6 |
| | 1-7 | 113 | 9.2 | 18.2 |
| | 8 | 109 | 10.0 | 15.4 |
| High School: | 1-3 | 84 | 16.7 | 24.3 |
| | 4 | 63 | 34.3 | 25.2 |
| College: | 1-3 | 54 | 12.5 | 8.8 |
| | 4 or more | 32 | 16.8 | 6.5 |

Source: Computed from data contained in U.S. Bureau of the Census, 1950 Census of Population, Special Report P-E No. 5B, *Education* (Washington, D.C.: U.S. Government Printing Office, 1953), Table 9, p. 73; U.S. Bureau of the Census, 1960 Census of Population, Special Report, PC(2)5B, *Educational Attainment* (Washington, D.C.: U.S. Government Printing Office, 1963), Table 4, p. 54; William V. Deuterman, "Educational Attainment of Workers, March, 1972," U.S. Department of Labor, Special Labor Force Report No. 148 (Washington, D.C.: U.S. Government Printing Office, 1973), Table D, p. A-10 and Table K, p. A-18.

overall unemployment rates. Because of the changing employment status of young workers, irrespective of schooling, this analysis is restricted to workers 25 years of age and over.

Comparing the unemployment rate in 1950 and 1960, among workers with various educational levels, the relative rate increased for those workers who lacked a high school diploma. However, the relative unemployment rate fell among workers who had obtained a high school education or more schooling. This change in relative unemployment rates is consistent with the Long hypothesis. On the other hand, the proportion of the labor force with 8 years of schooling or less fell by one-fourth. Thus, workers with 8 years of schooling or less accounted for only 54 percent of all unemployment in 1960 compared to 61 percent in 1950. The proportion of high school dropouts increased, and coupled with a rise in their relative rate of unemployment caused a 4 percent rise in the amount of unemployment accounted for by them. Thus, according to Gordon's criteria, the problem of structural unemployment among the less educated did not worsen between 1950 and 1960. Those workers with less than a high school education accounted for 80 percent of the unemployed in 1950 and 77 percent of the unemployed in 1960. In other words, the labor force was able to adapt, in terms of increased educational attainment, to the advancing technology of modern industry.

Between 1960 and 1972 the distribution of unemployment by level of schooling followed a pattern somewhat the opposite of that observed in the previous decade. In the more recent period the relative jobless rates for workers with educational levels below high school graduation declined, while those including high school graduation and beyond rose. This change in relative unemployment rates is contrary to the Long hypothesis since it implies a greater relative increase in the demand for less-educated labor and a smaller relative increase in demand for highly educated workers. Moreover, in the same period, the proportion of workers without a high school diploma fell sharply from 55 to 36 percent of the male labor force. As a result of a decline in the relative rate of unemployment for workers without a high school diploma, as well as a rapid drop in their share of the labor force, the proportion of unemployment accounted for by workers with less than 12 years of schooling declined from 77 to 60 percent.

Considering the entire period of 1950 to 1972, the relative rates of unemployment by years of schooling have shown little change. Because of this occurrence as well as the increase in the educational attainment of the labor force, the proportion of unemployment accounted for by the less-educated has fallen. However, the percentage of unemployment accounted for by high school graduates has nearly doubled. This is attributed to a slight rise in their relative unemployment rate and a 50 percent increase from 1950 to 1972 in the proportion of male high school graduates in the labor force.

An earlier chapter indicated that the labor force participation rates of less-educated males have declined substantially. Thus, unemployment rates for the less-educated segment of the work force have been significantly affected by the decline in their labor force participation rates. Suppose one made the assumption that all those individuals below retirement age who have dropped out of the labor force should be counted as unemployed. How would this affect the level of unemployment of the least educated?

The Council of Economic Advisors in its 1963 report stated that the "availability of jobs encourages the entry of many into the labor force who had not sought work in the knowledge that there was none to be had."[22] They estimated that a substantial improvement in economic prospects would pull back into the labor market about 800,000 people within a year, and more subsequently.[23]

The most important consideration is how the number of labor force dropouts is distributed among the various educational levels. There is a logical and straight-forward method for determining this distribution. Application of the 1960 and 1972 male population classified by age and educational attainment to the 1950 labor force participation rates for each age and schooling level category yields an adjusted labor force for each level of educational attainment. When actual employment for each educational level is deducted from the adjusted labor force, "real" unemployment is the result. Real unemployment is then expressed as a percentage of the adjusted labor force.[b]

We can assume that the extension and liberalization of social security and private pension plans during the postwar period would have decreased labor force participation rates in the 65 and older age bracket, even if there had been employment for everyone. For example, between 1950 and 1960 the decline in the participation rate for male college graduates 65 years of age and over was 12 percent. It is assumed that this decline measures the strength of influences other than job shortages that caused participation rates for these well educated older workers to decline.

Table 5-6 indicates the "real" unemployment rates in 1960 and 1972, by years of schooling. These rates were derived using the methodology described above. These statistics indicate that the percentage increase in the "real" unemployment rate for the less-educated is substantial. Considering all non-high school graduates, the "real" unemployment rate actually tripled between 1950 and 1972. Perhaps one weakness with this concept of "real" unemployment is that it indicates that there is a marked increase in "real" unemployment among high school graduates. It is difficult to believe that the slight decline in the

---

[b]This calculation also permits us to estimate what the size of the male labor force would be in 1960 and 1972, if a shortage of jobs had not squeezed out large numbers of people from the unemployment and labor force statistics. The concept of "real" unemployment was first discussed by Killingsworth. See Charles Killingsworth, "Automation, Jobs and Manpower," in *The Nation's Manpower Revolution*, U.S. Senate, Subcommittee on Labor and Public Welfare, 88th Congress, 1963, pp. 1475-1480 and "The Bottleneck in Labor Skills" in Arthur M. Okun (Ed.), *The Battle Against Unemployment* (New York: W.W. Norton, 1965), p. 35.

Table 5-6
**Real Unemployment Rates, 1950, 1960 and 1972 (Males 25 and Over)**

| Years of School Completed | 1950[a] Real Unemployment Rate | 1960 Official Unemployment Rate | 1960 Real Unemployment Rate | 1960 Official Unemployment Rate | 1972 Real Unemployment Rate | 1972 Percentage Increase Real Unemployment Rate 1950-1972 |
|---|---|---|---|---|---|---|
| 0 | 7.2 | 8.1 | 23.4 | 7.7 | 31.7 | 340 |
| 1-7 | 6.0 | 7.1 | 15.7 | 6.3 | 21.4 | 257 |
| 8 | 4.7 | 5.5 | 9.4 | 6.1 | 13.6 | 189 |
| 9-11 | 3.7 | 4.8 | 5.4 | 4.7 | 8.9 | 141 |
| 12 | 2.8 | 2.8 | 2.8[b] | 3.5 | 4.3 | 54 |
| 13-15 | 2.5 | 2.5 | 2.5[b] | 3.0 | 3.0[c] | 20 |
| 16 or more | 1.4 | 1.1 | 1.1[b] | 1.8 | 1.8[c] | 29 |

[a]Since 1950 is used as the base year, the official unemployment rate becomes the real unemployment rate.

[b]Between 1950 and 1960 the labor force participation rates for workers with 12 years, 13 to 15 years, and 16 years or more of schooling rose. Thus, there is no need to adjust the 1960 official unemployment rates to obtain the real unemployment rates.

[c]Between 1960 and 1972 the labor force participation rates for workers with 13 to 15 years of schooling and 16 years or more of schooling remained constant. Thus, there is no need to adjust the official unemployment rates to obtain the real unemployment rates.

Source: Computed from data contained in U.S. Bureau of the Census, 1950 Census of Population, Special Report P-E No. 5B, *Education* (Washington, D.C.: U.S. Government Printing Office, 1953), Table 9, p. 73; U.S. Bureau of the Census, 1960 Census of Population, Special Report PC(2)5B, *Educational Attainment* (Washington, D.C.: U.S. Government Printing Office,, 1963), Table 4, p. 54; William V. Deuterman, "Educational Attainment of Workers, March, 1972," U.S. Department of Labor, Special Labor Force Report No. 148 (Washington, D.C.: U.S. Government Printing Office, 1973), Table B, p. A-8, Table D, p. A-10, and Table K, p. A-18.

observed labor force participation rates and the concomitant rise in the "real" unemployment rate of high school graduates is due to lack of employment opportunities, although it certainly is possible.

Moreover, union retirement plans as well as provisions in Social Security legislation have likely encouraged early retirement, especially among blue-collar workers. Since these trends are not considered in calculating the "real" unemployment rate, this statistic is subject to some upward bias.

The data in Table 5-6 not only indicate the severe employment problems of the less-educated, but point out that official unemployment rates do not adequately reflect the shortage of job opportunities for these workers. This can be seen quite clearly by comparing Table 5-5 and Table 5-6. The former indicates that between 1960 and 1972 the measured rates of relative unemployment fell for those schooling categories below high school graduation. However, the actual change in employment opportunities for the less-educated was masked by a decline in the labor force participation rates of poorly educated workers. When the unemployment figures are adjusted for labor force withdrawal in the manner described above, it is clear that between 1960 and 1972 employment opportunities for the less-educated worsened substantially as indicated by the marked increases in real unemployment rates over that 12-year period.

Because the "real" unemployment rate for the less-educated rose far more rapidly than the proportion of less-educated workers declined (see Tables 5-5 and 5-6), the proportion of "real" unemployed workers who are less educated rose substantially indicating that structural unemployment worsened among poorly educated workers. (However, this does not confirm the Long "theory of creeping unemployment"; Long's hypothesis was formulated with respect to measured unemployment rates not the "real" unemployment rates being considered.)

To summarize the argument; the question of the existence of structural unemployment among the less educated depends in the last analysis on how one wishes to define unemployment. If one counts as jobless only those enumerated in the official unemployment statistics, then data presented above show no evidence of increasing structural unemployment among the less-educated. However, if one includes as unemployed those individuals who have dropped out of the labor force probably because they have been unable to find work, then the data clearly indicate the existence of structural unemployment among the less-educated.

Let us assume that the calculated "real" unemployment rates more accurately reflect the present employment opportunities for less-educated workers than the official unemployment statistics. What other factors beside lack of education per se can account for an increase in these unemployment rates from 1950 to 1972?

One factor which could be important is age. It may be that the burden of the increase in "real" unemployment has fallen on the older less-educated worker as opposed to his younger, less-educated counterpart. Thus, technological change and adolescence could make a man who completed 9 years of school in 1925 or 1930 about as qualified to compete on today's labor market as a younger individual with a recently acquired sixth-grade education. This would be especially true if there had been an increase in the productivity of schooling. Moreover, to the extent that there is age discrimination in employment, the burden of this discrimination would likely fall on the older, less-educated worker instead of his better-educated counterpart of the same age. The latter would be more likely to be protected by seniority provisions. This question is considered in Table 5-7 which indicates the "real" unemployment rates by age for each level of schooling below high school graduation. The data presented do not indicate that age has been a *major* factor in terms of its association with higher real unemployment rates. Only the statistics pertaining to individuals with 0 years of schooling show a consistently greater increase in "real" unemployment rates as one considers progressively older workers. Among the other schooling categories only workers in the 55 to 64 age group have experienced significantly greater increases in real unemployment than younger workers. This finding lends support to the argument that it is lack of education per se that has caused a rise in the "real" unemployment rate for these workers.

Another factor that could influence "real" unemployment is intellectual ability. As the work force has become more highly skilled, the mental demands placed on individuals have risen, likely making those individuals who are poorly equipped mentally less and less employable over time. Moreover, because of compulsory school attendance laws as well as a number of anti-dropout programs operated by state and federal agencies (such as the in-school and summer programs of the Neighborhood Youth Corps), it is likely that over time the ability level of those failing to complete grammar school or high school has fallen. For example, in 1925, when most individuals left school after the eighth-grade to take a job, there were undoubtedly many intelligent individuals who terminated their schooling at that point as well as those who were not mentally equipped to continue their education. However, in 1972 an individual leaving school at the age of 16—the minimum age for school-leaving in most states—having only completed the eighth grade, would have been kept in that or other grades several times and would tend to be of below average mental ability.

There is some limited evidence that tends to confirm this hypothesis. A study was undertaken by Viola Benson during which students in the sixth grade were given an I.Q. test and then followed up to determine their highest grade completed. The results indicated that the high school dropouts had a median I.Q. only 4 points lower than that of the entire group tested.[24] This is not surprising since the median years of schooling of the population at that time was about 9 years. However, in 1953 the Commission on Human Resources administered the AGCT Intelligence Examination to a large group of young people with varying amounts of schooling. This study indicated that the typical dropout had an average I.Q. which was 10 points below the median for the

Table 5-7
**Real Unemployment Rates, by Age and Level of Schooling, 1950 to 1972**

| Age/Education | 0 Years | | | 1-7 Years | | | 8 Years | | | 9-11 Years | | |
|---|---|---|---|---|---|---|---|---|---|---|---|---|
| | 1950 | 1972 | Percentage Points Difference | 1950 | 1972 | Percentage Points Difference | 1950 | 1972 | Percentage Points Difference | 1950 | 1972 | Percentage Points Difference |
| 25-29 | 7.3 | 19.4 | 12.1 | 8.1 | 12.9 | 4.8 | 6.4 | 10.8 | 4.4 | 5.9 | 6.1 | 0.2 |
| 30-34 | 7.0 | 20.7 | 13.7 | 6.1 | 11.5 | 5.4 | 4.7 | 9.4 | 4.7 | 4.4 | 9.2 | 4.8 |
| 35-44 | 6.7 | 25.8 | 19.1 | 5.4 | 11.1 | 6.7 | 4.3 | 8.1 | 3.8 | 3.8 | 6.8 | 3.0 |
| 45-54 | 7.1 | 26.6 | 19.5 | 5.7 | 11.6 | 5.9 | 4.1 | 7.1 | 3.0 | 3.8 | 4.4 | 0.6 |
| 55-64 | 8.0 | 28.2 | 20.2 | 6.0 | 28.2 | 22.2 | 4.7 | 11.6 | 6.9 | 3.2 | 11.6 | 8.4 |

Source: See Table 5-6.

entire group tested.[25] Because of the rapid decline in the number of high school dropouts during the 1960s, it is likely that the deterioration in the average mental ability of the high school dropout has continued although certainly other factors remain important influences regarding length of stay in school.

Thus, there is some evidence that a deterioration in the average ability of those failing to graduate from high school has occurred, which has likely contributed to the increase in the real unemployment rates of the less-educated. Moreover, the employment outlook for these poorly equipped individuals will likely continue to deteriorate. Not only are they falling further and further behind the average member of the labor force in terms of number of years of school completed, but the increasing complexity of modern production processes seems to indicate that mental requirements for blue-collar as well as many white-collar jobs may be rising. This phenomenon, coupled with an increasing social minimum wage, makes the low mental ability worker less and less employable.

## Summary

A number of major studies regarding the causes of the high jobless rates from 1957 to 1964 were reviewed. These studies generally found that unemployment in most sectors of the work force rose about as rapidly as the increase in the overall jobless rate. There was no tendency for unemployment to become more concentrated in certain occupations, industries, or regions. Thus, most of these studies concluded that inadequate aggregate demand and not structural unemployment was the primary factor accounting for excessive jobless levels during this period.

Using Gordon's definition to determine if structural unemployment worsened from 1956 to 1972, it was generally found that this did not occur. Although several sectors—such as white-collar workers—have experienced higher relative unemployment rates in recent years, it is clear that the high jobless rates experienced from 1970 to mid-1973 were primarily because of non-structural factors.

From 1950 to 1972 the relative unemployment rates of the less-educated have not increased in comparison with their better-educated counterparts, which contradicts the Long hypothesis. However, if the concept of unemployment is redefined to include labor force dropouts, then the "real" unemployment rates of the less-educated have risen sharply. Two factors besides lack of education per se likely account for this phenomenon, namely the increasing average age of the less-educated worker and a decline in the average ability of the poorly educated worker relative to the entire labor force.

# 6

# Unemployment, Poverty, and Economic Growth

The three previous chapters examined the characteristics and location of the unemployed. This chapter considers the interrelationships between the overall rate of unemployment and increases in Gross National Product and the price level. In addition, the association between the incidence of poverty and the rate of economic growth is explored.

Consider a situation in which, for a period of several consecutive years, aggregate demand is not sufficient to ensure full employment. The cause of the excessive joblessness may be frequent downturns in economic activity, or it may be the consequence of a slow rate of economic growth.

Suppose all the unemployment above frictional levels is attributable to insufficient aggregate demand, and moreover, any inadequacy of demand is the exclusive result of economic fluctuations. In this case, full employment will occur at cyclical peaks, but not during other phases of the business cycle.[1] Policies that *effectively* forestall or moderate any decline in economic activity will tend to keep the economy operating at reasonably close to full employment.

However, if all joblessness in excess of frictional levels is associated with an inadequacy of aggregate demand, but full employment does not exist even at cyclical peaks, the unemployment (above frictional levels) can be ascribed to a sluggish rate of economic growth. In a dynamic economy such as that of the United States, technological progress, additions to the stock of both physical and human capital, and additions to the total labor force make possible progressively higher levels of output. Thus, unemployment in excess of frictional levels may result, if economic growth has been insufficient to absorb all the new entrants into the labor force and to provide jobs for those displaced due to technical change. In this case, even if the appropriate monetary and fiscal policies are followed, and recessions are mild and of brief duration, unacceptably high rates of joblessness will persist. Policies designed to increase the rate of economic growth, however, may succeed in raising aggregate demand to a level consistent with full employment. Maintenance of full employment will then depend on whether the economy can continue to achieve a rate of growth sufficiently high to absorb the continually rising output made possible by both technical change with concomitant productivity advance and the ever increasing supplies of physical and human economic resources.

As indicated in the previous chapter, many economists believe that the high unemployment rates which occurred from 1957 to 1964 were primarily the result of inadequate demand. They point to the low rate of increase in real Gross

National Product that occurred during this period. Over the seven year interval the rate of economic growth was only about 70 percent of the average for the entire postwar period.[2] Moreover, those foreign countries that have consistently experienced lower levels of unemployment than the United States have generally had considerably higher rates of economic growth. In addition, the unemployment rate in Canada has been equal or above that of the United States through most of the last 25 years, and the former has had an even lower economic growth rate than the United States.

It is possible to determine the magnitude of the deficiency in aggregate demand responsible for any given amount of excess unemployment. This is accomplished by relating changes in total demand to data on recent changes in employment and unemployment.[3] For example, suppose a statistical analysis indicated that an increase of $1 billion in real Gross National Product has recently been associated with an increase in employment of 40,000 persons. Assuming the constancy of this relationship, one can estimate what level of real Gross National Product will be consistent with any given level of employment. To obtain a level of employment 400,000 higher than actually existed in any year, it would have been necessary for real Gross National Product to be $10 billion higher.

Moreover, if it can be assumed that the observed statistical relationship between real Gross National Product and employment will continue into the intermediate future, one can estimate the magnitude of the increase in real Gross National Product needed if employment is to increase by any given amount.

Because of growth in the labor force, however, an increase in the number of persons employed is not usually accompanied by an equivalent decrease in the number of persons unemployed. Moreover, the total labor force typically increases somewhat more rapidly in periods when employment opportunities are very plentiful than when jobless levels are high. Thus, if we wish to determine what magnitude of increase in GNP is needed in order to achieve a specified rate of unemployment, it is more useful to work directly with data on the unemployment rate, rather than with statistics on employment.

Using the latter approach, Arthur Okun developed an equation that could be used to measure the deficiency in aggregate demand or to determine the magnitude of the increase in aggregate demand that would be needed to achieve any given reduction in unemployment. His initial approach was to relate quarterly changes in the unemployment rate, expressed in percentage points, to quarterly percentage changes in real GNP. Using observations for 55 consecutive calendar quarters from 1947 to 1960, Okun obtained the following regression equation:[4]

$$Y = .30 - .30 \, X \, (r = .79)$$
$$Y = \text{percentage point change in unemployment rate}$$

where:

$X$ = percentage change in real GNP

$r$ = coefficient of correlation

The equation indicates that on the average, if real GNP remains unchanged, the unemployment rate increases 0.3 percent over the previous year's level. If real GNP increases 1.0 percent, the jobless rate remains the same. Should real GNP increase by more than 1.0 percent, the unemployment rate would decline by an amount equivalent to 0.3 times the additional percentage increase in real GNP. For example, if real GNP increases 3.0 percent, the unemployment rate declines 0.6 percent.

Partly because Okun's equation was fitted to data for the years 1947 to 1960, it does not accurately predict changes in the unemployment rate which occurred from 1961 to 1972. (See Table 6-1) In all but one case, the equation underpredicts the actual unemployment rate and in 5 cases the difference between the predicted and actual unemployment rate is greater than one percentage point.

It is possible to re-estimate the equation relating changes in unemployment to variations in real Gross National Product. Based on quarterly statistics on unemployment and real Gross National Product for the period of 1961 to 1972 the equation obtained is as follows:

**Table 6-1**

**Actual and Predicted Unemployment Rates, 1961 to 1972 (Okun's Equation)**

| Year | Actual Unemployment Rate | Predicted Unemployment Rate |
|------|--------------------------|------------------------------|
| 1961 | 6.7 | 5.2 |
| 1962 | 5.5 | 5.0 |
| 1963 | 5.7 | 4.6 |
| 1964 | 5.2 | 4.3 |
| 1965 | 4.5 | 3.6 |
| 1966 | 3.8 | 2.8 |
| 1967 | 3.8 | 2.9 |
| 1968 | 3.6 | 1.8 |
| 1969 | 3.5 | 3.5 |
| 1970 | 4.9 | 5.3 |
| 1971 | 5.9 | 4.9 |
| 1972 | 5.6 | 4.2 |

Actual data from U.S. Department of Commerce *Economic Report of the President, 1973* (Washington, D.C.: U.S. Government Printing Office, 1973), Table C-26, p. 223; Predicted unemployment rate based on Okun's equation Y = .30 −30 X fitted to 1947 to 1960 unemployment data.

$$Y = 1.3 - .30 \, X \, (r = .87)$$

where the symbols have the same meaning as indicated above. Notice that the percentage point decline in unemployment associated with changes in real Gross National Product is the same as that obtained by Okun. However, the autonomous component of the equation is a full percentage point higher. This means that if the real Gross National Product remained the same from one year to the next, the unemployment rate would increase by 1.3 percentage points compared with Okun's result of only 0.3 percentage point increase. The increase in the autonomous component of the equation probably reflects the more rapid increase of new labor force entrants which has occurred in the second as opposed to the first half of the postwar period. This implies that economic growth had to be considerably higher in the 1961 to 1972 period to reduce unemployment by an equivalent amount when compared to the 1947 to 1960 era. Table 6-2 indicates the actual and predicted unemployment rates for 1961 to 1972 on the basis of the equation obtained by the author.

Okun also developed an estimate of potential real Gross National Product. This equation was based on the assumption that when the unemployment rate was 4.0 percent (an estimate of the full employment, unemployment rate), actual GNP equals potential GNP. If the unemployment rate is above 4.0 percent, however, actual GNP is lower than potential GNP. The relationship between actual and potential GNP was given as follows:[5]

**Table 6-2**
**Actual and Predicted Unemployment Rates, 1961 to 1972 (Author's Equation)**

| Year | Actual Unemployment Rate | Predicted Unemployment Rate |
|------|--------------------------|------------------------------|
| 1961 | 6.7 | 6.2 |
| 1962 | 5.5 | 6.0 |
| 1963 | 5.7 | 6.1 |
| 1964 | 5.2 | 5.3 |
| 1965 | 4.5 | 4.6 |
| 1966 | 3.8 | 3.9 |
| 1967 | 3.8 | 4.4 |
| 1968 | 3.6 | 3.7 |
| 1969 | 3.5 | 4.2 |
| 1970 | 4.9 | 5.0 |
| 1971 | 5.9 | 5.5 |
| 1972 | 5.6 | 4.8 |

Source: Actual data from U.S. Department of Commerce, *Economic Report of the President, 1973* (Washington, D.C.: U.S. Government Printing Office, 1973), Table C-26, p. 223; Predicted unemployment rate based on equation Y = 1.30 −.30 X fitted to 1961 to 1972 unemployment data.

$$P = A [1 + .032 (U - 4)]$$
$P$ = Potential GNP
$A$ = Actual GNP
$U$ = Unemployment Rate

As an example of how the model works, suppose the unemployment rate is one percentage point above 4.0 percent (i.e., 5.0 percent), the size of the gap between actual and potential GNP is equal to 3.2 percent of actual GNP. If the unemployment rate is 2 percentage points above the 4.0 percent (i.e., 6.0 percent), the size of the gap is equal to 6.4 percent of actual GNP. Thus, for any period in which the unemployment rate is in excess of 4.0 percent, one can insert into this equation the actual unemployment rate and actual real GNP and determine what GNP would have been had the unemployment rate been only 4.0 percent. The gap between potential GNP and actual GNP may be regarded as the amount of unrealized output due to excessive joblessness.

George Perry has developed an alternative estimate of potential output that is based on a larger number of factors. Perry's estimates consider the composition and size of the labor force (shifting continually toward more women and teenagers), average hours of work, and productivity trends.[6]

Table 6-3 compares the estimates of potential GNP derived by applying Okun's single equation model with the results obtained in the more detailed investigation undertaken by Perry. The data presented indicate that except for the years 1969 and 1970 the two alternative estimates correspond rather closely. The higher estimates of potential GNP obtained by Perry for 1969 and 1970 than those calculated by employing Okun's model, are due to the unusually rapid rise in the size of the labor force during those years, a factor which Okun's equation does not consider.

In many respects the results presented above are disappointing. The only peacetime period in which the gap between actual and potential GNP was small was during the years 1955 to 1957. The only interval when the economy operated above its calculated potential level occurred when the United States military was heavily involved in Southeast Asia. Moreover, although the data is not presented, the only other period since 1948 during which the economy operated above its potential calculated level was during the period 1951 to 1953, at which time the military was involved in hostility in Korea.

The recessions of 1953-54, 1957-58, 1960-61, and 1969-70 are clearly indicated by sharp increases in the size of the gap between actual and potential output over the previous cyclical peak year. (See Table 6-3.) Thus, in 1958, a year in which the unemployment rate reached 7.5 percent in August, actual output was approximately 9 percent below potential levels.

The interval from 1957 to 1964, during which time the high rates of unemployment stimulated the debate over the relative importance of structural versus inadequate demand explanations of excessive joblessness, can be seen clearly as a period when the economy operated well below potential levels. Using

**Table 6-3**
**Alternative Estimates of Potential GNP and Actual GNP, 1954 to 1971**

| Year | Actual GNP (Billions of Current Dollars) | Potential GNP (Okun) | Potential GNP (Perry) | Gap (Percent) (Okun) | Gap (Percent) (Perry) |
|------|------|------|------|------|------|
| 1954 | 364.8 | 382.3 | 379.0 | 4.8 | 3.9 |
| 1955 | 398.0 | 402.8 | 399.0 | 1.2 | 0.2 |
| 1956 | 419.2 | 420.5 | 426.3 | 0.3 | 1.7 |
| 1957 | 441.1 | 445.5 | 458.1 | 1.0 | 3.8 |
| 1958 | 447.3 | 487.4 | 485.1 | 9.0 | 8.5 |
| 1959 | 483.7 | 506.9 | 510.3 | 4.8 | 5.5 |
| 1960 | 503.7 | 527.9 | 536.7 | 4.8 | 6.5 |
| 1961 | 520.1 | 565.0 | 562.7 | 8.6 | 8.2 |
| 1962 | 560.3 | 587.2 | 589.2 | 4.8 | 5.1 |
| 1963 | 590.5 | 622.6 | 617.8 | 5.4 | 4.6 |
| 1964 | 632.4 | 656.7 | 651.0 | 3.8 | 2.9 |
| 1965 | 684.9 | 695.9 | 688.9 | 1.6 | 0.6 |
| 1966 | 749.9 | 745.1 | 736.8 | −0.6 | −1.7 |
| 1967 | 793.9 | 788.2 | 792.3 | −0.7 | −0.2 |
| 1968 | 864.2 | 853.1 | 857.5 | −1.3 | −0.8 |
| 1969 | 929.1 | 914.2 | 937.2 | −1.6 | 0.9 |
| 1970 | 974.1 | 1002.1 | 1030.0 | 2.9 | 5.8 |
| 1971 | 1046.8 | 1110.4 | 1123.8 | 6.1 | 7.3 |

Source: Data on actual GNP from U.S. Department of Commerce, *Economic Report of the President, 1972*, (Washington, D.C.: U.S. Government Printing Office, 1972), Table B-1, p. 195; Perry's estimates from George L. Perry, "Labor Force Structure, Potential Output and Productivity," *Brookings Papers on Economic Activity* 2 No. 3, (1971): 534. Okun's estimates based on equation $P = A \left[ 1 + .032 \left( U - 4 \right) \right]$.

Perry's estimates, the average GNP gap in those years was 5.6 percent or over $30 billion, which meant that the rate of economic growth was too slow to absorb all the new entrants into the labor force, as well as those workers displaced by technical change.

Writing in 1971, Perry predicted that unemployment would be slow to fall in 1972 and 1973 because of an expected rapid rise in the rate of growth of productivity from the unusually low levels of 1965 to 1970. Thus, he predicted that even with an increase of real GNP of 7.0 percent in 1972 and 1973, unemployment would average 5.7 percent in 1972 and 4.8 percent in 1973.[7] Gross National Product grew by approximately 7 percent in 1972 and nearly at that rate during the first half of 1973. Unemployment averaged 5.6 percent in 1972 and 5.0 percent during the first half of 1973. Thus, Perry's predictions were quite accurate. In Table 6-2 the largest discrepancy between actual and predicted unemployment rates is for the year 1972, which occurs because the equation used to predict unemployment rates does not consider productivity changes resulting in an underestimate of the unemployment rate for that year.


## Poverty and Unemployment

The precise meaning of the term poverty is difficult to determine because some type of value judgment is required to specify a poverty level of income. The definition of a poverty level of income may be expressed in either relative or absolute terms. A relativistic approach to defining poverty could, for example, indicate that all those individuals in the lower 25 percent of the income distribution receive "poverty"-level incomes. In effect, however, this converts the problem of poverty into the more general issue of equality in the distribution of income. Therefore, unless the distribution of income becomes more equal, there can be no change in the relative number of people in poverty despite the fact that their incomes may be rising substantially over time.

Most of the poverty statistics used by government agencies are based on a so-called "poverty-index" that was developed by the Social Security Administration in 1964. For families of three or more persons, the poverty level was set at three times the cost of an economy food plan developed by the U.S. Department of Agriculture to provide minimum nutritional needs for "emergency or temporary use when funds are low." Annual revisions of the poverty-income cutoff, which in 1964 was $3,000 for a family of four, were formerly based upon price changes for the items in the economy food budget. Since 1969, the poverty-income levels have been revised upward to reflect similar movements in the overall consumer price index.[9] In 1971, the low-income or poverty threshold—the income level that separates "poor" from "non-poor" was $4,137 for a non-farm family of four.[10]

One difficulty with the standard government definitions of poverty is that being based upon an income criteria they do not consider the assets (liquid or illiquid) that an individual or family may own. Thus, equity in homes, landholdings, automobiles, stocks and bonds, and the cash value of life insurance policies are excluded, which results in large numbers of elderly retired persons being classified as earning incomes below the poverty level while their actual standard of living may be higher than that of many younger persons with greater earnings but fewer assets.

There are wide variations in the incidence of poverty among the various subgroups of the population. (See Table 6-4.) Thus, the likelihood that a family headed by a woman will have an income below the poverty level is five times greater than a family with a male head. Roughly 1 in 10 whites is below the poverty-income level, compared to one-third of all blacks. Thus, while only 11 percent of the population is black, this group accounts for nearly three-tenths of

**Table 6-4**
**Persons Below Poverty Level, by Status and Race, 1971**

| Status and Race | Total (Millions) | Below Poverty Level | |
|---|---|---|---|
| | | Number | Percent |
| All Persons | 204.6 | 25.6 | 12.5 |
| In Families | 188.2 | 20.4 | 10.8 |
|   Head | 53.3 | 5.3 | 10.0 |
|     Male | 47.1 | 3.2 | 6.8 |
|     Female | 6.1 | 2.1 | 33.9 |
|   Members Under Age 18 | 68.2 | 10.3 | 15.1 |
|   Other Members | 65.2 | 4.7 | 7.2 |
| Unrelated Individuals | 16.3 | 5.1 | 31.6 |
|   65 Years and Older | 6.1 | 2.6 | 42.3 |
| White | 179.4 | 17.8 | 9.9 |
| In Families | 165.2 | 13.6 | 8.2 |
|   Male Head | 151.7 | 9.5 | 6.2 |
|   Female Head | 13.5 | 4.0 | 30.4 |
| Unrelated Individuals | 14.2 | 4.2 | 29.6 |
|   65 Years and Older | 5.5 | 2.1 | 40.2 |
| Negro | 22.8 | 7.4 | 32.5 |
|   Percent of Total | 11.1 | 28.9 | — |
| In Families | 20.9 | 6.5 | 31.2 |
|   Male Head | 14.5 | 2.9 | 20.3 |
|   Female Head | 6.4 | 3.6 | 56.1 |
| Unrelated Individuals | 1.0 | 0.5 | 54.4 |
|   65 Years and Older | 0.3 | 0.2 | 68.4 |

Source: U.S. Department of Commerce, Bureau of the Census, *Consumer Income*, Series P-60, No. 82, "Characteristics of the Low Income Population: 1971," (Washington, D.C.: U.S. Government Printing Office, 1972), p. 1.

all persons classified as poor during 1971. (The census presently uses the words "poor" and "poverty" interchangeably; thus, a person with an income below the poverty level is classified as a "poor" person and one whose earnings are above the poverty level of income are categorized as "non-poor.") In spite of the nearly universal coverage of Social Security and private pension programs, over two-fifths of all older persons in 1971 received incomes below the poverty level. The high proportion of older unrelated individuals living below the poverty threshold occurred despite the fact that the poverty-income cutoff (separating "poor" from "non-poor") for these persons was only $1,931 in 1971. Families living on farms are twice as likely to be below the poverty-income level as those living elsewhere, and those family heads with an elementary school education were four times as likely to earn incomes below the poverty level as high school graduates.

The median income deficit for poverty families was about $1,100 in 1971. For white families the deficit was about $1,050, as compared to $1,250 for Negro families, a somewhat smaller difference than in the preceding year. The difference in the median deficit between white and Negro families is accounted for in part by the smaller average size of white families below the income level—3.6 persons for whites and 4.4 for Negroes.[11]

Poverty is increasingly becoming a phenomenon of our large metropolitan areas. Whereas in 1960 only about 43 percent of the poor lived in metropolitan areas, by 1971, 56 percent of the low-income families lived in these areas. In 1971, the South had 44 percent of all the nation's poor individuals, nearly the same percentage as in 1959.[12] The incidence of poverty is particularly high among southern blacks—they are between three and four times as likely to be poor as southern whites. Nevertheless, there are half a million more poor whites in the South than poor blacks.

There is an association between the unemployment rate and the proportion of families living in poverty. Since nearly seven-tenths of all poor families have at least one earner in the labor force, the tightness of the labor market should be one important factor in determining the proportion of families with incomes below the poverty level. Furthermore, it was observed earlier that there is a close relationship between changes in unemployment rates and increases in real GNP. Thus, one would expect that in years of low unemployment and concomitant rapid economic growth, more families would receive incomes above the poverty level than during periods of slow economic advance. This argument assumes that during rapid economic growth the share of income received by lower income groups does not decline. A comparison of the incidence of poverty with the overall unemployment rate is presented in Table 6-5.

Since 1953, the percentage of families who received incomes below the poverty level has fallen from nearly one-fourth of all families to one-tenth in 1971. However, this decline has been much more rapid in years of low unemployment than high unemployment. In those years when the annual unemployment rate was 4.5 percent or less, the average annual decline in the percent of families living in poverty was 1.2 percent compared to 0.3 percent in years when the unemployment rate was above 4.5 percent. The increases in the proportion of families in poverty (over the previous year) that took place in 1954, 1958, and 1970 reflect the impact of economic recession and its accompanying rise in unemployment. From 1956 to 1961 the incidence of poverty declined very slowly with the percentage of families in poverty falling by only two percentage points. Interestingly enough the poverty issue began to be articulated at just about the end of this period of very minimal change in the incidence of poverty. For example, Michael Harrington's book, *The Other America*, was published in 1962. Moreover, this period is almost the same time

Table 6-5

Percent of Families Living in Poverty and Unemployment Rate, 1953 to 1971

| Year | Percent of Families Living in Poverty | Unemployment Rate |
|------|---------------------------------------|-------------------|
| 1953 | 23.8 | 2.9 |
| 1954 | 25.4 | 5.6 |
| 1955 | 22.4 | 4.4 |
| 1956 | 20.2 | 4.2 |
| 1957 | 20.2 | 4.3 |
| 1958 | 20.5 | 6.8 |
| 1959 | 18.5 | 5.5 |
| 1960 | 18.1 | 5.6 |
| 1961 | 18.1 | 6.7 |
| 1962 | 17.2 | 5.6 |
| 1963 | 15.9 | 5.7 |
| 1964 | 15.0 | 5.2 |
| 1965 | 13.9 | 4.5 |
| 1966 | 12.7 | 3.8 |
| 1967 | 12.3 | 3.8 |
| 1968 | 10.9 | 3.6 |
| 1969 | 10.6 | 3.5 |
| 1970 | 10.9 | 4.9 |
| 1971 | 10.8 | 5.9 |

Note: Since poverty statistics were not collected for 1953 to 1958, these data are estimated on the basis of the percentage of families earning less than $3,000 (1959 constant dollars) during those years.

Source: Unemployment rates from 1953 to 1971, U.S. Department of Commerce, *Economic Report of the President, 1973* (Washington, D.C.: U.S. Government Printing Office, 1973), Table C-26, p. 223; data for 1953 to 1958 based on Lowell E. Gallaway *Manpower Economics* (Homewood, Ill.: Richard D. Irwin, Inc., 1971), p. 147; data for 1959 to 1971 from U.S. Department of Commerce, Bureau of the Census, *Consumer Income* Series P-60, No. 82, "Characteristics of Low Income Population: 1971" (Washington, D.C.: U.S. Government Printing Office, 1972), p. 4.

interval that brought into focus the unemployment controversy regarding the relative importance of structural change versus aggregate demand as explanations of high unemployment rates, which indicates the close association between the problems of poverty and unemployment.[13]

In 1969, the Council of Economic Advisors stated that if the rate of reduction in poverty obtained during the period of 1959 to 1968 could be maintained, poverty would be eliminated in about ten years.[14] Actually, even if the tight labor markets of the middle and late 1960s had continued, it is doubtful that this objective could have been achieved. The reason is that as poverty declines numerically, an increasing fraction of the remaining poor are members of households whose economic status is least affected by prosperity. For example, households headed by women with children, disabled persons, or elderly persons, presently account for about 60 percent of all poor households, and it is unlikely that these families would be helped significantly by low rates of aggregate unemployment.

While it is clear that economic growth and the tight labor markets of the middle and late 1960s have lowered the percentage of families living in poverty, as defined by an absolute income standard, "progress" has been quite different if another criteria of poverty is adopted. For example, suppose the poverty-income cutoff is stipulated to be an income level less than half of the median family income. Using this definition, Victor Fuchs has found that the proportion of families in poverty has remained constant at about 20 percent throughout the postwar period.[15]

Moreover, since 1945 there has been no major change in the proportion of national income received by various income groups. The following statistics indicate the percentage of income that went to various categories of families from 1950 to 1970:

| Group | 1970 | 1965 | 1950 |
|---|---|---|---|
| Lowest Fifth | 5.5% | 5.3% | 4.5% |
| Second Fifth | 12.0 | 12.1 | 12.0 |
| Middle Fifth | 17.4 | 17.7 | 17.4 |
| Fourth Fifth | 23.5 | 23.7 | 23.5 |
| Highest Fifth | 41.6 | 41.3 | 42.6 |

(Source: Federal Reserve Board data; from *Wall Street Journal*, February, 1972, p. 1.)

The slight increase in the share going to the lowest fifth of income recipients is consistent with the findings of Gallaway who observed that from 1959 to 1967 the incomes of low income families grew *more rapidly* than the growth in income of all families.[16] Thus, low unemployment and rapid growth reduced poverty by increasing the number of workers whose rising earnings permitted their families to obtain incomes above the poverty level; moreover, similar to what occurred during World War II, the income distribution shifted so that lower income families benefitted most in relative terms.

In addition to rapid economic growth and concomitant tight labor markets, two key policies can be used to reduce the incidence of poverty. The first involves utilizing the manpower training programs (See Chapter 7) as a means to help low income individuals to find jobs. Obviously such programs cannot be very helpful to mothers of small children with inadequate child-care facilities, elderly persons, or those severely physically and mentally disabled. While only a small percentage of the total number of persons on welfare are employable males (for example, in New York City about 4 to 5 percent), provision of adequate jobs for such men would have a multiple effect by removing their families from the welfare rolls. This proportion has been estimated at 20 to 25 percent of all welfare recipients in New York City.[17]

Thus, training programs may be an important tool in reducing poverty especially for the working poor and those whose attachment to the labor force can be described as marginal. This group consists largely of those with less than high school educations, unskilled workers, many blacks, Mexican-Americans, and American Indians. Their number was estimated to be about 7.9 million in 1966 with a projected decline to a little more than 5 million in 1975.[18] Although manpower training programs would seem a useful form of assistance for these individuals, in fact less than 5 percent of the funds for the poor have been allocated to training programs. The bulk of assistance has been in the form of cash grants, such as the income received by welfare recipients or the payments received by poor farmers under a variety of agricultural subsidy programs. However, in the case of farmers, most of the payments have been to those whose incomes are considerably above the poverty level.

Another possible approach to reducing poverty is through various types of income transfer payments in which funds are taken by taxation from higher income individuals and given to the poor as grants. Thus, in 1971, it would have taken approximately $12 billion to raise the income of all persons above the poverty line.

One possible income transfer mechanism is the negative income tax. Persons with incomes higher than minimum support levels would pay tax while persons with incomes below this figure would receive a benefit payment through the tax system. Thus, a "break-even" level would be designated as the dividing line between those who receive payments and those who do not. This payment would be computed by applying a negative tax rate (or rates) to the difference between the individual's income and the break-even level.[19] For example, if the rate is 50 percent and the break-even level is $3,000, a family with an income of $1,000 would receive $1,000 (i.e., half of the difference between $3,000 and $1,000) as the negative tax allowance, as shown in Table 6-6.

The following characteristics of the negative income tax are significant from the standpoint of an income maintenance strategy:

a. The allowances would go to all persons with income below the break-even level, regardless of their age, employment status, or source of income;
b. The allowances would be adjusted to family size as well as to income;
c. Expenditure of the funds by the recipients would not be subject to scrutiny by the government; and
d. The allowances would not be given in the spirit of the dole—the system is structured to avoid the stigma associated with the receipt of government assistance.[20]

**Table 6-6**

**Illustrative Negative Tax Allowances for a Family of Four, on Assumption of a Break-Even Level of $3,000 and a Negative Tax Rate of 50 Percent (In Dollars)**

| Annual Income | Negative Tax Allowance | Disposable Income[a] |
|---|---|---|
| $    0 | 1,500 | 1,500 |
| 500 | 1,250 | 1,750 |
| 1,000 | 1,000 | 2,000 |
| 1,500 | 750 | 2,250 |
| 2,000 | 500 | 2,500 |
| 2,500 | 250 | 2,750 |
| 3,000 | 0 | 3,000 |

[a]Annual income plus negative tax allowance.

The major income maintenance initiative proposed by the Nixon Administration would have combined income supplements for poor families with funds for job-training and child-care services for the heads of poor families. Under this Family Assistance Plan, the basic benefit for each family with no income would have been $500 for each of the first two members and $300 for each additional one. Thus, a family of four without income would have received federal payments of $1,600 annually. The first $60 a month (up to $720 a year) of other income, earned or unearned, would not have caused a cut in the basic payment. For each dollar of income above that level the payment would have been reduced, but by only 50 cents; assistance to the family would have continued until its total income rose to $3,920. The plan thus would have provided a modest incentive to obtain and hold a job, since earning an income would not have brought a sudden end to welfare payments. Those who accepted job training would have received a bonus of $30 per month. Employable recipients, except for mothers of preschool-age children would have been required to accept suitable jobs or training. Those who refused would have lost their benefits, but their family would have continued to receive payments.

Although this piece of legislation was passed by the House, it was not accepted by the Senate, partly because liberals thought its benefits too meager and conservatives found unacceptable the idea of adding millions to the welfare rolls.

A controversial aspect of income-maintenance programs is their effect upon work incentives. It is difficult to devise an adequate income-maintenance program with income guarantees that are just and at the same time to provide sufficient work incentives so that individuals do not receive a higher income by not working than they would if employed. Thus, the measurable value of belonging to the public assistance system for a family of four with no other income in Chicago, is equal to an income received from full-time work of $2.30 per hour. The addition of public housing to those who qualify is worth another 70 cents. Allowances for work expenses and payroll deductions probably raise the equivalent wages by another 25 or 50 cents. Such levels hardly constitute opulence, but they do compare favorably with the earnings of many full-time workers in Chicago.[21]

According to the Office of Economic Opportunity, the early findings of an experimental project in New Jersey designed to determine the impact of an income-maintenance program on work incentives produced positive results. In fact, there was an indication that the work effort of participants receiving payments *increased* relative to the work effort of those not receiving payments.[22]

However, a subsequent investigation by the General Accounting Office found that the available data were inadequate to permit independent evaluation and that the findings were questionable because the various guarantee and incentive schemes had no measurable different effects on incentives, that many had dropped out of the experiment, and that the experimental group had more room for improvement in earnings since 11 percent were unemployed.

**Inflation and Unemployment**

As unemployment declines and labor reserves are diminished, firms must increase their wage rates and lower their hiring standards in order to recruit sufficient workers. This policy raises unit labor costs, which are passed on to consumers in the form of higher prices. The generally accepted policy for reducing inflationary pressure is to diminish aggregate demand, which will result in the layoff of the least productive workers. There will be a moderation in union demands for wage increases and hence labor costs and consumer prices will rise more slowly. Price stability is achieved at the cost of a higher jobless rate.

Thus, there is a "trade-off" relationship between a given rate of price increase and the rate of unemployment. It has become customary to speak of this relationship in terms of the "Phillips Curve," which is shown in Figure 6-1. The latter is an analytical tool developed by a British Economist, A.W. Phillips, who related changes in money wages to the levels of unemployment in Great Britain during the period of 1861 to 1957.[23]

As pointed out by Rees:

The Phillips Curve should in principle be convex as viewed from the origin. Frictional unemployment prevents it from ever reaching the vertical axis, and wages could be expected to rise very rapidly if demand were strong enough to make unemployment lower than normal frictional levels. This makes the curve very steep at the far left. In this region, unemployment is subject to two conflicting influences. The strength of demand reduces the duration of job

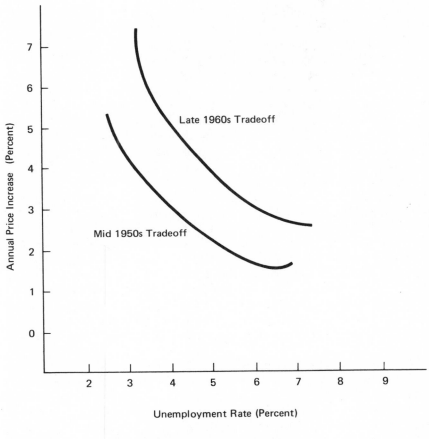

Annual Price Increase (Percent)

Late 1960s Tradeoff

Mid 1950s Tradeoff

Unemployment Rate (Percent)

**Figure 6-1.** Phillips Curve

search for each unemployed worker, since there are many unfilled vacancies. However, the voluntary quit rate rises, so the number of people frictionally unemployed may rise. The first tendency outweighs the second for if the opposite occurred, the Phillips Curve would have a positive slope.[24]

As unemployment increases, the Phillips Curve is flattened due to the downward rigidity of money wages. Because wages are not falling in any sector, the average wage will rise to some extent as long as there is excess demand in any submarket, and this may be true even when the aggregate level of unemployment is quite high.

While there are powerful theoretical arguments for expecting convexity in the

Phillips Curve, a curve does not generally fit the data better than a straight line, especially if there are few observations at the extremes. In particular, a Phillips Curve fitted to American data seldom seem to have any appreciable curvature.[25]

For example, Darnell has derived a modified Phillips Curve indicating the trade-off in the United States between unemployment and changes in the *price level*. He obtained a regression equation based upon percentage changes in quarterly values of the Consumer Price Index ($P$), the dependent variable, and the inverse of the quarterly value of the unemployment rate ($UR^{-1}$), the independent variable.[26] The resultant equation is $P = -.828 + 6.371\ UR^{-1}$. Based on this relationship, the economy would have to tolerate at least a three percent annual increase in the consumer price index in order to achieve full employment (an unemployment rate of 4 percent).

However, recent investigations indicate a worsening trade-off between inflation and unemployment. In Phillips Curve terminology, the curve has shifted to the right. (See Figure 6-1.) Perry found that a 4 percent overall unemployment rate would produce about 1.5 percentage points more inflation per year than was the case in the mid 1950s.[27] Perry's conclusion was based on an equation that used, instead of the overall unemployment rate, two other measures of labor market conditions: (1) a weighted unemployment rate, in which the unemployment rate for each age-sex group is weighted by the relative hours of work and wage levels of that group; and (2) an unemployment dispersion index, which measures the variance of unemployment rates among different age-sex groups.

The use of a weighted unemployment variable simply recognizes that a given percentage increase in wages of low paid and part-time workers has less impact on an aggregate wage index than does the same increase obtained by higher-paid full-time workers. Moreover, Perry's use of the dispersion index reflected two reasonable hypotheses: Substitution among different age-sex groups in the labor market is imperfect; and the elasticity of wage response to unemployment increases as the unemployment rate decreases. As a consequence, the overall rate of wage increase associated with any given unemployment rate will be higher the greater the dispersion of sector unemployment rates about the mean.

The upward shift in the Phillips Curve found by Perry is related to two structural changes: (1) Relative to prime-age male workers, young people and women now make up a higher proportion of the labor force than they did 15 years ago; because their wages and working hours are below the average, the weighted unemployment index has fallen relative to unweighted unemployment. (2) Unemployment rates for young people and teenagers have risen relative to the rate for prime-age male workers; as a consequence, for any given level of unemployment, the dispersion of that unemployment is higher than it was in the mid-1950s.

Schultze has identified another factor responsible for the shift in the Phillips Curve—that is, an increase in the quit rate in manufacturing.[28] Generally speaking, there is an inverse relationship between the overall unemployment rate and the quit rate, the latter falling to low levels during high unemployment. With an autonomous rise in the quit rate, employers must raise wages in order to minimize turnover putting upward pressure on prices even in a period of high unemployment.

Between 1952 and 1965 the relationship between the quit rate and unemployment was stable but from 1966 to 1971 the quit rate rose sharply relative to unemployment. Moreover, this autonomous upward shift in the quit rate provided evidence of an increase in the level of *excess demand* associated with any given level of unemployment. In addition, the number of unfilled job vacancies relative to unemployment has risen.

A fourth factor associated with the recent shift in the Phillips Curve may be the extension of unionism to new sectors of the economy. During this period there was a rapid spread of collective bargaining to the public sector, and a new militance and willingness to strike appeared among public-employee unions.[29] Similarly, unionism spread to such previous unorganized employers as nonprofit hospitals and private universities.

Many economists, noting the difficult policy choice that is represented by a trade-off between inflation and unemployment, advocate a variety of policies that would shift the Phillips Curve to the left. For instance, rehabilitation and training programs might reduce structural unemployment by preparing technologically displaced or educationally disadvantaged workers for productive employment. Improved labor market services that increase the rate of job placement reduce the idle time between jobs and thus the level of unemployment. Measures that improve mobility will tend to reduce frictional unemployment resulting in a decline in prices and unemployment.[30] Finally, manpower programs, which improve the supply of skilled workers through vocational training, will reduce the pressure on prices and wages resulting from shortages of skilled labor. Helping those with the most severe labor market problems and the highest rates of unemployment will lower the dispersion of unemployment rates and in turn reduce the pressure on wages so that there will be less price rise at any level of joblessness.[31] However, Hall has recently argued that proposals of this sort would in fact do little to shift the Phillips Curve.[32] For example, examining the functions and clientele of the U.S. employment service, he concluded that it was already doing a fairly complete job of listing openings in certain sectors of the economy and was not well suited for job placement in other sectors (those involving higher-paid employees). Neither intensive or extensive expansion of this agency would have much prospect for decreasing unemployment. Moreover, according to Hall, training programs—both those designed to increase occupational mobility, as well as those designed to make disadvantaged workers more productive—have been a serious disappointment even at their present scale. He argues that the Manpower Development and Training Act, like the innovative Concentrated Employment Program, and the

Jobs Opportunity in the Business Sector effort, all suffer from excessive turnover and inability to place graduates in good jobs.[33] While Hall does find some encouragement in the apparent success of limited programs in offering well-paying jobs to disadvantaged workers, it is not clear that these programs would operate as efficiently if they were greatly expanded.

## Summary

One major cause of excessive joblessness in the postwar period has been a relatively slow rate of economic growth. Equations developed by Arthur Okun and this writer indicate that during the second half of the postwar period, a rising number of labor force entrants required that the rate of economic growth be accelerated to maintain the jobless rate at a constant level.

Two estimates of potential GNP were presented as well as information on actual GNP. It was noted that the gap between actual and potential GNP has been substantial in most peacetime years.

There is a close association between the rate of decline in the incidence of poverty and the unemployment rate. Using an absolute income criteria for determining poverty, the statistics show considerable progress in reducing the proportion of poor families since 1953. However, if a relative index of poverty is employed, the data indicate substantially less reduction in the incidence of poverty.

Two key policies that can be useful in fighting poverty were discussed. These were manpower training programs and income maintenance. One major difficulty with the latter is the difficulty of retaining sufficient work incentives.

The Phillips Curve relates the percentage of unemployment to changes in either wages or prices. This curve has shifted upward in recent years indicating that low rates of joblessness can only be achieved with more rapid inflation than previously. Factors such as increased dispersion of sector unemployment rates, a rise in the quit rate in manufacturing, as well as union activity in the public sector, have all contributed to the shift in the Phillips Curve.

**Manpower Training Programs for the Development of Human Resources**

While it was determined in Chapter 5 that there was no *general* tendency for structural unemployment to worsen in the postwar period, several sectors of the work force did experience sharply higher relative unemployment rates. These sectors included teenagers, the inexperienced unemployed, and for the first half of the postwar period, blacks. This chapter focuses on a number of manpower programs designed to alleviate the employment problems of these groups as well as other structurally unemployed workers. In addition, some attention is given to training programs for welfare recipients, the majority of whom are not in the labor force.

Before 1961, only limited federal funds were spent to remove imperfections in the labor market and to provide remedial services for disadvantaged workers. At the beginning of the decade, there was no federal manpower policy, or even a distinguishable set of manpower programs to assist those whose work history showed repeated spells of joblessness. During the 1960s, however, federal manpower programs underwent enormous expansion. A wide range of new programs and approaches were initiated, providing training for the technologically displaced; public employment for youths, the aged, and those on welfare; subsidies to private employers to hire, train, and employ disadvantaged workers; residential vocational education for teenagers; basic education for adults, as well as other services.[1]

### Evaluation of Manpower Programs

There are a variety of dimensions of program effectiveness that must be considered to attempt a comprehensive evaluation of federal manpower programs. These measures can assist in determining which programs most effectively meet their overall objectives. One important factor used to assess program effectiveness is the ratio of benefits to costs. Benefits are generally measured by focusing on the increment in participants' lifetime earnings that is attributable to the program. Individuals who took part in a particular program are compared with a control group—that is, a comparable group of individuals who did not participate. Control groups are often obtained from a sample of individuals who applied for a program, were eligible to enter it, but for one reason or other did not choose to enroll.[2] In determining the costs of the project most studies have concentrated on determining the total resource costs (including administrative costs), as well as the participants' foregone earnings (income a trainee would have presumably earned had he not participated in the program). Subsistence payments or allowances given during training have been excluded. The reason for the exclusion is that the cost of the subsistence payment can be assumed to be counterbalanced by the immediate gains to the recipient.[3]

One of the uncertainties in cost-benefit analysis is the problem of the appropriate discount rate. Benefits (in dollar terms) that will accrue in the future, have a present value that is less than their absolute amount. The level of expected benefits depends on the interest (discount) rate just the same as the present value of a bond, which matures in the future, is a function of the rate of interest. Since higher discount rates lower the value of future earnings, programs with a longer-run payoff will have a relatively higher cost-benefit ratio compared with shorter-run programs, if the discount rate applied is low.

Extreme care must be exercised in interpreting the results obtained from benefit-cost analysis. For example, suppose one found that a cost-benefit study of the Manpower Development and Training Act and Job Corps programs indicated that the former was more efficient. This fact would not necessarily justify a redistribution of funds from the Job Corps to MDTA. The Job Corps has served a seriously disadvantaged clientele, while the MDTA has a moderately large proportion of skilled, experienced workers. No sophisticated analysis is required to indicate that the cost to train those with the most serious employment problems is higher, while the measurable benefits in terms of increased potential earnings per dollar invested may be lower than for clients who need little help.[4]

A second dimension of program effectiveness is the number of participants who are removed from a poverty-income status as a result of the manpower program. It is quite possible for a number of very low-income participants to experience substantial increases in income, resulting in the calculation of a favorable benefit-cost ratio, despite the fact that these persons may not be able to earn sufficient income to bring their family above the poverty income level. For example, a number of manpower programs operated by the Bureau of Indian Affairs for reservation Indians obtain extremely high benefit-cost ratios but many of the participants still earn poverty incomes.[5]

Another factor to be considered is the change in the employment status of participants as a result of the training and education received. Hopefully the program should result in a reduction of the proportion of individuals who were unemployed or not in the labor force and an increase in the proportion with full-time, year-round employment. In addition, one would hope that the occupational status of those trainees who were employed prior to training would be enhanced.

A fourth measure of efficiency is the proportion of trainees who actually complete the program. It is likely that a brief experience with a manpower program leaves little lasting benefit. One might expect that a project exclusively serving a disadvantaged clientele would have a higher dropout rate than one in which the enrollees were skilled, experienced workers. Therefore a comparison of non-completion rates would not be particularly meaningful. However, one can usefully compare the dropout rates for programs with the same length of training that serve similar kinds of clients.

A fifth aspect of manpower assessment is the percentage of participants who obtain jobs related to the training they have acquired, which is a function not only of the quality of training received but the effectiveness of the placement service as well as its follow-up efforts. Moreover, successful placement also depends on general economic conditions. It is more difficult to place graduates in training-related jobs during recession than prosperity.

An issue that is often not considered by manpower evaluators is the displacement effect of a program. Displacement occurs when participants are placed in jobs that other persons would have obtained in the absence of the manpower effort. Such displacement might be justified on equity grounds, if workers of average income were replaced by the poor or by some other group for whom it was socially desirable to increase earnings and employment. (An example of this kind of program might be the training of black instead of white youth to enter apprenticeship programs.) However, the manpower programs may replace one group of marginal workers with a similar group resulting in no equity gain.[6] If the program is training persons for occupations in which there is a shortage of qualified persons or unfilled vacancies, the displacement effect is minimized.

Most evaluators of manpower programs analyze only one or two dimensions of effectiveness, which is primarily a result of a lack of comprehensive data. However, the shortcomings of measurement and evaluation lie deeper than the lack of adequate data. A basic problem is that measurement and evaluation are often focused on variables that do not lend themselves to improved program effectiveness. In other words, emphasis has been on the form of programs rather than their substance. Most programs feature a package of services. For example, the Job Corps offers enrollees counseling, health care, food and shelter, vocational training, basic education, work experience, and placement assistance.[7] Little effort has been focused on the relative benefit of each of these services or their optimal mix in terms of the total program.

### The Manpower Development and Training Act

In spite of the passage of the Employment Act of 1946, which declared that it was the responsibility of the federal government to undertake policies to promote maximum employment, production, and purchasing power,[8] unemployment rates in the early 1960s were at nearly the highest levels in 20 years. Manufacturing employment was declining as production levels rose, and there was a strong fear of technological displacement of production workers by modern, highly automated capital equipment.

To combat the problem of technological unemployment, Congress passed the Manpower Development and Training Act in 1962 to be administered by the Department of Labor. The program initially concentrated on retraining, within an institutional or classroom setting, those individuals whose skills had become obsolete as a result of automation. Occupations in which employment opportunities were growing were identified, and unemployed, experienced workers were trained to fill them. As concern grew for the high rate of teenage unemployment, special youth programs were developed to provide young people with skills prior to their entrance into the work force. When a widespread need for basic education prior to vocational training became apparent, Congress responded by authorizing basic literacy training.

In 1966, because of the decline in the national unemployment rate, a diminished fear of automation, and a national commitment to eliminate poverty, a redirection of the MDTA program was undertaken. Thus, it was decided that about 65 percent of the entire training effort should be focused on the hard-core unemployed.[9] Groups with special employment difficulties—such as persons with low educational achievement, members of racial minorities, and the rural poor—were to be recruited. Informal quotas were established to insure a distribution of training opportunities among these groups.

The balance of the training effort—approximately 35 percent of the total— was to be "job oriented," focusing on the need for trained persons in skill shortage categories.

Since it was recognized that the new emphasis on the disadvantaged would require more intensive effort, the training program was altered so that the enrollment would be equally divided between the institutional and on-the-job-training components of the program. The latter training, which enrolled very few MDTA participants until 1966, is conducted through private industry—local employers, unions, or non-profit organizations. The private firms are reimbursed by the federal government, either directly or through the states, for costs of instruction. Moreover, the trainees are on the payrolls of the employers.

Has the changed legislative emphasis of the programs been translated into reality? Table 7-1 indicates a variety of statistics relevant to this question. As indicated, there is fairly persuasive evidence that the intent of the 1966 amendments was achieved. After 1966, a more disadvantaged group of trainees (in terms of the characteristics enumerated) was selected. However, partly because of some reluctance on the part of employers to participate, there have been nearly twice as many enrollees in the institutional portion of the MDTA program as compared to the on-the-job-training component. Thus, the intended equal division of trainees between the institutional and on-the-job-training components has not been achieved.

In 1968, the MDTA Act was amended again to provide for the establishment

**Table 7-1**

**Characteristics of Institutional Trainees, Selected Statistics, MDTA Program, 1963 to 1966 and 1967 to 1971**

| Characteristics | 1963-1966 Trainees | 1967-1971 Trainees |
|---|---|---|
| Percent Black | 28.8 | 39.7 |
| Percent with 8 Years of School or Less | 5.9 | 7.5 |
| Percent with 11 Years of School or Less | 48.1 | 55.2 |
| Percent Receiving Unemployment Insurance | 21.1 | 9.0 |
| Percent with Less than 3 Years of Employment | 34.3 | 45.1 |
| Percent Receiving Public Assistance | 9.9 | 13.4 |

Source: Computed from U.S. Department of Labor, *Manpower Report of the President, 1972* (Washington, D.C.: U.S. Government Printing Office, 1972), Table F-5, p. 265.

of Manpower Skills Training Centers. These centers, which have become a major source of occupational training under the institutional training effort, also provide a comprehensive program of basic education, job counseling, job placement, and employment follow-up.

Several skills centers have been established at community colleges. Use of the college's facilities has meant broader course offerings and the possibility of obtaining college credits for MDTA trainees, while the basic education offered under the MDTA has been useful to other students. Because many disadvantaged persons are receiving training in an institution with large numbers of other students, there is much less risk of stigma being attached to the disadvantaged participants.

Ribich evaluated the benefits and costs of the MDTA programs that operated in the states of Connecticut, Massachusetts, and West Virginia. Using a 5 percent discount rate, he found that the ratio of benefits to costs was 10.1:1 in Connecticut; 4.2:1 in Massachusetts, and 15.0:1 in West Virginia.[10] These results indicate that the MDTA program was quite efficient in these three states. However, Ribich assumed that the income differences between the trainees and the control group would persist over their entire working lifetime (about 40 years). If one assumed the training would become obsolete after ten years and its effectiveness would cease, benefits would no longer accrue to the participants. Thus, the total level of calculated benefits, and hence the benefit-cost ratio would be considerably lower. Moreover, the data collected for Ribich's study were obtained in the period of 1962 to 1963, when the MDTA was almost exclusively a program for the technologically unemployed. In order to consider its effectiveness as a program for the disadvantaged another study is examined.

Main studied a sample of 1,200 trainees who had completed MDTA courses in the mid-1960s. Of this group, 40 percent were black and slightly less than half were high school graduates.[11] Among those who held a full-time job anytime since the training period, the MDTA program had no effect on income; completers and non-trainees (controls) reported about the same weekly wages on their most recent full-time jobs. However, more completers than non-trainees were employed when interviewed. The average amount of full-time employment for trainees and controls combined was 55 percent of the time interval since training. The net effect of MDTA institutional training on full-time employment was estimated to be between 13 and 23 percent of the period after training for completers (and between 7 and 19 percent for dropouts).[12] Thus, it appears that for this sample of trainees the MDTA program increased employment, even if it did not lead to better paying jobs.

On the basis of the two studies, one can conclude that the benefit-cost ratio declined dramatically (in fact to 0) partly because a higher percentage of the trainees in the latter study were disadvantaged. However, both investigations were based on a small sample of trainees and therefore, such a conclusion must be extremely tentative.

From 1963 to 1972, 67 percent of all participants in the MDTA program (including institutional trainees as well as on-the-job trainees) actually completed their training. Of those completing training, 74 percent were employed when contacted 6 months after training. However, on-the-job trainees are more likely to remain in training-related jobs than participants in institutional training. A survey undertaken by the Department of Labor indicated that 85 percent of the on-the-job trainees were in training related employment one year after training. However, an intensive survey of 500 completers of MDTA institutional training found that only 34 percent of these persons were in training related positions 18 months after they left the program.[13]

By the early 1960s youth unemployment rates had reached critically high levels. The federal response was limited to the addition of a youth component to the MDTA training program and a feeble attempt through the Vocational Education Act of 1963 to revamp the machinery for employment preparation.[14]

However, the Economic Opportunity Act of 1964, which became known as the War on Poverty, established two major manpower programs for youth—the Job Corps and the Neighborhood Youth Corps. Both programs will be described and evaluated.

**The Job Corps**

The Job Corps was created as part of the Economic Opportunity Act in order to prepare youths, aged 16 through 21, "for the responsibility of citizenship and to increase [their] employability by providing them in rural and urban residential centers with education, vocational education, useful work directed toward conservation of natural resources, and other appropriate activities." The assumption underlying this statement was that many youths from poor families had to be removed from their home environment before they could be made productive through training and education.

Although the antecedents of the Job Corps may be traced back to the Civilian Conservation Corps of the 1930s, the contrasts between the two institutions are more significant than the similarities. The CCC was a product of the Great Depression, and its 2.5 million enrollees represented a broad cross-section of the population.[15] The Job Corps, on the other hand, focuses upon the special needs of a small minority of youths who, because of educational deficiency and debilitating environment and lack of work skills, are at a competitive disadvantage in the labor market.

The main Congressional opposition to the Job Corps focused on the establishment of conservation centers. Such work experience, it was argued, had little relevance to preparing youths for jobs. Moreover, the relatively high cost of operating the centers was considered unjustified. However, Congress specified that 40 percent of male Job Corps enrollees be assigned to conservation centers. The Job Corps delegated responsibility for the operation of its conservation centers to the Department of Agriculture and the Department of the Interior. The two agencies assumed day-to-day responsibility for administration but the Office of Economic Opportunity (coordinator of the War on Poverty) retained the authority to formulate policy and develop training and educational curricula.

To operate the urban centers, the Job Corps turned to private contractors. By mid-1967 university or non-profit organizations operated 7 of the 28 urban centers. Private corporations operated the other 21. The profits were small, but contractors had no financial risk since they operated on a cost-plus-fixed-fee basis. Moreover, operation of a center provided the opportunity to enter the expanding market of developing techniques for the education and training of the disadvantaged.

The average cost per Job Corps enrollee has been approximately $7,500, roughly 3 times the cost of MDTA institutional training. Women's centers have cost approximately $1,000 more per trainee to operate than centers for males located in urban areas. The cost per participant in the Job Corps is the highest of any manpower program.

*Characteristics of Trainees*

The Job Corps has consistently recruited youths from a disadvantaged background, as shown in Table 7-2. The administrators have made a concerted effort to attract youths who would have difficulty finding permanent employment even when overall labor markets were tight. However, by avoiding "creaming"—

**Table 7-2**
**Corpsmen Characteristics, 1967 and 1971**

| Characteristics | 1967 Entrants | 1971 Entrants |
|---|---|---|
| Median Years of Schooling | 9.5 | 10.4 |
| Median Educational Attainment | | |
| Reading | 5.3 | – |
| Arithmetic | 5.4 | – |
| Family | | |
| Broken Home | 60 | – |
| Unemployed Head of Family | 63 | – |
| Relief | 39 | 36 |
| Median Family Income | – | $2800 |
| Percent Black | 56 | 60 |

Source: Data for 1967 computed from Sar A. Levitan, *Anti-Poverty Work and Training Efforts: Goals and Reality*, Policy Papers in Human Resources and Industrial Relations, No. 3, (Ann Arbor, Mich.: Institute of Labor and Industrial Relations, 1967), p. 9; Data for 1971 from U.S. Department of Labor, *Manpower Report of the President, 1972* (Washington, D.C.: U.S. Government Printing Office, 1972), Table F-8, p. 268.

that is, by not enrolling those most likely to succeed after training is completed—the administrators of the Job Corps accepted the risk that standard evaluation measures would not place this manpower program in a particularly favorable light.

*Evaluation of Job Corps*

The Job Corps was quite different from other manpower programs (mainly because of the residential center concept). Because of its relatively high cost per enrollee, considerable data was collected in an attempt to justify or discredit the program.

The first evaluative factor to be considered is changes in earnings. Levitan found in 1967 that those who completed training earned 32¢ an hour more, 6 months after graduation, than they did prior to entering the Job Corps.[16] Pichler in 1969 obtained nearly identical results.[17] However, the relevant question is not what Job Corps trainees earned before and after training, but how much more do Job Corps completers earn than a comparable group of controls. The available data indicate that the average hourly wage gain of former Corpsmen exceeded that of a control group by only 12 cents per hour.[18]

Cain undertook a cost-benefit analysis of the Job Corps. He concluded that the "realistic" ratio of benefits over costs was 1.18, but estimates ranged from 1.05 to 1.69, depending upon the assumptions made.[19] However, in calculating the benefits of the Job Corps, Cain included the increased earnings during the potential lifework of the former Corpsmen—a period of 48 years. This would seem too long a period over which to stretch the benefits. (However, no gains are attributed by Cain to the probable side effects of the Job Corps experience benefits resulting from social development and family stability, which cannot presently be measured.)

A relatively high dropout rate has plagued the Job Corps ever since its inception. From 1964 to 1969 only 35 percent of all enrollees completed the program, with the majority of dropouts leaving within three months after their arrival at the centers.[20] The older the youth, the longer he tended to stay in the Job Corps. The median length of stay for 16- and 17-year-old enrollees was 3.0 months; but for older Corpsmen, the median stay was 5.6 months.[21] While there is little information available as to why the dropout rate is so high, it seems that part of the reason would be the location of centers so far from friends and relatives. Thus, homesickness is probably an important factor in an enrollee's decision to leave the Job Corps.

Table 7-3 indicates changes in the labor force status of enrollees who completed the program in 1966 and 1969. Although these data show considerable employment gains in a "before-after" comparison, over a quarter of the graduates were unemployed 6 months after termination. Moreover, this information does not tell us what would have happened to the employment status of these individuals if they had not entered the Job Corps at all—in other words,

**Table 7-3**

**Labor Force Status of Corpsmen Before Entering Job Corps and Six Months After Job Corps, Enrollees in 1966 and 1969**

| | Before Job Corps | | | After Job Corps | | |
|------|----------|------------|----------------------|----------|------------|----------------------|
| Year | Employed | Unemployed | Not in Labor Force | Employed | Unemployed | Not in Labor Force |
| 1966 | 47 | 42 | 11 | 65 | 27 | 9 |
| 1969 | 33 | 47 | 20 | 58 | 26 | 14 |

Source: Computed from Sar A. Levitan, *Anti-Poverty Work and Training Efforts: Goals and Reality*, Policy Papers in Human Resources and Industrial Relations, No. 3 (Ann Arbor, Mich.: Institute of Labor and Industrial Relations, 1967), p. 31; Joseph A. Pichler, "The Job Corps Transition," *Industrial and Labor Relations Review* 25, No. 3 (April 1972): 341. Copyright ©1972 by Cornell University. All rights reserved.

there is no control group. However, unemployment rates for teenage blacks were 20 to 25 percent for males and 30 to 35 percent for females in the 1965 to 1972 period, with ghetto unemployment rates for teenagers even higher. Thus, it is likely that the Job Corps has resulted in improvement in the employment status of enrollees, but the results are not particularly encouraging.

There is very little information available regarding the relevance of Job Corps education and training to subsequent employability. A Labor Department report written in 1969 severely criticized the conservation centers for providing rudimentary work activities, which did not substantially improve trainee employability, and for their failure to emphasize high school equivalency curricula.[22] Basic education programs at rural sites were found to be less effective than at urban centers: aptitude tests indicated that verbal and mathematics grade levels had risen only 80 percent and 50 percent as much, respectively, as had the levels at urban centers.[23]

Partly because the evaluations of various aspects of the Job Corps have been unfavorable, the Nixon administration has reduced the emphasis of this program and transferred it from the Office of Economic Opportunity to the Department of Labor. The maximum number of participants has been cut from 60,000 to 50,000 and over half the 106 centers were closed. These were to be replaced by 30 new centers that would provide more comprehensive manpower services and would hopefully be more effective and somewhat less expensive. As of mid-1973 most of these new centers had not been established. Moreover, attempts to reduce program costs and increase trainee retention levels have been unsuccessful. Since the reorganization of the Job Corps the average cost per enrollee man year has declined by only 4 percent and the total dropout rate has increased slightly. (When the Job Corps was originally established, one argument for placing the residential training centers in remote areas was that students would be more likely to attend classes than would be the case if they commuted. The new centers have been located close enough to trainees' homes that they are able to commute; and, as predicted earlier, absenteeism rates have increased markedly.)

Considerable effort has been recently directed toward the goal of developing linkages between the Job Corps and other sources of manpower training. Two-thirds of the conservation centers now offer preapprenticeship programs conducted by trade unions. Local union officials have been appointed to the advisory councils of the newly established centers and have assisted in recruiting instructional staff, as well as in placing graduated Corpsmen into area apprenticeship programs. A number of centers have concluded substantial on-the-job-training contracts with local firms, providing Corpsmen with potential employment opportunities as well as increased familiarity during the training period. Finally, closer relations with employment service offices have been developed since the transition. A number of local offices have stationed personnel at center sites to assist in job placement. However, during 1970 the employment service offices accounted for less than 30 percent of all Job Corps placement—a level not materially different from the pretransition levels.[24]

## The Neighborhood Youth Corps

The Neighborhood Youth Corps became a reality with the passage of the Economic Opportunity Act of 1964. The program, which is the nation's largest manpower program (both in terms of participants and federal outlays), has enrolled nearly 4 million youths age 16 to 21 in its various components. At first, NYC had two separate but related components: a part-time job creation program for youths attending school and a separate full-time work program for idle 16 to 21 year olds, mostly high school dropouts. As the program evolved a third component—provision of summer employment opportunities has been added. Enrollees, who must be from low-income families, work an average of 26 hours a week during the summer and 8 to 15 hours a week during the school year at a minimum wage of $1.60 per hour. Thus, this manpower effort, which is administered by the Department of Labor, is not only a job creation program but a drop-out prevention effort as well.

### Characteristics of Enrollees

By definition NYC enrollees come from impoverished families, though a number of project sponsors have occasionally stretched the family income limit for enrollees. (See Table 7-4.) The typical enrollee comes from a large family whose median income is approximately $3,000 per year. He has completed the sophomore year of high school, though no data are available on his actual

**Table 7-4**
**Characteristics of Neighborhood Youth Corps Enrollees, 1966 and 1972**

|  | 1966 | | | 1972 | |
| Characteristic | In School | Summer | Out of School | In School[a] | Out of School |
| --- | --- | --- | --- | --- | --- |
| Percent Black | 41 | 51 | 42 | 53 | 43 |
| Median Years of School | 10 | 10 | 10 | 10 | 10 |
| Median Number of Persons in Family | 6 | 6 | 6 | – | 5.5 |
| Public Assistance Recipient | 26 | 27 | 27 | 30 | 38 |
| Percent of Families Living in Poverty | 69 | – | 71 | – | 99 |
| Percent Male | 53 | 59 | 57 | 57 | 50 |
| Median Family Income | – | – | – | $3,200 | $2,800 |

[a]Includes those participating in the summer program.
Source: Data for 1966 computed from Sar A. Levitan, *Anti-Poverty Programs: Goals and Reality*, Policy Papers in Human Resources and Industrial Relations, No. 3 (Ann Arbor, Mich.: Institute for Labor and Industrial Relations, 1967), p. 51; data for 1972 from U.S. Department of Labor, *Manpower Report of the President, March, 1973* (Washington, D.C.: U.S. Government Printing Office, 1973).

achievement level. One of three families of NYC participants was on public assistance in 1972.

The costs per enrollee are $500 for the summer program, $740 for the in-school NYC and $3,000 for the out-of-school component. This is far less than the expenditures per person in the Job Corps and MDTA institutional training programs.[25] Seventy percent of the cost per enrollee consists of wages paid to participants.

*Evaluation*

The crucial test of the effectiveness of the in-school and summer programs is whether they provide sufficient incentives for enrollees to complete their high school education. Most in-school work assignments consist of performing various chores around the schools, including clerical and custodial work, or serving as a teacher's aide or library assistant. Summer work assignments include cleaning up neighborhoods, lawn mowing, and other outdoor activities.

Two separate surveys undertaken by the District of Columbia and Pittsburgh school systems produced positive findings. The Washington study examined dropout rates, attendance, scholarship and conduct of 122 NYC students during the next academic year. Because the District of Columbia school system gave priority for NYC enrollment to eligible students who were "judged to be potential dropouts" and who had other problems, it was assumed that the potential dropout rate would be at least as high as that for the rest of the students in the three high schools studied. The actual dropout rate for the NYC enrollees was only 10 percent of the predicted rate. As for the other variables, the study concluded that NYC participation had no impact upon attendance, scholarship, or deportment.[26]

The Pittsburgh results, though less dramatic than those obtained in the Washington study, are considerably more comprehensive and constituted a strong argument for expansion of in-school NYC. The survey, which included all 16 public senior high schools, compared the dropout rate among the 2,100 NYC enrollees during the summer of 1965 and the academic year 1965 to 1966, with the dropout rate among the remaining 19,000 high school students in the city. In 14 of the 16 schools the NYC dropout rate was lower than for those not participating in the program. The 4.2 percent dropout rate for NYC enrollees was exactly half the 8.4 percent rate for the other students.[27]

However, a study of Somers and Stromsdorfer based on a nationwide sample survey of in-school and summer NYC enrollees found no difference in the rate of high school completion for the 442 participants in the sample in comparison to 338 persons in the control group. They did find that black women and American Indians had lower dropout rates than comparable members of the control group.[28]

Finally, a survey by NYC noted that "counseling and remedial education were largely ineffectual or non-existent in many projects visited." The study also suggested that "the NYC summer program is not an effective vehicle for attracting young dropouts *back* to school."[29] The same report indicated that one of every four enrollees dropped out of the project before completion. But the same proportion of this group returned to school as those who stayed with their projects until termination.

These divergent findings imply that the in-school and summer NYC programs are more effective in some locations than others. Whether this occurs because of differences in the structure of the programs, the quality of administration, or the motivation of the applicants is impossible to determine.

## Out-of-School NYC

Although comprehensive data are not available, it appears that 50 to 60 percent of all participants leave before their assignments are completed.[30] The majority of the girls were assigned to clerical and health work, while the boys were most often assigned to maintenance, custodial, and clean-up duties. About 1 in 6 individuals who terminated, left because they found employment, with 1 in 5 terminating because of behavior problems. An equal number left to enter other training programs, the military, or to return to school. The average stay in the out-of-school NYC was only 4 months.

Because the average enrollee in the out-of-school NYC remained in the program such a short time and since the support services that were offered were limited, the program did not have a major employment impact upon enrollees. Table 7-5 indicates the labor force status of former enrollees by duration of stay.

**Table 7-5**
**Employment Status of Enrollees in Out-of-School Neighborhood Youth Corps, by Length of Time in Program, 1967**

|  | Less Than 4 | 5-12 | 13-20 | 21-28 | 29 or More |
|---|---|---|---|---|---|
| Employed | 38.4 | 38.8 | 42.1 | 43.3 | 52.9 |
| In School | 13.8 | 13.6 | 10.1 | 8.9 | 10.0 |
| In Other Training Program | 5.7 | 3.3 | 6.5 | 5.5 | 0.4 |
| Unemployed | 16.5 | 15.9 | 15.4 | 19.8 | 13.1 |
| Not in Labor Force or School or Training | 25.6 | 28.4 | 25.9 | 22.5 | 24.2 |

Source: Computed from data contained in Dunlap and Associates, "Survey of Terminees from Out-of-School NYC Projects, May, 1967," mimeographed (Darien, Conn.).

While a higher proportion of those who remained in NYC 6 months or longer were employed and fewer unemployed in comparison to enrollees who remained in the program only a few weeks, the incidence of unemployment remained very high among all participants. Moreover, 1 in 4 was not even looking for work or taking part in another training program. In a sense, they were "doing nothing." However, the proportion of unemployed among former NYC enrollees is no greater than for youths who have completed MDTA institutional courses.

Borus, Brennan and Rosen undertook a cost-benefit analysis of the out-of-school NYC program in Indiana. Their results were based on the earnings of 604 participants and 166 eligible non-participants (the control group).[31] They determined the effectiveness of the program for individuals with different levels of schooling. (See Table 7-6.)

The authors assumed that the benefits (income differential between participants and controls) would last for 10 years. The program was more efficient for men than women and more effective for high school dropouts than for graduates. The finding of greater benefits for men than women contradicts the findings of Walther and Magnusson who came to the opposite conclusion.[32] However, the geographic location of the participants in the samples, the racial composition of the enrollees, as well as the methods of analysis were so different in each of the studies that no firm conclusion can be drawn.

Borus, et al., found that for individual participants, the longer they remained in the program, the greater was the increase in post-program earnings. This indicates the importance of encouraging youths to remain in NYC for some months. Long-term participation in the NYC program may be considered by employers an indication of stability. Therefore, the youths with the longest participation are more likely to get good jobs. Moreover, the individual who remains in NYC for some time probably obtains certain work skills, such as the ability to communicate effectively, neatness of appearance, and perhaps the desire to accept responsibility.

## Table 7-6
**Benefit-Cost Ratio for the Out-of-School Program in Indiana**

| Years of Education Completed | Benefit/Cost Ratio | |
|---|---|---|
| | Males | Females |
| 8 years | 3.0 | 0.7 |
| 9 years | 3.3 | 1.0 |
| 10 years | 3.3 | 1.0 |
| 11 years | 3.0 | 0.6 |
| 12 years | 2.4 | 0.0 |

Source: Michael E. Borus, John P. Brennan, and Sidney Rosen, "A Benefit-Cost Analysis of the Neighborhood Youth Corps: The Out-of-School Program in Indiana," *Journal of Human Resources* 5, No. 2 (Spring 1970): 156.

One major criticism of the out-of-school NYC is that it has distributed funds among too many beneficiaries, primarily by cutting unit costs drastically and foregoing various supportive services that would increase costs and limit the number of participants.[33] Thus, having decided to forego rehabilitative efforts under this program, it would appear that Congress has undertaken a fairly large scale commitment to make the government the employer of last resort for poor youth. The out-of-school program fulfills the immediate need for jobs but provides only minimal work skills.

## Work Programs for Relief Recipients

In this section two programs focusing on the manpower needs of welfare recipients and other needy persons are considered. The first is the Work, Experience, and Training Program that operated from 1966 to 1968 and was succeeded by the Work Incentive Program.

The purpose of the Work, Experience, and Training Program, as expressed by section 501 of the Economic Opportunity Act, was to "expand the opportunities for constructive work experience and other needed training available to persons who are unable to support or care for themselves or their families." Those eligible for enrollment included all those individuals who were receiving public assistance under the aid to families of dependent children program, those unemployed heads of families who did not qualify for public assistance, and single able-bodied needy adults.

Because of the welfare aspects of the program, the responsibility for administration was given to the Department of Health, Education, and Welfare, and the states where the projects were located. This decision caused vigorous and continuing objections from the Department of Labor, which maintained that they were better equipped to operate a training program than an agency that was essentially "welfare oriented."

Pressure to develop projects was strong. Nearly all states participated by 1966 with enrollment varying from less than a dozen to nearly 10,000 persons. However, most projects had fewer than 200 enrollees. Some project administrators emphasized training and preparation for jobs in the regular labor market, while others stressed the more immediate goal of providing income and work relief for the poor. Because the latter objective was more readily accomplished, it is not surprising that many projects were limited to providing some form of work relief.

### Trainee Characteristics

Given the goal of enhancing the employability of relief recipients and other poor individuals, and the importance placed by program administrators on strengthening family life, it might be expected that work experience and training for male family heads would be emphasized. However, this was not the case. (See Table 7-7.) The primary reason was that project administrators tended to draw enrollees from the immediately available welfare population. Since female heads of families comprise the majority of those on welfare, they tended to be selected for the program.

The typical participant was older and less educated in comparison to enrollees in other programs. However, the percent of black enrollees was similar to that of other manpower efforts.

Total costs of the program in 1968 (the last year of its operation) was $2,100 per enrollee, if the individual was not receiving public assistance, and $700 per enrollee, if the individuals were receiving welfare payments.

*Evaluation*

While the enrollees' work assignments featured a certain amount of informal vocational instruction, the bulk of these tasks was limited to low-paying, unskilled occupations. This phenomenon was understandable in view of the trainees' limited skills and educational attainment. There is little or no evidence that the occupational training resulted in upgrading of skills. In fact, only 1 of 4 enrollees received vocational education and only about one-third of the participants received adult basic education or high school equivalency training. The enrollees seemed to lack interest in the training as 75 percent dropped out of the program before course completion. Of course the high proportion of female participants with family responsibilities, as well as the limited educational background of many of the male participants, may have resulted in a high dropout rate even if the program content had been improved. About one-third

Table 7-7
**Characteristics of Enrollees, Work, Experience, and Training Program, 1966**

| Characteristic | |
|---|---|
| Percent Head of Household | 92 |
| Percent Male | 51 |
| Percent Black | 36 |
| Median Age | 35 |
| Median Years of Schooling | 8 |

Source: Computed from, Sar A. Levitan, *Anti-Poverty Work and Training Efforts: Goals and Reality*, Policy Papers in Human Resources and Industrial Relations, No. 3 (Ann Arbor, Mich.: Institute of Labor and Industrial Relations), 1967, p. 87.

of those terminating prematurely left to take a job and another third were involuntarily dismissed.

Of those who graduated from the program in 1966 (a rather select group since 75 percent dropped out), only 50 percent were employed one year later; 43 percent were unemployed. Only 22 percent of the dropouts were employed. Those who were employed graduates earned $248 a month compared to $238 a month for employed dropouts.[34]

This program did little to improve the employment status and earnings of the enrollees. Actually one-half of relief recipients remained on public assistance after separating from the program and a fifth earned inadequate wages to provide self support. Whether this record is significantly better than could be expected for non-participants is, of course, a major, unanswered question.

It probably would have been beneficial had more private employers been utilized rather than relying almost exclusively upon public and non-profit institutions. However, this was against HEW policy. "Provisions must be made for adequate supervision by the public welfare agency to assure that such on-the-job training is constructive from the standpoint of up-grading the employability . . . and that there is no exploitation of participants. . . . It is not the purpose of [this program] to provide labor for private employers paid for by the federal government."[35] The decision missed the potentialities of placing trainees with private employers. A temporary government subsidy during the initial period of training, covering part of the trainees' wages, might have provided adequate incentive for employers to hire enrollees. Such a subsidy would have resulted in a saving to the government, which paid full support of trainees on assignments to public and non-profit organizations.

Because of poor results, the Work, Experience, and Training Program effort was terminated in 1968. It was replaced by the Work Incentive Program (WIN). Under this program certain welfare recipients are referred by their welfare offices to training or work programs operated by the state employment offices under the direction of the Department of Labor. Thus, the training aspects of the program were given much greater emphasis than was the case with the defunct Work, Experience, and Training Program. The WIN program has three phases—on-the-job training, institutional and work experience training, and special work projects for those who cannot be found regular jobs or for whom training is not appropriate. Recipients receive $30 per month plus 30 percent of any earnings without offsetting reductions in the relief payments they receive.

The program got off to an extremely slow start—nearly one year after the program was authorized, less than 30,000 welfare recipients were enrolled, or fewer than 2 percent of all adults on the welfare rolls.[36] One reason for this occurrence was that the overall responsibility was divided between the Departments of Labor and Health, Education, and Welfare. Moreover, the state employment offices were unable to set up training programs, and potential clients were often not interested because of the inadequate child-care programs and the lack of implementation of special work projects. However, after overcoming these initial problems, the program expanded rapidly and by 1972 had enrolled 400,000 individuals.

Even though participation is limited to those actually receiving public assistance, the characteristics of enrollees do not differ greatly from those who were in the defunct Work, Experience, and Training Program. In WIN, 60 percent of the enrollees are women, the average age is 35, and 36 percent of the participants are black. The typical enrollee has 10 years of school, lives in a family with a median income of $2,600 per year, and has been unemployed over 6 months.[37]

There is a limited amount of information available that can be utilized for program assessment; however, the available data do not permit a favorable evaluation. In the first 2 years of program operation, less than 20 percent of those participating left the welfare rolls. Moreover, from 1968 to 1971, nearly 80 percent of the enrollees left the program before completing their projects.[38] This dropout rate is similar to that which occurred among participants in the antecedent Work, Experience, and Training Program. Moreover, of the 50,000 individuals placed in jobs between July 1970 and September 1971, only 27,000 remained employed for 6 months.[39] Many of those who found jobs were unemployed fathers who could likely have obtained employment without the program.

Finally, did WIN enhance the earnings potential of the graduates? Among males the median gain, over previous employment was $.12 per hour compared to $.60 per hour for women.[40] Although these earnings increases seldom allow graduates to earn enough to be removed from the welfare rolls, they are more often sufficient to permit reductions in assistance payments.

This manpower effort would probably be more effective if several legislative changes were enacted. At present, mothers receiving welfare payments who work can retain only the first $30 of their monthly earnings, plus one-third of the remainder, without reduction in benefits. These participants could be allowed to keep a higher proportion of their earnings. Secondly, the working poor could be included in the program. This would eliminate the present inequity whereby many full-time workers obtain a smaller total income than people on welfare. Finally, day-care facilities could be greatly expanded and improved. This would not only permit more welfare recipients to enter the program but would allow them to take a full- or part-time job after completing their training project. Under WIN at present, child-care support generally terminates when the enrollee is separated from the program. It could be continued for an employed mother with the fee charged being related to her income.

## Other Federal Manpower Programs

Although the manpower programs evaluated above constitute the major federal efforts regarding the development of human resources, others will be discussed briefly.

**The JOBS Program.** This program provides training and employment for disadvantaged persons. It is administered through the Department of Labor in cooperation with the National Alliance of Businessmen. The program consists of a contract component and a non-contract, or voluntary component. Under the former, private employers enter into contracts with the Department of Labor, either individually or in groups, for the employment and training of disadvantaged persons. The contracts provide for reimbursement by government for the relatively high costs of hiring, training, and retaining such individuals. Under the non-contract component, private employers pledge to hire specific numbers of disadvantaged persons without cost to the government.

**The Opportunities Industrialization Centers Program (OIC).** This program provides motivational and basic work orientation, basic education, skills training, and job placement assistance to unemployed and underemployed persons. It attempts to reach persons who are not interested in manpower programs sponsored by public agencies. OIC is unique in that it was started by a group of private citizens without federal funding. The program emphasizes minority group leadership. As of July 1971, 68 centers were in operation, of which 62 received some federal funds.[41]

**The Emergency Employment Act of 1971.** This program has provided funds to state and local governments for a 2-year program to hire an estimated 150,000 to 200,000 unemployed or underemployed persons for public service jobs. During the first year, expenditures totalled 1 billion dollars.[42] These jobs were to be transitional in nature and the participants were expected to return to regular employment as soon as possible. Unlike most of the other programs discussed and evaluated, this one is not aimed at the disadvantaged or the less-educated. In fact, the "typical" person hired under the Emergency Employment Act in 1972 was a white male high school graduate.[43] In 1971-72 a major objective of the program was to provide transitional employment for engineers and highly skilled persons who lost their jobs as a result of the scaling down of defense and aerospace work.

### Manpower Programs: Enrollment and Costs

A substantial increase in new enrollments in federally assisted work and training programs in 1972 brought the total to 3.1 million, an increase of 27 percent from the previous year. (See Table 7-8.) It was clearly the administration's desire to reduce the enrollment in many of the manpower programs during 1973. While the decline in the Public Employment Program (Emergency Employment Act) is consistent with legislative intent and improving business conditions, it is not clear why the NYC program was so sharply curtailed or why some other categorical programs were cut. The administration expects these enrollment declines to be replaced by new state and local programs funded through

Table 7-8

**New Enrollments in Federally Assisted Work and Training Programs, 1964 and 1971 to 1973 (Thousands)**

| Programs | 1964 | 1971 | 1972 | 1973 (Estimated) |
|---|---|---|---|---|
| MDTA Institutional Training | 69 | 156 | 151 | 140 |
| JOBS | 9 | 192 | 234 | 167 |
| Neighborhood Youth Corps | — | | | |
| In-School and Summer | — | 562 | 779 | 145 |
| Out-of-School | — | 53 | 65 | 60 |
| Operation Mainstream | — | 22 | 31 | 27 |
| Public Service Careers | — | 45 | 63 | 37 |
| Concentrated Employment Program | — | 77 | 69 | 58 |
| Job Corps | — | 50 | 49 | 49 |
| Work Incentive Program | — | 112 | 121 | 120 |
| Public Employment Program | — | — | 231 | 97 |
| Veterans Programs | — | 76 | 81 | 79 |
| Vocational Rehabilitation | 179 | 468 | 497 | 533 |
| Other Programs | 21 | 652 | 744 | 837 |
| Total | 278 | 2,465 | 3,115 | 2,350 |

Source: U.S. Department of Labor, *Manpower Report of the President, March, 1973* (Washington, D.C.: U.S. Government Printing Office, 1973), p. 51.

manpower revenue sharing. However, it is not clear how these programs are to be developed or whether all localities will be interested in supporting such efforts.

About 1.3 million young people 16 to 21 years of age were first-time enrollees in federal manpower programs during fiscal 1972. About three-fourths were in the Neighborhood Youth Corps' in-school and summer programs. These programs had a considerable impact on jobless rates. For example, in July 1971, there were 499,000 unemployed black youths 16 to 21 years of age in the labor market, indicating an unemployment rate of 28 percent. At the same time, more than 415,000 black youths were enrolled in manpower programs. It is not known whether all of these people would have been active job seekers, but if the manpower programs represented an alternative to unsuccessful job seeking for only two-thirds of the enrollees, the jobless rate for young blacks would have been 43 percent in the absence of these programs.[44] (Enrollees in manpower programs are not counted as unemployed irrespective of their previous employment status.) Cohen estimated that in 1967 the NYC, MDTA (OJT), Community Action and Work Study Programs reduced the unemployment rate among 16 to 21 year olds from 13.5 percent to 11.0 percent.[45] This study considered only these four programs and excluded any reduction in unemployment caused by the increasing skill of the labor force and the multiplier effects of government spending. Thus, irrespective of whether these programs are as efficient as they should be, they certainly do act to reduce youth unemployment.

Manpower training has been costly. From 1963 to 1972 the Department of Labor spent over $9 billion on such programs, including $2.7 billion during 1972. (See Table 7-9.) The total outlay for manpower and related programs in 1972 was $4.2 billion. During 1972 the Emergency Employment Act, the MDTA and Neighborhood Youth Corps, accounted for two-thirds of total expenditures.

## Overall Assessment of Manpower Programs

The first major point to be considered is the relatively poor performance of most of the programs in terms of the evaluative criteria employed. Low benefit-cost ratios, high dropout rates, and little improvement in employment status seem to be an all too common result. However, one should remember that these manpower efforts are designed to assist the disadvantaged individual or the structurally unemployed worker who could not find a job even in a tight labor market. Because these programs have made a serious attempt to reach these hard-core unemployed (often alienated youth) one should expect the results to be less positive than would occur if the programs had "creamed" the most highly motivated individuals. To what degree these major efforts to reach disadvantaged, often uninterested individuals, excuse the poor results of many of these projects is a matter of judgment.

**Table 7-9**
**Expenditures in 1972 for Major Manpower Programs Administered by the Department of Labor**

|  | Expenditures (Thousands) |
| --- | --- |
| MDTA | |
| Institutional Training | $ 355,708 |
| On-the-Job Training | 68,845 |
| Job Corps | 202,185 |
| Neighborhood Youth Corps | 517,244 |
| Operation Mainstream | 85,164 |
| Concentrated Employment Program | 154,602 |
| JOBS Program | 118,224 |
| Public Service Careers Program | 58,301 |
| WIN Program | 174,788 |
| Emergency Employment Act | 961,879 |
| Total | $2,696,940 |

Source: U.S. Department of Labor, *Manpower Report of the President, March, 1973* (Washington, D.C.: U.S. Government Printing Office, 1973), Table F-1, p. 227.

Secondly, considering the amount of money being spent on manpower programs, very little has been devoted to research and evaluation. For example, in 1969 over $1.5 billion was spent on manpower efforts, with 0.6 percent spent on research and evaluation.[46] Moreover, many of the government sponsored surveys are of limited relevance because of inadequate use of control groups and limited follow-up of trainees. Virtually no studies examine trainee performance more than 1 year after training has been completed. However, the long-term effects of manpower programs are extremely important for public policy. Moreover, most evaluation studies are commissioned while the program is relatively new, and there is pressure by Congress for quick results. Since most of these programs go through a "shake-down" period, an emphasis on early assessment may actually give a bleaker picture of the long-term effectiveness than is actually the case. Moreover, political factors often far outweigh research results in determining program priorities. For example, the summer NYC expanded rapidly becoming NYC's largest component. Each year, expansion has been fostered as a form of urban "riot insurance." It has never been demonstrated that this program increases the probability of returning to school, or that the work experience increases post-program earnings.[47] Instead, growth has been linked to a crisis atmosphere, with little attention to improving the employability or education of enrollees.

Thirdly, it appears that the reaction of government to weak programs has been to create a new program instead of attempting to improve existing efforts. This proliferation of specific programs has caused rigidities to develop that frustrate efforts to allocate limited resources and use them most effectively. The existence of categorical programs limits the ability of local communities to adapt and design manpower development efforts to meet their particular needs. Furthermore, although each program is supposed to meet the needs of a definite client group, many persons requiring training could qualify for several programs because of similar conditions of eligibility. Thus, a disadvantaged high school dropout would be eligible for the Job Corps, the out-of-school NYC, or the on-the-job training component of MDTA, which creates a problem for the individual, because he may not be able to ascertain which program is best suited to his needs. In extreme cases, this variety of programs has resulted in personnel competing with each other to fill available slots rather than being concerned with fitting the enrollee to the course of training best suited for him. For example, the OJT component of MDTA has suffered a decline in enrollment because the JOBS program also features on-the-job training for similar clientele. The JOBS program offers larger subsidies than MDTA-OJT, and the former has less federal monitoring of projects. JOBS is more costly, and it has not been shown that the additional cost has resulted in better training and employment opportunities.

Finally, it is clear that manpower programs have not been modified to meet changing economic conditions. From 1965 to 1969, when federal manpower programs grew rapidly, unemployment was low and the economy grew rapidly. A tight labor market made it somewhat easier to place disadvantaged persons. However, in 1971-72 nearly 5 million people were unemployed, including many with strong educational qualifications and superior skills. With a pool of competent unemployed workers, business became less interested in hiring the disadvantaged, whether they had completed a training program or otherwise. To continue to process disadvantaged persons through training programs with little prospect of employment is not only a waste of public funds, but is likely counter-productive because of the bitterness and disillusion created.

Manpower programs oriented toward the private sector are likely to be more effective in tight labor market conditions than when slack occurs. Subsidies to hire and train disadvantaged workers will have their greatest impact when qualified workers are not readily available. However, when firms are forced to lay off employees because of declining demand, subsidies or on-the-job training programs will be less effective.

Public sector training and employment is imperative in slack times. Institutional training provides income maintenance and the enrollees are more likely to complete the program because there are few jobs to entice them to terminate prematurely. Because placements and employment rates are related to lengths of stay, institutional programs should become more effective.

However, when employment levels are stable or declining, manpower participants who obtain jobs are likely displacing non-participants generally resulting in little equity gain.

## Summary

During the 1960s a large variety of manpower programs were developed to meet the needs of the technologically unemployed as well as the disadvantaged worker. These programs, which have concentrated their efforts primarily on young people, have generally not lived up to the expectations of their initial proponents. High dropout rates and the inability of most of these programs to place graduates in good jobs seem to be the rule and not the exception for most of these manpower efforts.

However, these programs have served to reduce youth unemployment and may be partly responsible for the absence of major urban violence in the United States since 1969. Moreover, since many of these programs such as the Job Corps made a serious effort to reach extremely disadvantaged young people, the poor performance of these programs, in terms of the standard assessment criteria, should be considered in this light.

Some consolidation of existing programs seems in order, which would eliminate duplication of effort that is extremely wasteful of scarce administrative talent. It would also terminate the practice of a number of manpower programs competing for the same clientele.

**A Look Ahead: The Labor Force in 1980**

Should present trends continue, what will be the size and composition of the labor force in 1980? What will be the labor force participation rate of married women? How many individuals will be unemployed? Questions such as these, though they are important, cannot be intelligently discussed unless one is willing to make some basic assumptions.

Three of the more pertinent factors one must consider are demographic shifts in the population as a whole and changes in both technology and social conditions.

By far the most important demographic development of the past decade has been the shift from the three-child to the two-child family. This consequence of an unusually steep decline in the number of children born to American women since 1958 may be expected to have a profound impact on manpower policies in future years. Its influence will be apparent in an increase in the number of working wives, and somewhat later, in an aging of the labor force in the form of a gradual decline in the proportion of younger workers and a corresponding increase in the proportion of workers in the highly productive 35 to 55 age group.

In addition to its impact on the size and composition of the labor force, a slower rate of population growth has wide ranging implications for social and economic institutions. The educational system and the teaching profession, for example, are not expected to continue the exuberant expansion of the past two decades, while the health care delivery system may have to concentrate an increasing proportion of available resources on services to older citizens. Residential patterns and housing requirements may change as the proportion of two-career/two-child families increases, and the social climate may be altered perceptably as the prevailing emphasis on the young gives way to greater involvement in the needs and aspirations of those over 30.

With respect to technology economists differ widely in their assessment of future changes. The Labor Department generally has assumed that technological change in the near future will not be radically different from that of the past decade. Thus, from 1962 to 1972 output per man hour (one measure of technical change) increased at a rate of 3.0 percent per year.[1] (However, when the age-sex distribution of man hours is weighted by its relative wage in the 1950 to 1970 period, productivity tends to decline slightly during the 1970 to 1980 decade because women workers—whose relative wages have always been lower than those of men—now contribute a more important part of total hours.)

Official projections indicate little change from the 3.0 percent per year rate for the remainder of the 1970s, but not all private economists share this expectation, especially if a somewhat longer time horizon is indicated. Robert Theobald, one of the more articulate and persuasive spokesmen for the view that the pace of technological change will quicken dramatically, argues that in the years ahead most structured jobs—white-collar as well as blue-collar—will be performed by machines not by men.[2] (The structured job, as defined by Theobald, is one in which the decision-making rules can be set out in advance.) Automation, which involves the replacement of human judgment and effort by electronic machines, may make it possible to eliminate the jobs of vast numbers of clerical as well as production workers. Cybernation, which involves the use of the computer as a decision-making device to control the operation of an automatic process, may make it possible to replace many technical and professional workers.

Thus, Theobald and others who accept the same assumptions about technological change foresee mass unemployment unless our present institutions and attitudes concerned with employment are drastically modified. If their assumptions are valid, there would be little point in attempting to estimate the size or composition of the labor force in 1980 by projecting the trends of the recent past.[3]

Finally, government manpower projections assume no *major* change in the propensity of work force groups to seek employment. In addition, it is assumed that no major wars or social upheavals will occur and no basic legislative or social changes will take place that could alter the conditions under which individuals choose to enter or remain out of the labor force.

## Uses of Manpower Projections

Manpower projections are used for a variety of planning purposes, some of which require a high degree of specificity and accuracy, while others require only that the projections be approximately correct. For vocational guidance purposes, for example, projections do not have to be expressed in precise quantitative terms but merely need to give a general idea of the relative growth rate of the occupation and of the employment opportunities available. For other purposes, such as revising vocational curriculums to meet changing manpower needs, the projections should be more specific and their assumptions must be fully presented. Other uses of manpower projections include:

1. *Identification of critical occupations.* Projections of the requirements for and the supply of workers are used by industry and government to determine which occupations face severe manpower shortages. This information is used by both government and industry in determining salary scales, developing training

programs, formulating immigration policy and determining who, if anyone, should be deferred from military service because he possesses a critical skill.

2. *Developing education and training programs.* Public and private institutions of higher learning need the best possible estimates of requirements for trained workers in various categories to determine which activities should be expanded and which should be reduced. The failure of these institutions to do this kind of manpower planning has resulted in an oversupply (hopefully temporary) of persons with graduate school training in the United States.

3. *Developing other projections.* The statistics on U.S. Gross National Product are commonly projected on the basis of expected trends in the labor force, hours of work, and average output per man hour. Projections of employment by industry have been used in estimating industrial demand for electric power, income payments and numbers of income taxpayers.

**Projection Methodology**

The labor force projection is based on Bureau of the Census projections of population and is developed through separate projections of labor force participation for the various age, sex, and color groups in the population. The detailed participation rates are then applied to the projected levels in each population group.

The industry and occupational employment projections are determined by utilizing two projection techniques. Total industry employment, which includes wage and salary workers, unpaid family workers, and the self-employed, is obtained by calculations involving projected changes in demand, interindustry relationships, and output and productivity. The employment projections are initially developed for about 82 industries or industry groups, covering the entire economy.[4] The employment estimates are also distributed into much greater detail (about 250 industries) by using regression analysis to estimate employment in each industry consistent with the basic assumptions of the economic projections. The results obtained by the two methods are then reconciled for consistency. Finally, the employment projections are converted into estimates of occupational requirements by projecting detailed occupational patterns, industry by industry. By summing over all industries one obtains the occupational projections.

It should be noted that all of the manpower projections presented in this chapter as well as the supporting information, are directly based on official Department of Labor estimates. The projections are not derived by the author. The estimates and their justification are synthesized from a number of Department of Labor publications including the *Manpower Report of the President, March 1973; The Occupational Outlook Handbook, 1973;* "The U.S. Economy in 1980," (Bulletin 1673; U.S. Department of Labor), as well as a number of

Special Labor Force Reports that provide projections of the occupational and industrial distribution of the work force in 1980.

## Projections of the Size and Composition of the Labor Force

Although the declining birth rate is likely to have a marked influence on manpower resources of the future, the major impact prior to 1980 will be more qualitative than quantitative; because all persons who will be in the labor force in 1980 have already been born, it is not too difficult to make the basic projections of the number of persons eligible for labor force participation and their age distribution. As shown in Table 8-1, from 1970 to 1980 the labor force is expected to grow by about 15 million—from 86 to 101 million workers. The absolute increase in the number of female workers is expected to be nearly as great as the increase in the male labor force, in spite of the fact that the latter was 60 percent greater than the former in 1970. Labor force projections for women

**Table 8-1**
**Age-Sex Distribution and the Labor Force, 1970 and Projection for 1980**

|  | Numbers (Thousands) | | Rates (Percent) | |
| --- | --- | --- | --- | --- |
| Male | 1970 | 1980 | 1970 | 1980 |
| 16 years and over | 54,343 | 62,590 | 82.4 | 78.0 |
| 16 to 19 years | 4,395 | 4,668 | 58.6 | 56.0 |
| 20 to 24 years | 7,378 | 8,852 | 88.9 | 83.0 |
| 25 to 34 years | 11,974 | 17,523 | 96.4 | 94.6 |
| 35 to 44 years | 10,818 | 11,851 | 96.4 | 95.1 |
| 45 to 54 years | 10,487 | 9,908 | 94.3 | 91.9 |
| 55 to 64 years | 7,127 | 7,730 | 85.2 | 79.1 |
| 65 years and over | 2,164 | 2,058 | 32.2 | 21.2 |
| Female |  |  |  |  |
| 16 years and over | 31,560 | 39,219 | 42.8 | 45.0 |
| 16 to 19 years | 3,250 | 3,669 | 43.7 | 45.5 |
| 20 to 24 years | 4,893 | 6,592 | 57.5 | 63.4 |
| 25 to 34 years | 5,704 | 9,256 | 44.8 | 50.2 |
| 35 to 44 years | 5,971 | 6,869 | 50.9 | 53.2 |
| 45 to 54 years | 6,533 | 6,537 | 54.0 | 56.2 |
| 55 to 64 years | 4,153 | 5,057 | 42.5 | 44.7 |
| 65 years and over | 1,056 | 1,239 | 9.2 | 8.6 |

Source: U.S. Department of Labor, *Manpower Report of the President, March, 1973* (Washington, D.C.: U.S. Government Printing Office, 1973), Table E-2, p. 220.

workers, which are based on a continuation of the two-child family norm, indicate a nearly 70 percent increase in the potential female labor force from 25 to 34 years of age during the 1970s, compared to a 48 percent increase for men of that age group. Thereafter, the projected labor force potentials of women aged 35 and over parallel those projected among working men.

Maintenance of the two-child norm has an important effect on the size of the labor force. Thus, an immediate return to a three-child norm would lower the size of the female labor force by 1.7 million in 1980. The projected 1980 labor force of women 16 to 24 years old is nearly 500,000 larger and that of women 25 to 54 years old 1.2 million larger, with the assumption of a two-child family as compared to a three-child family.[5]

Actual levels of female labor force participation will be more closely related to employment opportunities than the above projections of labor supply would indicate. While the two-child norm frees additional numbers of women from child-care responsibilities, it also reduces their need for supplementary income. On balance, the higher labor force participation rates for women projected under the two-child norm reflect the assumption that the decision to seek employment by family members other than the principal wage earner is not motivated solely by the need for supplementary income. For example, higher levels of education-al attainment and greater equality of access to professional-level employment are likely to induce many women to enter the labor force, with or without the added incentive of financial need.

### Manpower Planning for Women Workers

The anticipated increase in the proportion of married women in the labor force has serious implications for manpower policies in the years immediately ahead. There is every reason to expect that substantial numbers of these potential workers—especially those in the disadvantaged sector of the population—will require remedial and/or refresher job training in an increasing range of occupa-tions. In addition, any increase in the number of occupations potentially open to all women can be expected to alter present patterns of job matching and placement. Moreover, the fact that many of these women are in the younger age groups may complicate the hiring and promotion process for men in similar age groups who are competing for the same jobs and advancement opportunities; this latter development is one that could add somewhat to the handicaps of disadvantaged male job seekers. Although low birth rates will contribute to an aging of the labor force, which is expected to result in a gradual restriction of opportunities for promotion of both men and women, this phenomenon is not expected to have its main effect until after 1980.

Finally, there is the urgent problem, discussed earlier, of providing adequate child-care services for working mothers. The statistics on family income indicate that children in families headed by women derive major financial benefits if their mother is in the labor force and, as indicated in Chapter 2, Table 2-6, married women make a substantial contribution to family income. Nevertheless, a continuing scarcity of child-care arrangements may discourage some of these women from seeking work.

Male workers in the central age group (25 to 54) years are expected to continue to be the most stable part of the nation's labor force, comprising about 40 percent of it in both 1970 and 1980. In projecting to 1980, the participation rates were only slightly lower than those observed during 1970, when the unemployment rate was 4.5 percent—a more or less full employment level. The projections for men 55 to 64 years old represent the net effect of two major assumptions: labor force participation rates for those 55 to 59 years old will decline slightly from the levels observed during 1970 with a somewhat larger decline for men in the 60 to 64 age group, as the trend toward early retirement continues to outweigh somewhat the assumed continuing demand for the skills and experience of working men in this age group. The slight decline in the labor force participation rates of younger males are due primarily to an increase in school enrollment rates.

In determining the labor force participation rates presented in Table 8-1, the Department of Labor assumed full employment—that is, a rate of unemployment that could not be lowered without the likelihood of substantial increases in the price level. In 1956—a peacetime year of high employment and low inflation—the aggregate unemployment rate was 4.1 percent. As stated in Chapter 3, during 1971 the aggregate unemployment rate would have been 4.5 percent if the 1956 rate for each age/sex group had remained at the same level in the intervening years. This increase in the full-employment unemployment rate is due to the effect of larger numbers of young and female job seekers whose jobless rates are relatively high. Thus, the jobless rate equivalent to that of 4.1 percent in 1956 is 4.5 percent in 1971 and the projected equivalent rate for 1980 is also 4.5 percent.

## Occupational Changes

Important changes in occupational employment patterns may be expected in the United States, owing to the differing growth trends in different industries, a continuation of technological change, and a maintenance of a rate of economic growth that permits the economy to produce at near capacity levels. An assessment of future employment trends in major occupations is consequently essential if we are to appraise future manpower needs and the adequacy of present and prospective labor supply.

In assessing the demand for workers in a particular occupation, account must be taken of both the number needed because of net growth in employment and those required to replace workers who are separated from the occupation because of death, sickness, transfer or other reasons.

Table 8-2 indicates the occupational distribution of workers in 1960 and 1970 as well as the expected distribution in 1980. Employment of professional and technical workers, which was the fastest growing occupational group from 1960 to 1970, is expected to grow at a slightly slower rate during the 1970s. Manpower requirements are expected to increase substantially in nearly every professional field such as the health professions, the social sciences, the law and the natural sciences. However, employment in teaching will grow more slowly than in the past two decades.

In engineering and the natural sciences, employment requirements may be about three million by 1980, nearly double the number actually employed in 1970. It is expected that interdisciplinary areas such as the fields of oceanography, biophysics, engineering physics, and metallurgy will show the most rapid gain.

The number of technicians working with engineers and scientists is expected to increase at about the same rate as the growth of the latter occupations leading probably to a doubling of requirements by 1980 and the employment of over 2 million technical specialists.

The rapid growth in the employment of technicians is due to two basic factors. First, because of the rapid pace of modern technology, a need has been created for workers who have some basic scientific and mathematical knowledge and also specialized training in some aspect of technology. Secondly, the long-term shortage of scientists and engineers has created a need for technicians to relieve the professional workers of tasks that can be performed by less highly trained persons.

Because of the slower increase in school age population, the 1970s will witness a drop in the demand for additional elementary and secondary school teachers, in spite of increasing replacement requirements. An average annual increase of 23,000 elementary and secondary school teachers was required between 1967 and 1971 to serve mounting numbers of pupils. Between 1972 and 1981 the increase will fall to 13,000 new jobs because of declining enrollments.[6] For college teachers the situation is similar. From 1967 to 1971 the annual increase in demand was 26,000 teachers per year. From 1972 to 1981 the additional demand is expected to decline to 18,000 per year. The problem of prediction is most difficult at the college level, where enrollment trends, and hence teacher demand, are less dependent of general population increases, and where the shifting needs and interest of students could result in major revision of curriculums.

Relatively slow growth in the number of proprietors is expected during the 1970s, primarily because the trend toward formulation of larger businesses is expected to continue and will greatly restrict the growth in the total number of firms. However, the number of managers and other salaried officials in business organizations and government is likely to continue increasing fairly rapidly.

**Table 8-2**

**Employment by Occupation Group, 1960, 1970, and Projected 1980 Requirements (Thousands)**

| Occupation Group | 1960 | | Actual 1970 | | Projected Requirements in 1980 | |
|---|---|---|---|---|---|---|
| | Number | Percent Distribution | Number | Percent Distribution | Number | Percent Distribution |
| Professional and Technical Workers | 7,469 | 11.4 | 11,140 | 14.2 | 15,000 | 16.3 |
| Managers, Officials and Proprietors | 7,067 | 10.7 | 8,289 | 10.5 | 9,500 | 10.0 |
| Clerical Workers | 9,762 | 14.8 | 13,714 | 17.4 | 17,300 | 18.2 |
| Sales Workers | 4,224 | 6.4 | 4,854 | 6.2 | 6,000 | 6.3 |
| Craftsmen and Foremen | 8,554 | 13.0 | 10,158 | 12.9 | 12,200 | 12.8 |
| Operatives | 11,950 | 18.2 | 13,909 | 17.7 | 15,400 | 16.2 |
| Service Workers | 8,023 | 12.2 | 9,712 | 12.4 | 13,100 | 13.8 |
| Non-Farm Laborers | 3,553 | 5.4 | 3,724 | 4.7 | 3,500 | 3.7 |
| Farmers and Farm Laborers | 5,176 | 7.9 | 3,126 | 4.0 | 2,600 | 2.7 |
| Total | 65,778 | 100.0 | 78,626 | 100.0 | 95,100 | 100.0 |

Note: A 3 percent unemployment rate in 1980 is assumed.

Source: U.S. Department of Labor, *Manpower Report of the President, March, 1973* (Washington, D.C.: U.S. Government Printing Office, 1973), Table E-9, p. 225.

The net result of these divergent trends will probably be a slower increase in employment in the manager-proprietor group as a whole than in any other major group of white-collar workers. Nevertheless, the relative increase in the combined group is expected to be only slightly less than for all occupations.

Employment of clerical workers is expected to increase rapidly during the 1970s due to the ever mounting volume of communications, record-keeping, and other paperwork that is characteristic of our economy. This development is likely to more than offset the widespread use of such labor saving devices as electronic computers and other new office equipment. By 1980 clerical employment is expected to reach 17.3 million, nearly double the number of clerical workers in 1960.

One reason for anticipating this employment growth is the expected rapid expansion of the finance and insurance industries—which employ a large number of clerical workers. Moreover, clerical employment will also increase because of the trend toward transferring to clerical workers' functions which were formerly performed by sales personnel and proprietors. For example, the trend toward self service in retail stores will mean the elimination of some sales jobs but the creation of new positions for cashiers and checkers (who are now classified as clerical workers).[7]

Population growth and rising per capita income are the major factors that will tend to bring about the projected increase in sales employment. The expected further growth in the numbers of part-time workers in sales positions will also tend to increase total employment in this occupational group. These factors are expected to outweigh the negative effects of self service techniques and other labor saving innovations which will occur in retail establishments.

Among blue-collar workers, the craftsmen, foremen, and kindred workers continue to have the most favorable employment outlook. Increased employment of mechanics and repairmen, building trades craftsmen, skilled metal workers and foremen will probably account for most of the growth in the skilled worker group. Because of the mounting need for mechanics and repairmen to install and maintain the ever-increasing amount of complex equipment used by industry, government agencies, and private households, employment of these workers is expected to reach 3.25 million in 1980 compared to only 2 million in 1960.

The anticipated large volume of construction activity is expected to cause a sharp increase in the number of building trades craftsmen from 3.25 million in 1970 to 4 million in 1980. The trades expected to experience the fastest growth are operating engineers, cement masons, bricklayers, construction electricians, sheet metal workers, and plumbers and pipefitters.

Operatives and kindred workers, currently the largest occupational group are expected to have a slower than average rate of growth of employment in the 1970s. Increasing automation of production processes will eliminate many operative jobs in the coming decade. However, it is expected that the introduction of automated machinery in factories and other business establishments will be gradual, easing the adjustment process. Moreover, the expected continued growth of the use of motor vehicles for transport will result in increasing employment of truck and bus drivers—one of the largest groups of workers in the operative category.

Service workers are expected to have the second most rapid total employment growth of the nine occupational groups during the 1970s. A relatively rapid rise in employment of protective service workers, such as policemen and firemen, is expected as the population increases, especially in suburban communities. In addition, as a result of increased demands for health services, very substantial expansion in the demand for practical nurses and for attendants in hospitals and other institutions is anticipated. Other categories of service workers expected to experience rapid employment growth include waiters and waitresses, cooks, and charwomen and cleaners. The chief reason for anticipating growth in these latter occupations is the expected expansion in the food service business and the need for such persons in hospitals and other types of public buildings and institutions.

**Industrial Employment**

The overall growth in civilian jobs will be accompanied by significant changes in the industrial distribution of employment. (See Table 8-3.) Many industries will grow more rapidly or more slowly than the economy-wide average because of changes in patterns of demand. Future demand for industrial products not only reflects changes in the purchasing pattern of consumers but also is a function of the type and volume of business investment. Moreover, decisions by government about public expenditures for highways, public buildings, defense production, and education all impinge on the growth in output and employment of a wide variety of industries.

The only broad industry sector in which an actual decline in employment is expected during the 1970s is agriculture. The rise in output per farm worker, which underlies the long-term decline in farm employment, is expected to continue as a result of the increased use of machinery, fertilizers, feed activities, pesticides, and other technological advances. The continuing decrease in the number of farms—particularly the small, low-income producing units—will result in a significant decrease in the number of farmers. Thus, during the 1970s agricultural employment is expected to fall by nearly a half million workers.

**Service-Producing Industries**

Employment in the transportation, communications, and public utilities industries is expected to increase slowly during the 1970s, and the share of total

**Table 8-3**

**Employment by Industry Division, 1960, 1970, and Projected 1980 Requirements (Thousands)**

| Industry Division | 1960 | | Actual 1970 | | Projected Requirements in 1980 | |
|---|---|---|---|---|---|---|
| | Number | Percent Distribution | Number | Percent Distribution | Number | Percent Distribution |
| Agriculture | 5,458 | – | 3,462 | – | 3,000 | – |
| Total Non-Agricultural Wage and Salary Workers | 54,234 | 100.0 | 70,616 | 100.0 | 86,000 | 100.0 |
| Goods-Producing Industries | 20,393 | 37.6 | 23,336 | 33.0 | 27,085 | 31.3 |
| Mining | 712 | 1.3 | 622 | 0.9 | 550 | 0.6 |
| Contract Construction | 2,885 | 5.3 | 3,345 | 4.7 | 4,600 | 5.3 |
| Manufacturing | 16,796 | 31.0 | 19,369 | 27.4 | 21,935 | 25.3 |
| Durable Goods | 9,459 | 17.4 | 11,198 | 15.9 | 13,015 | 15.0 |
| Non-Durable Goods | 7,336 | 13.5 | 8,171 | 11.6 | 8,920 | 10.3 |
| Service-Producing Industries | 33,840 | 62.4 | 47,281 | 67.0 | 59,515 | 68.7 |
| Transportation, Communication and Public Utilities | 4,004 | 7.4 | 4,504 | 6.4 | 4,740 | 5.5 |
| Wholesale and Retail Trade | 11,391 | 21.0 | 14,922 | 21.1 | 17,625 | 20.4 |
| Finance Insurance and Real Estate | 2,669 | 4.9 | 3,690 | 5.2 | 4,260 | 4.9 |
| Service and Miscellaneous | 7,423 | 13.7 | 11,630 | 16.5 | 16,090 | 18.6 |
| Government | 8,353 | 15.4 | 12,535 | 17.8 | 16,800 | 19.4 |

Note: A 3 percent unemployment rate in 1980 is assumed.

Source: U.S. Department of Labor, *Manpower Report of the President, March, 1973* (Washington, D.C.: U.S. Government Printing Office, 1973), Table E-10, p. 225.

employment is expected to fall to 5.5 percent from 6.4 percent in 1970. Transportation employment has long been dominated by the long, slow decline in railroad employment during the postwar period. However, trucking and air transportation are expected to increase sufficiently fast to slightly more than offset whatever further small railroad declines occur.[8] If the present fuel shortage continues, there may be a resurgence in passenger rail traffic and a concomitant decline in air travel causing increases in the number of rail employees and declines in the number of airline workers. Thus a long term energy shortage would cause the employment projections for 1980 to be inaccurate with respect to these two industries.

Public utilities and communications are highly productive service industries. Thus, even with the expected rapid increase in output in these industries the number of jobs will expand only moderately.

Total employment changes in wholesale and retail trade are expected to generally parallel those of the entire economy, and this industry's share of total employment is thus expected to show little change. Retail trade employment will expand most rapidly in general merchandise stores and eating and drinking establishments. Technological developments such as vending machines, other self-service gadgets, and electronic computers for inventory control and billing will tend to retard employment growth.

A large part of the increased employment in trade is expected to be among part-time workers, including many women and younger workers. The development of suburban shopping centers and the trend toward keeping stores open during night-time hours is creating a demand for part-time workers.

Wholesale trade employment is expected to increase more rapidly than retail trade. Employment in motor vehicles, automotive equipment, and machinery equipment and supply will be among the faster growing areas.

Employment in the finance, insurance, and real estate fields will grow somewhat slower than the level of total employment resulting in a small decline in the proportion of employed workers in this industry.

Banking employment is expected to grow at a slower pace than in the last decade as advancing automation eliminates many clerical functions. Electronic data processing equipment is also expected to slow employment growth in the security dealers and exchanges sector, a rapid growth area within the overall financial sector. Increase in the size of firms, due to growth and mergers, may also limit employment gains.

Although restrained somewhat by the computerization of record-keeping functions, insurance employment will continue to grow at about the same pace as during the 1960s because of the steadily rising population. Real estate employment will grow at a slightly faster pace than in the past decade: it is little affected by technological advances but highly responsive to the number of family formations and the price of new and used housing.

Employment growth in the service industries will be more rapid during the

1970s than in any other industry. This industry is somewhat heterogeneous including personal, business, health and educational services. Employment growth in this industry will be related to a substantial increase in population, a rapid rise in personal disposable income, expanding economic activity, and a growing demand for medical, educational, and other services. The output of these labor-intensive industries is less affected by technological change than many other industries, hence their employment growth is not restrained very much by productivity advances.

Growth in employment in business services is expected to be quite rapid as firms rely increasingly on advertising services to sell their products; on accounting, auditing, bookkeeping, and computing services to handle their record-keeping; on contract firms to provide maintenance services; and on audit bureaus and agencies to cope with mushrooming consumer credit.

During the 1970s employment among federal government workers is expected to rise only slightly, but state and local employment will continue to expand rapidly especially if the president's revenue sharing proposals are fully implemented. Although the rate of increase in state and local government will be higher than almost any other industrial sector, the growth will be slower than during the 1960s, mainly because of a decline in the rate of growth of educational employment, which accounts for roughly half of the jobs in state and local government.

**Goods-Producing Industries**

Mining is projected to have the lowest rate of increase in output among all non-farm industries. Continued employment declines are projected through the 1970s, although at a reduced rate because of some resurgence in the demand for coal. The magnitude of this increased demand will be a function of the severity of the shortage of oil and gas. Furthermore, manpower requirements will be affected by the increasing use of new and improved labor saving devices and techniques, such as continuous mining machinery systems and more efficient exploration and recovery techniques in crude oil and natural gas extraction.

The construction industry may benefit from intensive application of existing technology that would increase the output per man hour. Already, prefabricated panels and shells for houses show promise of more widespread use, which would slow the increase in employment. However, the national housing goal for the decade 1968 to 1978, calling for the construction of 20 million new housing units in the private market and the production of 6 million new and rehabilitated units with public assistance in one form or other, will continue to spur growth in the construction industry. Additional demand will come from an expansion in state and local government needs, particularly for highway construction and from expanding investment in industrial plants.

Manufacturing is still the biggest industry but growth is expected to be slower than overall employment with the share of total employment accounted for by manufacturing falling to one-fourth by 1980.

Growth in the durable goods sector will be accelerated by the significantly increased demand for building materials for housing construction. The increasing application of technological innovations to manufacturing processes is expected to continue to reduce unit labor requirements in manufacturing. Major technological developments that will continue to limit growth in manufacturing employment include numerical control of machine tools, new metal processing methods, electronic computers, and instrumentation and automatic controls.

Large increases in output will occur in those industries producing instruments and industrial electrical equipment that are involved in the production of automated capital equipment. Among the non-durable goods industries, the fastest growing will be chemicals, printing, and paper.

Because of offsetting tendencies, the labor force projections previously discussed assume little change in the geographic mobility of the labor force. The decreasing proportion of workers 16 to 24 years of age, the most mobile age group, will tend to reduce overall mobility. Similarly the reduction of agriculture to a relatively small sector of the economy indicates that another source of mobility—farmworkers—will be of less importance in the future. Finally, the movement of southern blacks to northern cities, while still continuing, is doing so at a much reduced rate. This decline in South-North migration is expected to continue.

However, there are indications of increasing intercity mobility, especially among the professional-technical, managerial, and skilled groups in the work force, as well as a continuing shift of population from cities to suburbs, accompanied (or preceded) by a corresponding shift by industry. These trends are expected to continue well beyond 1980. This latter development may have serious implications for labor force mobility among blacks. Because of segregated housing patterns, blacks generally cannot purchase suburban housing and are forced to remain residents of central cities. However, the industrial shift discussed above means that a substantial proportion of urban job opportunities will have relocated to portions of the metropolitan area that may be poorly serviced by mass transit systems.

There are two factors that will tend to increase the mobility of the American work force. First, since highly educated workers tend to have higher mobility rates than less-educated workers, the continued upward shift in the educational distribution will tend on balance to increase worker mobility. In addition, childless couples and small families tend to be more geographically mobile than larger family units.

## Educational Attainment of the Labor Force

The nation's labor force will have higher educational qualifications in 1980 than in 1970: the proportion of workers with at least 4 years of high school will be rising among workers at all ages. (See Table 8-4.) By 1980, only 1 in 16 adult workers (25 and over)—about 5 million—will have less than 8 years of schooling; and 7 in every 10 adult workers—about 52 million—will have completed at least 4 years of high school. In contrast about 1 in 10 adult workers in 1970—nearly 7 million—had completed less than 8 years of schooling while 6 in every 10 adult workers—about 37 million—had completed 4 years of high school or more.[9]

Nearly 1 in 6 workers, 25 years and over—about 13 million—will have completed at least 4 years of college in 1980; in 1970 about 9 million or 1 in 7 workers, 25 years and over, had a similar amount of education.

## Highly Educated Manpower

The nation's colleges and universities are presently turning out record numbers of graduates and are expected to continue to do so through the 1970s. The number of persons earning bachelor's degrees will climb by two-thirds, and those earning master's and doctoral degrees are expected to double by 1980.[10]

The large output of highly educated workers is expected to eliminate many long-time occupational shortages in such fields as physics, biology, and nursing. The anticipated surplus of applicants trained for elementary and secondary teaching, the biggest single source of professional opportunity for women, will mean that many college-educated women will need to enter previously male-dominated professions such as engineering, law, medicine, dentistry, and pharmacy, if they are to effectively utilize their schooling.

Professional health occupations are expected to continue to be in short supply. If the number of engineering graduates were to keep pace with the expected growth in total college graduates, the new supply would be adequate to meet projected requirements. Recent trends, however, indicate that bachelor's degrees in engineering continue to become a *smaller* proportion of total bachelor's degrees awarded.

Other areas for which potential shortages are in prospect include counseling, social work, urban planning, and state and local government administration.

## Quality of Projections

How much confidence can we place in the projections that have been presented? One way of approaching this question is to compare past projections with actual results. In 1960, the Department of Labor issued a report entitled *Manpower Challenge of the 1960's* which projected the size and composition of the labor force to 1970.[11]

The labor force changes by age group are compared with the projections made in 1960 in Table 8-5. The overall projection was quite accurate. However, there was an overestimate of the additional number of workers over 45. Earlier retirements resulting, in part, from changes in social security eligibility as well as

**Table 8-4**

**Projected Educational Attainment of the Labor Force, 25 Years and Over, Both Sexes, 1980 (Thousands)**

| Years of School Completed | Total 25 Years and Over | 25 to 34 Years | 35 to 44 Years | 45 to 54 Years | 55 to 64 Years | 65 Years and Over |
|---|---|---|---|---|---|---|
| Total: Number | 76,327 | 25,474 | 18,386 | 16,252 | 12,947 | 3,268 |
| Percent | 100.0 | 100.0 | 100.0 | 100.0 | 100.0 | 100.0 |
| Less than 4 years of High School | 28.7 | 17.8 | 25.6 | 35.2 | 39.5 | 53.1 |
| 4 years or more of High School | 71.3 | 82.2 | 74.3 | 64.7 | 60.5 | 46.8 |
| Less than 5 years | 1.8 | 0.7 | 1.4 | 2.4 | 2.8 | 4.4 |
| 5 to 7 years | 4.0 | 1.3 | 3.1 | 5.5 | 6.7 | 11.0 |
| 8 years | 6.1 | 2.2 | 4.3 | 7.9 | 10.8 | 19.3 |
| 9 to 11 years | 16.8 | 13.6 | 16.8 | 19.4 | 19.2 | 18.4 |
| 12 years | 42.4 | 47.3 | 44.7 | 39.4 | 37.8 | 24.4 |
| 13 to 15 years | 12.0 | 14.2 | 12.1 | 10.6 | 10.1 | 9.9 |
| 16 years or more | 16.9 | 20.7 | 17.5 | 14.7 | 12.6 | 12.5 |
| Median Years of School Completed | 12.5 | 12.7 | 12.5 | 12.4 | 12.3 | 11.5 |

Source: U.S. Department of Labor, *Manpower Report of the President, March, 1973* (Washington, D.C.: U.S. Government Printing Office, 1973), Table E-11, p. 226.

**Table 8-5**

**Comparison of Labor Force Changes, by Age Group, with Projections Made in 1960 (Millions of Workers)**

| Age | 1970 Projection | 1970 Actual |
|---|---|---|
| Under 25 | 6.2 | 6.8 |
| 25 to 34 | 1.8 | 2.5 |
| 35 to 44 | −0.2 | 0.0 |
| 45 and over | 5.7 | 4.0 |
| Total | 13.5 | 13.3 |

Source: Computed from Sol Swerdloff, "How Good Were Manpower Projections for the 1960s," *Monthly Labor Review* 92, No. 11 (November 1969): 19.

greater numbers than expected receiving social security disability retirements both contributed to this smaller than projected growth.

An underestimate for younger workers occurred because no increase in the labor force participation rate of women 20 to 24 years of age was projected. In fact, the participation rate for this group increased from 46.2 in 1960 to 57.8 in 1970, partly because school enrollment rates for this age group were lower than expected.

The broad occupational trends projected in 1960 report have also been quite accurate, as shown in Table 8-6. The biggest discrepancy between the projection for 1970 and actual employment is the occupational group, farmers and farm workers. Because of productivity advances and the decline of subsistence agriculture employment fell more rapidly than expected. In addition, professional and technical occupations grew more rapidly than envisioned partly in response to defense needs created by the war in Vietnam as well as the rapid

**Table 8-6**

**Percent Change in Employment, by Occupational Group, 1960 to 1970**

| Occupation | 1970 Projection | 1970 Actual |
|---|---|---|
| Profession and Technical | 41 | 51 |
| Managers, Officials and Proprietors | 25 | 17 |
| Clerical and Sales | 30 | 32 |
| Skilled | 24 | 20 |
| Semiskilled | 19 | 22 |
| Service | 24 | 20 |
| Unskilled | 0 | 0 |
| Farmers and Farmworkers | −18 | −42 |

Source: Sol Swerdloff, "How Good Were Manpower Projections for the 1960s?" *Monthly Labor Review* 93 (November 1969): 22.

development of the aerospace industry. The growth in the number of managers and proprietors was slower than expected. Because of the financial benefits that accrue to corporate enterprises, many small businesses have incorporated, thereby shifting the owner's occupational classification from self-employed proprietor to the salaried and official group or even to the sales, professional, or craftsmen occupational groups.

While some improvements may be expected in the field of manpower projections, it would be unrealistic to assume that any forecasting procedure can ever be developed that would enable labor force developments to be accurately predicted. Any forecasting procedure is more appropriately viewed as an attempt to assemble the relevant information that would facilitate decision-making in the face of uncertainty than as a precise projection methodology.[12] Because of the importance of manpower projections in educational planning, vocational guidance, as well as forecasting of economic growth, these exercises will grow in importance and hopefully in accuracy.

## Summary

Manpower projections are used by business and government to forecast changing manpower needs as well as to pinpoint shortages and surpluses. They assume a large degree of stability in the general social and economic climate.

The labor force growth in the 1970 to 1980 decade is expected to be equally divided between male and female workers. This implies a continuing increase in the labor force participation rate of women and a decline in the participation rate for men. Major industrial and occupational changes during the 1970s will result in large increases in professional and service workers (particularly government employees) and sharp declines in the number of agricultural workers and miners and among the unskilled generally.

A comparison of 1970 labor force projections (made in 1960) with actual 1970 statistics on the age distribution of the labor force and its distribution by occupation indicate that the errors were quite small. This indicates that barring unforeseen circumstances we may place reasonable confidence in the projections made in this chapter.

**Notes**

# Notes

Chapter 1
The Anatomy of Employment
and Unemployment

1. President's Committee to Appraise Employment and Unemployment Statistics, *Measuring Employment and Unemployment* (Washington, D.C.: U.S. Government Printing Office, 1962), p. 1.

2. Ewan Clague, *The Bureau of Labor Statistics* (New York: Praeger, 1968), pp. 50-51.

3. John E. Breggar, "Unemployment Statistics and What They Mean," *Monthly Labor Review* 94 (November 1971): 23.

4. Ibid.

5. Betty·G. Fishman and Leo Fishman, *Employment, Unemployment and Economic Growth* (New York: Crowell, 1969), p. 18.

6. *Measuring Employment and Unemployment*, op. cit., p. 25.

7. See, for example, Susan S. Holland, "Adult Men Not in the Labor Force," *Monthly Labor Review* 90 (March 1967): 5-15.

8. Gordon F. Bloom and Herbert R. Northrup, *Economics of Labor Relations* (Homewood, Ill.: Richard D. Irwin, 1973), p. 429.

9. U.S. Department of Labor, *Manpower Report of the President, March, 1973* (Washington, D.C.: U.S. Government Printing Office, 1973), p. 190.

10. Maurice Preston, "Unemployment: Why We Need a New Measurement," *Lloyds Bank Review* 104 (April 1972): 3.

11. Jean Mouly, "Some Remarks on the Concepts of Employment, Underemployment and Unemployment," *International Labor Review* 105 (February 1972): 156.

12. U.S. Congress, Joint Economic Committee, *The Extent and Nature of Frictional Unemployment* (Washington, D.C.: Bureau of Labor Statistics, 1959), p. 1.

13. Eleanor G. Gilpatrick, *Structural Unemployment and Aggregate Demand: A Study of Employment and Unemployment in the United States, 1948-1964* (Baltimore, Md.: The Johns Hopkins Press, 1966), p. 39.

14. Curtis L. Gilroy, "Job Losers, Leavers and Entrants: Traits and Trends," *Monthly Labor Review* 96 (August 1973): 7.

15. Ibid.

16. See John E. Breggar, op. cit., p. 13, for a discussion of the statistical techniques utilized in seasonal employment adjustments.

17. U.S. Department of Labor, *Manpower Report . . . 1973*, Table A-6, p. 35 and Table A-19, p. 152.

18. United Nations, *Measures for the Economic Development of Underdeveloped Countries* (New York: United Nations, 1951), p. 9.

19. N.S. Buchanan and H.S. Ellis, *Approaches to Economic Development* (New York: Twentieth Century Fund, 1955), p. 45.

20. Warren Robinson, "Disguised Unemployment Once Again: East Pakistan, 1951-1961," *American Journal of Agricultural Economics* 51 (August 1969): 592.

21. T.W. Schultz, "The Role of Government in Promoting Economic Growth," in L.D. White (ed.), *The State of the Social Sciences* (Chicago, Ill.: University of Chicago Press, 1956), p. 375.

22. See Carol Rosen, "Hidden Unemployment and Related Issues," *Monthly Labor Review*, Vol. 96, No. 3, March 1973, pp. 31-37, for an excellent bibliography on the subject of discouraged workers.

23. Paul O. Flaim, "Discouraged Workers and Changes in Unemployment," *Monthly Labor Review* 96 (March 1973): 31-37.

24. Ibid.

25. U.S. Department of Labor, *Manpower Report of the President, 1972* (Washington, D.C.: U.S. Government Printing Office, 1972), p. 38.

## Chapter 2
## The American Labor Force

1. U.S. Department of Labor, *Manpower Report of the President, March, 1973* (Washington, D.C.: U.S. Government Printing Office, 1973), Table A-13, p. 144.

2. U.S. Department of Labor, op. cit., Table C-2, p. 189.

3. U.S. Bureau of the Census, *Income in 1970 of Families and Persons in the United States*, Current Population Reports, Series P-60 (Washington, D.C.: U.S. Government Printing Office, 1971), p. 117.

4. Sar A. Levitan, Garth L. Mangum and Ray Marshall, *Human Resources and Labor Markets: Labor and Manpower in the American Economy* (New York: Harper and Row, 1972), p. 68.

5. Clarence D. Long, *The Labor Force Under Changing Income and Employment* (Princeton, N.J.: Princeton University Press for the National Bureau of Economic Research, 1959), p. 287; U.S. Department of Labor, *Manpower Report . . . March, 1973*, p. 128.

6. Long, op. cit., p. 141.

7. Stuart H. Garfinkle, *Job Changing and Manpower Training*, U.S. Department of Labor, Manpower Administration, Office of Manpower, Automation and Training, Manpower Report No. 10, (Washington, D.C.: U.S. Government Printing Office, 1964), p. 1.

8. Robert L. Stein, "Reasons for Nonparticipation in the Labor Force," *Monthly Labor Review* 90 (July 1967): 23; and U.S. Department of Labor, *Manpower Report . . . March, 1973*, Table A-8, p. 137.

9. Stein, op. cit., p. 28.

10. William G. Bowen and T. Aldrich Finegan, *The Economics of Labor Force Participation* (Princeton, N.J.: Princeton University Press, 1969), p. 561 and p. 565.

11. James N. Morgan, Ismail A. Sirageldin and Nancy Baerwaldt, *Productive Americans* (Ann Arbor: University of Michigan, 1966), p. 48.

12. Jacob Mincer, "Labor Force Participation of Married Women: A Study of Labor Supply" in *Aspects of Labor Economics*, (New York: National Bureau of Economic Research, 1962), pp. 63-105.

13. Glen G. Cain, *Married Women in the Labor Force: An Economic Analysis* (Chicago, Ill.: University of Chicago Press, 1966), p. 118.

14. Levitan, et al., op. cit., p. 29.

15. Valerie K. Oppenheimer, "The Female Labor Force in the United States," population Monograph Series No. 5 (Berkeley: University of California, 1970), p. 160.

16. Juanita Kreps, *Sex in the Marketplace: American Women at Work*, Policy Studies in Employment and Welfare, No. 11 (Baltimore, Maryland: Johns Hopkins Press, 1971), p. 38.

17. U.S. Department of Labor, *Manpower Report . . . 1973*, Table B-4, p. 168.

18. Seth Low and Pearl Spindler, U.S. Department of Labor and U.S. Department of Health, Education, and Welfare, *Child Care Arrangements of Working Mothers in the United States* (Washington, D.C.: U.S. Government Printing Office, 1968), pp. 15-16.

19. U.S. Department of Labor, Women's Bureau, "Day Care: An Employer's Plus," Women's Bureau Release 71-112 (Washington, D.C.: U.S. Government Printing Office, March 1971), p. 1.

20. Levitan, et al., op. cit., p. 47.

21. Elizabeth Waldman and Kathryn R. Gover, "Marital and Family Characteristics of the Labor Force," *Monthly Labor Review* 95 (April 1972): 4.

22. Sophia Cooper and Denis F. Johnston, "Labor Force Projections by Color, 1970-1980," *Monthly Labor Review* 89 (September 1966): 969.

23. Cain, op. cit., p. 119.

24. For further information, see Alan Sorkin, "Education, Occupation and Income of Nonwhite Women," *Journal of Negro Education*, Vol. XLI, No. 4, Fall 1972, pp. 343-351.

25. Computed from U.S. Bureau of the Census, 1940 Census of Population, *The Labor Force* (Washington, D.C.: U.S. Government Printing Office, 1943), Table 68, p. 111; U.S. Department of Labor, *Manpower Report of the President, 1971* (Washington, D.C.: U.S. Government Printing Office, 1971), Table B-1, p. 234.

26. Gary Becker, *Human Capital* (New York: National Bureau of Economic Research, 1964), p. 101.

27. U.S. Department of Commerce, *Statistical Abstract, 1970* (Washington, D.C.: U.S. Government Printing Office, 1971), Table 75, p. 60.

28. U.S. Department of Labor, Bureau of Labor Statistics, *Case Studies of Displaced Workers*, Bulletin 1408 (Washington, D.C.: U.S. Government Printing Office, 1962).

29. Richard C. Wilcock and Walter H. Franke, *Unwanted Workers*, (New York: The Free Press of Glencoe, 1963), p. 68.

30. U.S. Bureau of the Census, 1970 Census of Population, Subject Reports, final Report PC(2)–5B, *Educational Attainment* (Washington, D.C.: U.S. Government Printing Office, 1973), Table 8, p. 182.

31. For a further elaboration of this hypothesis, see Long, op. cit., pp. 267-270.

32. For the statistical evidence see Long, op. cit., Chapter 10.

33. Jacob Mincer, "Labor Force Participation and Unemployment: A Review of Recent Evidence," in Robert and Margaret Gordon (eds.), *Prosperity and Unemployment* (New York: John Wiley, 1966); and Bowen and Finnegan, op. cit., p. 483.

34. Joseph D. Mooney, "Urban Poverty and Labor Force Participation," *American Economic Review* 57, No. 1 (March 1967): 117.

**Chapter 3**
**The Nature and Composition**
**of Postwar Unemployment**

1. For further information see Robert E. Hall, "The Market for Professional and Technical Workers," *Brookings Papers on Economic Activity* 2, No. 1 (1971): 213-218.

2. Gordon F. Bloom and Herbert R. Northrup, *Economics of Labor Relations* (Homewood, Ill.: Richard D. Irwin, 1973), p. 444.

3. For two good studies of the "sex-typing" of occupations, see Valerie K. Oppenheimer, "The Sex-Labeling of Jobs," *Industrial Relations*, Vol. 7, May 1968, pp. 219-234; and Janet M. Hooks, *Women's Occupations Through Seven Decades*, U.S. Department of Labor, Women's Bureau, Bulletin No. 218 (Washington, D.C.: U.S. Government Printing Office, 1947), pp. 65-70.

4. Ray Marshall, "The Job Problems of Negroes," in Herbert R. Northrup and Richard L. Rowan (eds.), *The Negro and Employment Opportunity* (Ann Arbor: University of Michigan, 1965).

5. Arthur M. Ross, "The Negro in the American Economy," in Arthur M. Ross and Herbert Hill (eds.), *Employment, Race and Poverty* (New York: Harcourt, Brace and World, 1967), p. 17.

6. Robert C. Weaver, *Negro Labor: A National Problem* (New York: Harcourt, Brace and World, 1946), p. 14.

7. Nathan Glazer and Daniel Moynihan, *Beyond the Melting Pot* (Cambridge, Mass.: MIT Press, 1963), especially Chapter 3.

8. U.S. Bureau of the Census, *The Social and Economic Status of Negroes in the United States, 1970* (Washington, D.C.: U.S. Government Printing Office, 1971), p. 11.

9. U.S. Commission on Civil Rights, "Equal Protection of the Law," *Public Higher Education* (Washington, D.C.: U.S. Government Printing Office, 1960), Appendix H, p. 298.

10. Clarence D. Long, "A Theory of Creeping Unemployment and Labor Force Replacement," *Congressional Record* (Washington, D.C., July 25, 1961), pp. 13422 and 13434.

11. Computed from data contained in U.S. Bureau of the Census, 1950 Census of Population, Subject Report PE No. 4B, *Migration Between State Economic Areas* (Washington, D.C.: U.S. Government Printing Office, 1953), Tables 19 and 20.

12. See U.S. Bureau of the Census, 1960 Census of Population, PC(2)-2C *Mobility for Metropolitan Areas* (Washington, D.C.: U.S. Government Printing Office, 1963), Table 4.

13. U.S. Bureau of the Census, *The Social and Economic Status of Negroes, 1970* (Washington, D.C.: U.S. Government Printing Office, 1971), p. 21.

14. David E. Kaun, "Negro Migration and Unemployment," *Journal of Human Resources* 5, No. 2 (Spring 1970): 191.

15. *Report on the National Advisory Commission on Civil Disorders* (New York: Bantam Books, Inc., 1968), p. 269.

16. Lowell E. Gallaway and Zachary Dyckman, "The Full Employment-Unemployment Rate: 1953-1980," *Journal of Human Resources*, 5 (Fall 1970): 506-508.

17. Yale Brozen, "The Effect of Statutory Minimum Wage Increases on Teenage Unemployment," *Journal of Law and Economics* (April 1969).

18. Arthur F. Burns, *The Management of Prosperity* (New York: Columbia University Press, 1966).

19. Marvin Kosters and Finis Welch, "The Effects of Minimum Wages on the Distribution of Changes in Aggregate Employment," *American Economic Review* 62 (June 1972).

20. Edward Kalachek, "Determinants of Teenage Employment," *Journal of Human Resources* 4 (Winter 1969); 3-21.

21. U.S. Department of Labor, *Employment and Earnings* 18 (Washington, D.C.: U.S. Government Printing Office, March, 1972): 3.

22. Bloom and Northrup, op. cit., p. 438.

23. U.S. Department of Labor, *Manpower Report . . . 1973*, p. 25.

24. Ibid., p. 26.

25. Bureau of Labor Statistics, "Analysis of Layoff, Recall and Work Sharing Procedures in Union Contracts," Bulletin 1209 (Washington, D.C.: U.S. Government Printing Office, 1957).

26. National Industrial Conference Board, *Seniority Systems in Non-unionized Companies*, Studies in Personnel Policy, No. 110 (New York: National Industrial Conference Board, 1950).

27. Betty G. Fishman and Leo Fishman, *Employment, Unemployment . . .* , p. 43. This includes all workers 18 years and over.

28. William V. Deutermann, "Educational Attainment of Workers, March 1972," U.S. Department of Labor, Special Labor Force Report, No. 148 (Washington, D.C.: U.S. Government Printing Office, 1972), Table K, p. A-18.

29. Howard Hayghe, "Employment of High School Graduates and Dropouts," U.S. Department of Labor, Special Labor Force Report, No. 145 (Washington, D.C.: U.S. Government Printing Office, 1972), Table A, p. A-9.

30. Data derived from U.S. Department of Labor, *Manpower Report . . . 1973*, Table A-22, p. 157.

31. Ibid., p. 19.

32. Robert A. Gordon, *The Goal of Full Employment* (New York: Wiley, 1967), p. 68.

33. U.S. Department of Labor, *Manpower Report . . . 1972*, p. 43.

34. See "Heath Tightening Unemployment," *Washington Post*, December 6, 1971, p. D-12; and "Britain's Jobless: A Rapid Rise," *U.S. News and World Report*, May 24, 1971, pp. 84-85.

35. Constance Sorrentino, "Unemployment in Nine Industrialized Countries," *Monthly Labor Review* 95 (March 1972): 31.

36. Ibid.

37. Fishman and Fishman, op. cit., p. 11.

## Chapter 4
## The Geographic Incidence
## of Unemployment

1. Paul M. Schwab, "Unemployment by Region and in Ten Largest States," *Monthly Labor Review* 93 (January 1970): 4.

2. Betty G. Fishman and Leo Fishman, *Employment, Unemployment . . .* , p. 53.

3. Otto Eckstein, "Aggregate Demand and the Current Unemployment Problem," in Arthur M. Ross (ed.), *Unemployment and the American Economy* (New York: John Wiley, 1964), p. 120.

4. Ibid.

5. U.S. Bureau of the Census, *The Social and Economic Status of Negroes*, 1970 (Washington, D.C.: U.S. Government Printing Office, 1971), Table 7, p. 13.

6. *The New York Times*, March 6, 1972, p. 22.

7. Edward D. Kalachek and John M. Goering (eds.), "Transportation and

Central City Unemployment," Institute for Urban and Regional Studies, Washington University, Working Paper INS5, March 1970, p. 8.

8. Bennett Harrison, "Education and Underemployment in the Urban Ghetto," *American Economic Review* 62 (March, 1972): 799.

9. Harrison, op. cit., p. 800.

10. Computed from U.S. Bureau of the Census, 1970 Census of Population, *American Indians*, Subject Report No. PC(2)-1F (Washington, D.C.: U.S. Government Printing Office, 1973), Table 9, p. 120.

11. U.S. Public Health Service, *Indian Health Highlights* (Washington, D.C.: U.S. Government Printing Office, June 1966), p. 7.

12. U.S. Department of the Interior, Bureau of Indian Affairs, "Employment Assistance Programs," unpublished manuscript, 1972, p. 9.

13. U.S. Department of Commerce, *Annual Report of the Economic Development Administration, 1968* (Washington, D.C.: U.S. Government Printing Office, 1968), p. 7.

14. Interview with Ray E. Tanner, Special Assistant for Indian Affairs, Economic Development Administration, November 30, 1972.

15. U.S. Department of Commerce, *Annual Report of the Economic Development Administration, 1970* (Washington, D.C.: U.S. Government Printing Office, 1970), p. 6.

16. Ibid.

17. Niles Hansen, "Growth Centers, Human Resources and Rural Development," unpublished manuscript (University of Texas, 1971).

## Chapter 5
## Structural Change or Inadequate
## Demand: Two Explanations of
## Excessive Unemployment

1. U.S. Congress, Joint Economic Committee, Subcommittee on Economic Statistics, *Higher Unemployment Rates 1957-1960: Structural Transformation or Inadequate Demand*, 87th Congress, 1st Session (Washington, D.C.: Government Printing Office, 1961).

2. Eleanor G. Gilpatrick, *Structural Unemployment and Aggregate Demand: A Study of Employment and Unemployment in the United States, 1948-1964* (Baltimore, Md.: The Johns Hopkins Press, 1966), pp. 75-76.

3. Walter W. Heller, "The Administration's Fiscal Policy," in A.M. Ross (ed.), *Unemployment and the American Economy* (New York: John Wiley and Sons, 1963), p. 103.

4. Lowell E. Gallaway, "Labor Mobility, Resource Allocation and Structural Unemployment," *American Economic Review* 53 (September 1963): 712.

5. The same results apply to the Canadian labor market. See Mahmood A.

Zaidi, "Structural Unemployment, Labor Market Efficiency and the Intrafactor Allocation Mechanism in the United States and Canada," *Southern Economic Journal* 35 (January 1969): 212.

6. Lowell E. Gallaway, "Proposals for Federal Aid to Depressed Industrial Areas: A Critique," *Industrial and Labor Relations Review* 14 (April 1961): 363-378.

7. Otto Eckstein, "Aggregate Demand and the Current Unemployment Problem," in A.M. Ross (ed.), *Unemployment and the American Economy* (New York: John Wiley and Sons, 1963), p. 120.

8. Eckstein, op. cit., p. 123.

9. See for example, Barbara Bergmann and David E. Kaun, *Structural Unemployment in the United States* (U.S. Department of Commerce, Washington, D.C.: U.S. Government Printing Office, 1966); Kalachek and Knowles, op. cit., pp. 49-58; Gallaway, "Labor Mobility, Resource, Allocation and Structural Unemployment," op. cit., p. 712; Walter Heller, op. cit., pp. 97-103.

10. Gilpatrick, op. cit., p. 182.

11. N.J. Simler, "Long Term Unemployment, The Structural Hypothesis, and Public Policy," *American Economic Review* 54 (December 1964): 988 and 996.

12. D.E. Diamond, "New Jobs for the Structurally Unemployed," *Challenge* 12 (November 1963): 34-37.

13. Simler, op. cit., p. 997.

14. Gilpatrick, op. cit., p. 181.

15. Gilpatrick, op. cit., p. 202.

16. Bergmann and Kaun, op. cit., p. 108.

17. R.A. Gordon, "Has Structural Unemployment Worsened?" *Industrial Relations* 4 (May 1964): 55.

18. Gordon, op. cit., pp. 55-56.

19. Gordon, op. cit., pp. 66-67.

20. C.D. Long, "A Theory of Creeping Unemployment and Labor Force Replacement," *Congressional Record* (July 25, 1961), p. 13432.

21. Alan Sorkin, "Education, Ability and the Distribution of Wages," unpublished doctoral thesis, The Johns Hopkins University, 1966, pp. 306-319.

22. U.S. Department of Commerce, *The Economic Report of the President, 1963* (Washington, D.C.: U.S. Government Printing Office, 1963), p. 26.

23. Ibid.

24. Viola Benson, "The Intelligence and Later Scholastic Success of Sixth Grade Pupils," *School and Society* 55 (1942): 163-167.

25. Dael Wolfe, *America's Resources for Specialized Talent* (New York: Harper and Brothers, 1954), p. 314.

Chapter 6
Unemployment, Poverty, and
Economic Growth

1. Betty G. Fishman and Leo Fishman, *Employment, Unemployment...* p. 81.

2. Calculated from data contained in U.S. Department of Commerce, *Economic Report of the President, 1973* (Washington, D.C.: U.S. Government Printing Office, 1973), Table C-2, p. 194. The average rate of economic growth from 1947 to 1972 was not particularly unusual or unsatisfactory if judged by prewar standards.

3. Fishman and Fishman, op. cit., p. 83.

4. Arthur M. Okun, "Potential GNP: Its Measurement and Significance," *1962 Proceedings of the Business and Economic Statistics Section* (Washington, D.C.: American Statistical Association, 1962), pp. 98-104.

5. Ibid.

6. George L. Perry, "Labor Force Structure, Potential Output and Productivity," *Brookings Papers on Economic Activity* 2, No. 3 (1971): 533-561.

7. Perry, op. cit., p. 561.

8. Lowell E. Gallaway, *Manpower Economics* (Homewood, Ill.: Richard D. Irwin, Inc., 1971), p. 146.

9. Gordon F. Bloom and Herbert R. Northrup, *Economics of Labor Relations* (Homewood, Ill.: Richard D. Irwin, Inc., 1973), p. 448.

10. U.S. Department of Commerce, Bureau of the Census, *Consumer Income*, Series P-60, No. 82, "Characteristics of the Low Income Population: 1971" (Washington, D.C.: U.S. Government Printing Office, 1972), p. 1.

11. U.S. Department of Commerce, op. cit., p. 2.

12. Ray Marshall, "Some Rural Economic Development Problems in the South," *Monthly Labor Review* 95 (February 1972): 28.

13. Gallaway, op. cit., p. 148.

14. U.S. Department of Commerce, *Economic Report of the President, 1969* (Washington, D.C.: U.S. Government Printing Office, 1969), p. 159.

15. Victor Fuchs, "Redefining Poverty and Redistributing Income," *The Public Interest* 9 (Summer 1967): 88.

16. Gallaway, op. cit., p. 153.

17. Chase Manhattan Bank, *Business in Brief*, p. 4.

18. Leonard A. Lecht, *Poor Persons in the Labor Force: A Universe of Need*, Report Prepared for the U.S. Department of Labor, Manpower Administration, October 1970, pp. 1-5.

19. Joseph A. Pechman, Henry J. Aaron, and Michael K. Taussig, *Social Security: Perspectives for Reform* (Washington, D.C.: The Brookings Institution, 1968), p. 198.

20. Pechman, Aaron and Taussig, op. cit., p. 199.

21. Sar A. Levitan, Martin Rein and David Marwick, *Work and Welfare Go Together* (Baltimore, Md.: The Johns Hopkins Press, 1972), pp. 3-4.

22. Office of Economic Opportunity, "Preliminary Results of the New Jersey Graduated Work Incentive Experiment," mimeographed (February 1970), p. 3.

23. A.W. Phillips, "The Relation Between Unemployment and the Rate of Change of Money Wage Rates in the United Kingdom, 1861-1957," *Economica* 25 (December 1958): 283-299.

24. Albert Rees, *The Economics of Work and Pay* (New York: Harper and Row, 1973), p. 229.

25. Ibid.

26. Jerome C. Darnell, "Another Look at the Trade-Off Between Inflation and Unemployment," *Conference Board Record* 7 (January 1970): 18-19.

27. George L. Perry, "Changing Labor Markets and Inflation," *Brookings Papers on Economic Activity* 1, No. 3 (1970): 411-441.

28. Charles L. Schultze, "Has the Phillips Curve Shifted? Some Additional Evidence?" *Brookings Papers on Economic Activity* 2, No. 2 (1971): 452-467.

29. For further information see, Harry H. Wellington and Ralph K. Winter, Jr., *The Unions and the Cities* (Washington, D.C.: The Brookings Institution, 1971).

30. Sar A. Levitan, Garth L. Mangum, and Ray Marshall, *Human Resources . . . ,* pp. 514-515.

31. George L. Perry, *Inflation and Unemployment* (Washington, D.C.: The Brookings Institution, 1970), p. 42.

32. Robert E. Hall, "Prospects for Shifting the Phillips Curve Through Manpower Policy," *Brookings Papers on Economic Activity* 2, No. 3 (1971): 659-701.

33. Hall, op cit., pp. 696-697.

Chapter 7
Manpower Training Programs for the
Development of Human Resources

1. Sar A. Levitan and Robert Taggert, III, *Social Experimentation and Manpower Policy: The Rhetoric and the Reality* (Baltimore, Md.: The Johns Hopkins Press, 1971), p. 1.

2. Michael E. Borus and Charles G. Buntz, "Problems and Issues in the Evaluation of Manpower Programs," *Industrial and Labor Relations Review* 25, No. 2 (January 1972): 238.

3. Thomas I. Ribich, *Education and Poverty* (Washington, D.C.: The Brookings Institution, 1968), p. 37.

4. Levitan and Taggert, op. cit., p. 26.

5. Alan Sorkin, *American Indians and Federal Aid* (Washington, D.C.: The Brookings Institute, 1971), pp. 113 and 116.

6. Borus and Buntz, op. cit., pp. 241-242.

7. Levitan and Taggert, op. cit., pp. 26-27.

8. N.N. Franklin, "Employment and Unemployment: Views and Policies, 1919-1969," *International Labor Review* 99 (March 1969): 300.

9. U.S. Department of Labor, *Manpower Report of the President, 1967* (Washington, D.C.: U.S. Government Printing Office, 1967), p. 51.

10. Thomas I. Ribich, *Education and Poverty* (Washington, D.C.: The Brookings Institution, 1968), p. 49.

11. Earl D. Main, "A Nationwide Evaluation of MDTA Institutional Job Training," *Journal of Human Resources* III, No. 1 (Spring 1968): 162.

12. Main, op. cit., pp. 166-167.

13. H.H. London, *How Fare MDTA Ex-Trainees? An Eighteen Months Follow-Up Study of Five Hundred Such Persons* (Columbia: University of Missouri, 1967), p. 8.

14. Garth L. Mangum, "The Why, How, and Whence of Manpower Programs," in Louis A. Ferman (ed.), *Evaluating the War on Poverty, The Annals of the American Academy of Political and Social Science* 385 (September 1969), p. 53.

15. Sar A. Levitan, *Antipoverty Work and Training Efforts: Goals and Reality* Policy Papers in Human Resources and Industrial Relations, No. 3 (Ann Arbor, Mich.: Institute for Labor and Industrial Relations, 1967), p. 5.

16. Levitan, op. cit., p. 35.

17. Joseph A. Pichler, "The Job Corps Transition," *Industrial and Labor Relations Review* 25, No. 3 (April, 1972): 342.

18. Levitan, op. cit., p. 35.

19. Glen G. Cain, "Benefit-Cost Estimates for Job Corps," (Madison: University of Wisconsin, Institute for Research on Poverty, 1967).

20. Pichler, op. cit., p. 337.

21. Levitan, op. cit., p. 28.

22. U.S. Department of Labor, "Report of the Secretary of Labor on Restructuring Job Corps," mimeographed (April 11, 1969), p. 16.

23. Ibid.

24. U.S. Department of Labor, "Job Corps Placement Performance, 1970" (Washington, D.C.: U.S. Government Printing Office, 1970), p. 14.

25. U.S. Department of Labor, *Manpower Report . . . , 1973*, Table F-1, p. 227.

26. District of Columbia Board of Education, Department of Research, Budget, and Legislation, "Work Scholarship Program Evaluation," mimeographed (April 25, 1967).

27. Pittsburgh Public Schools, "Neighborhood Youth Corps: Holding Power Study, School Year 1965-1966," mimeographed (March 1967), p. 4.

28. Gerald G. Somers and Ernst Stromsdorfer, "A Cost-Effectiveness Analysis of In-School and Summer Neighborhood Youth Corps: A Nationwide Evaluation," *Journal of Human Resources* VII, No. 4 (Fall 1972): 456.

29. U.S. Department of Labor, Neighborhood Youth Corps, "An Analysis of the NYC Summer Program," mimeographed (March 21, 1967).

30. Dunlap and Associates, "Survey of Terminees from Out-of-School Neighborhood Youth Corps Projects," (Darien, Conn.: Dunlap and Associates, May 1967).

31. Michael E. Borus, John P. Brennan and Sidney Rosen, "A Benefit-Cost Analysis of the Neighborhood Youth Corps: The Out-of-School Program in Indiana," *Journal of Human Resources* (Spring 1970): 139.

32. R. Walther and M. Magnusson, *A Retrospective Study of the Effectiveness of the Out-of-School Neighborhood Youth Corps Programs in Four Urban Sites*, report submitted to the Manpower Administration, U.S. Department of Labor (Washington, D.C., 1967), pp. 44-47.

33. Levitan, op. cit., p. 64.

34. Levitan, op. cit., pp. 95-96.

35. U.S. Department of Health, Education, and Welfare, Welfare Administration, Policy Decision No. 11, April 5, 1965.

36. Frederick B. Arner, "The Work Incentive Program: Establishment and Early Implementation," mimeographed (June 1969), p. 4.

37. U.S. Department of Labor, *Manpower Report . . . , 1973*, Table F-8, p. 234.

38. Sar A. Levitan, Martin Rein and David Norwick, *Work and Welfare . . . ,* p. 97.

39. Levitan, Rein and Morwick, op. cit., p. 98.

40. Analytic Systems, Inc., *Analysis of WIN Program Termination Data*, mimeographed (1970), p. 33.

41. Comptroller General, *Federal Manpower Training Programs* (Washington, D.C.: U.S. Government Printing Office, 1972), p. 18.

42. Sar A. Levitan and Robert Taggert, "The Emergency Employment Act: An Interim Assessment," *Monthly Labor Review* 95, No. 6 (June 1972): 3.

43. Levitan and Taggert, op. cit., p. 7.

44. U.S. Department of Labor, *Manpower Report . . . , 1972*, p. 95.

45. Malcolm S. Cohen, "The Direct Effects of Federal Manpower Programs in Reducing Unemployment," *Journal of Human Resources* IV (Fall 1969): 504.

46. Derived from Sar A. Levitan and Robert Taggert, III, *Social Experimentation and Manpower Policy: The Rhetoric and the Reality*, Policy Studies in Employment and Welfare No. 9 (Baltimore, Md.: The Johns Hopkins Press, 1971), pp. 110-111.

47. Somers and Stromsdorfer, op. cit., p. 459.

## Chapter 8
## A Look Ahead: The Labor
## Force in 1980

1. U.S. Department of Labor, *Manpower Report . . . , 1973*, Table 6-2, p. 242.

2. See "The Background to the Guaranteed Income Concept," in Robert Theobald (ed.), *The Guaranteed Income* (Garden City, N.J.: Doubleday, 1966), pp. 83-96.

3. Betty G. Fishman and Leo Fishman, *Employment, Unemployment . . . ,* p. 128.

4. U.S. Department of Labor, *The U.S. Economy in 1980: A Summary of BLS Projections,* Bulletin 1673 (Washington, D.C.: U.S. Government Printing Office, 1970), p. 3.

5. U.S. Department of Labor, *Manpower Report . . . , 1973,* p. 66.

6. U.S. Department of Labor, op. cit., p. 77.

7. U.S. Department of Labor, "Employment Projections to 1975," *Monthly Labor Review* 86, No. 3 (March 1963): 246.

8. Maxine G. Stewart, "The U.S. Economy in 1980: A Preview of BLS Projections," *Monthly Labor Review* 93 (April 1970): 15.

9. U.S. Department of Commerce, Bureau of the Census, 1970 Census of Population, Subject Report No. PC(2)-5B, *Educational Attainment* (Washington, D.C.: U.S. Government Printing Office, 1973), Table 5, p. 105.

10. Stewart, op. cit., p. 32.

11. For details regarding the assumptions made in deriving the projections see Sol Swerdloff, "How Good Were Manpower Projections for the 1960's," *Monthly Labor Review* 92, No. 11 (November 1969): 18-19.

12. Martin O'Donoghue, *Economic Dimensions in Education* (New York: Aldine, 1971), p. 147.

# Index

# Index

# About the Author

**Alan Sorkin** is Associate Professor of International Health and Economics at the Johns Hopkins University, where he received the Ph.D. in economics in 1966. He is the author of *American Indians and Federal Aid* (The Brookings Institution, 1971). Dr. Sorkin's articles on the relationship between schooling and earnings, economic problems of minorities, and the quality of American colleges and universities have appeared in professional economic and social science journals.